*Every Employee
a Manager*

Every Employee a Manager

MORE MEANINGFUL WORK THROUGH JOB ENRICHMENT

M. Scott Myers

McGRAW-HILL BOOK COMPANY

New York   St. Louis   San Francisco   Düsseldorf   Johannesburg
Kuala Lumpur   London   Mexico   Montreal   New Delhi
Panama   Rio de Janeiro   Singapore   Sydney   Toronto

EVERY EMPLOYEE A MANAGER

Library of Congress Catalog Card Number 79-111991

ISBN 07-044268-1

67890 KPKP 79876543

For Susan

IF JUST A BUSINESS CONTRACT*

Maybe
our relationship is just a business contract—
you give me something
and I give you something in turn.

If that is all that you want,
you need not take any additional effort;
you can go about as you ever did.

You can try to get the most from me
and I can try to get the most from you.

When effort is thus called for on either's part,
it becomes a sort of a tug-of-war—
I try to give you the minimum
and you try to extract the maximum
and give me the minimum.
Being generally clever,
both of us succeed in this game,
up to a point.

Of course, with unfortunate effects on
business purpose,
namely, utilization of resources
and creation of wealth.

* Nagam Atthreya, *The You and I in Business,* K. Venkataraman, MMC School of Management, Sahakaar Bhavan, Kurla Industrial Estate, Bombay 77, May, 1966, pp. 32, 33.

Foreword

The most important continuing challenge to industry in the years ahead will be to establish innovative programs that encourage the achievement of compatible employee and company goals. In a society that continues to change through the introduction of new technologies, a better educated and younger workforce, and an increase of leisure time, it is necessary to know what these goals should be, what the measurable checkpoints are, and what has been and still needs to be accomplished. Management's role in attracting, challenging, and retaining the members of the coming generations is as vital to an organization's success as any breakthrough in technology or newly designed production equipment.

The truly successful growth organization of the future will require a marriage of industry's richest assets—the capabilities of human beings and the efficiency of operational systems. As high-volume, repetitive, and rigidly paced manufacturing systems place unyielding demands on people, management must show the same dedication to improving job satisfaction that it has in the past to improving equipment design and satisfying people's pay requirements.

The "involvement" type of organizational climate is essential to successful management. Modern problems are too complex and diversified for one man or one approach. Therefore, we need a blending of skills and perspectives in the form of effective problem-sharing and problem-solving teams to achieve our goals. However, we need to remember that synergy through the effectiveness of people cannot be achieved instantaneously or through directives—that people require time and opportunity for the development of trust, communications, interaction, and commitment.

The concept of every employee a manager through meaningful work requires supervisory sophistication not common in today's organizations. Involvement of people in the planning and controlling as well as the doing of their work must be understood not as an act of good "human relations" nor as a means of exploitation but, rather, as a sound business practice that benefits both the organization and its members. The supervisor of the future knows he is not managing a technique or a program, but a way of life at work that finds expression in all levels of the create, make, and market functions of the organization. Through this way of life, people gradually become more knowledgeable and competent, and migrate and polarize toward a total commitment which leads to continuing growth, success, and self-renewal for both the organization and its members.

Mark Shepherd, Jr.
Dallas, Texas

Preface

Textbooks are rich in case histories of industries that have started from modest beginnings and progressed to the industrial giants listed in the *Fortune* 500. These case histories are testimonials of managerial innovation in research and engineering, product design, manufacturing, distribution and marketing, financial management, and growth strategy. Successful corporations are often used as models for planning the development of other companies. But planning through extrapolation can lead to obsolescence.

Managers are finding old blueprints inadequate for planning new organizational success. New variables include the changing preceptions of employees and the increased rate of technological and social change. The knowledge explosion, coupled with increasing affluence, is enabling the oppressed to discover their latent talents and new freedoms. Wage earners are disregarding traditional guidelines or finding ways of circumventing them. Docile conformists are transformed into indignant reactionaries. Disaffection has extended beyond the factory work force to include teenagers, college students, schoolteachers, minority groups, soldiers, civil servants, and even citizens of totalitarian countries and their satellites. Attempts to suppress nonconformity evoke more reactive behavior.

Thus, today's manager finds himself in a ground swell of a quiet revolution—quiet only in the sense that many are not aware of it or have failed to recognize its symptoms. Many managers are only now beginning to realize the potential of the workplace for giving expression to unused or misdirected talent. The challenge of increasing human effectiveness is emerging as the remaining frontier, offering competitive advantage to organizations most successful in channeling human talent and energy into constructive outlets. The reservoir is vast, as talent at all levels is poorly utilized, but the largest and most underutilized resource consists of the 80-some percent of the nation's work force, classified as hourly nonexempt under the terms of the Fair Labor Standards Act. Tomorrow's manager will manage through the influence of competence, organizing materiel and manpower to give expression to talent and individuality in the pursuit of synergistic personal and organizational goals.

A major purpose of this book is to bridge the gap between theory and practice. Textbooks, research reports, and professional journals are rich in theory, but too often written in a jargon unfamiliar to those who need and wish to understand them. At the expense of some of the detail and comprehensiveness reflected in many of these published resources, this book attempts to explain in everyday language how theory can be translated into managerial styles and management systems.

Theory is presented, rather briefly, as a foundation for building managerial effectiveness, and an attempt is made to show that most theories, though differing in terminology, share the common purpose of defining conditions in which talent can find expression. These conditions are defined in terms of the relationships among people and the characteristics of their goals and physical environment.

Job enrichment is defined as a process for developing employees so that they think and behave like managers in managing their jobs, and a process for redefining the job and the role of the job incumbent to make such development feasible. Examples and techniques of job enrichment are presented.

The changing role of the management process is defined in terms of supervisory style, organizational climate, and management systems. Through these media, the manager's role in increasing human effectiveness is defined, both at home and in his American operations abroad.

The role of the industrial relations specialist is defined to show him as a change agent in integrating concern for the individual with concern for mainstream organizational goals. Emphasis is placed on the industrial relations specialist's educative role in qualifying managers to apply behavioral theory in anticipating, understanding, and coping with human behavior. As a bona fide member of the management team, the personnel man escapes his traditional enslaving role of dealing only with symptoms.

This book was made possible through my ten years with Texas Instruments. I am indebted to Pat Haggerty, Chairman of the Board, and Mark Shepherd, President, for providing a climate in which personnel research could be undertaken, for taking an active interest in research results, and for providing support and leadership in implementing innovations.

Most of the management innovations in Texas Instruments were developed by managers in pursuit of organizational goals. It is to their credit that they are integrating concepts of human effectiveness with traditional concepts in evolving ever-improving management practices. Innovative leadership of the type provided by Fred Bucy in mainstream operations and by Earl Weed as a behavioral change agent is an essential ingredient.

In an organization of more than 50,000 members it is impossible to name all who have contributed directly and indirectly to the content of this book, particularly since the book describes a strategy which involves all members of the work force. However, a list of persons who also have been particularly helpful through either words or action would include Ted Beers, Warren Bowles, Tom Clark, Bill Dees, Roy Fuller, Bill George, Earl Gomersall, Phil Gomez, John Grooms, Joe Halbach, Gary Holmgren, Jerry Junkins, Bob Kastendiek, Bob Kelly, Charles Kettler, Bill Latham, Bill Lawrence, Neil MacKinnon, Katherine Matthews, Lucinda Monett, Fred Ochsner, Chuck Neilsen, Ray Newby, Gil Perkins, Bill Polleys, Scotty Prescott, Bill Rigsby, Bill Roche, Mark Smith, Graham Sterling, Jack and Peggy Stroud, Bill Tony, Don Wass, Pat Weber, and Gil Wood.

The perspective of this book has been broadened through my involvement as a consultant with managers in other organizations including Cominco, Continental Can, Control Data, Dow Chemical,

DuPont, General Motors, Hughes Aircraft, IBM, Monsanto, Polaroid, Procter & Gamble, Steinberg's, Tektronix, Weyerhaeuser, and various school boards and teacher federations in the province of Ontario, Canada.

My wife Susan helped me write and edit portions of the book, and Sandi McCaskill prepared the original manuscript and most of the artwork.

M. Scott Myers

Contents

*Every Employee
a Manager*

chapter one

Theories of Human Effectiveness

People's behavior stems from their interpretations of what they think they perceive. These perceptions influence and become crystallized or incorporated into their values or assumptions and, ultimately, their habits. Broadly speaking, then, individuals' values and assumptions may be thought of as their own personal theories.

The term "theory" implies a tentativeness which, if removed, would either invalidate the theory or establish it as a law. However, because ambiguity is uncomfortable for many people, they tend to defend their values and theories and act on them as though they were laws. The quality of human relationships is directly or indirectly a function of people's values or personal theories. Thus, harmony or conflict between individuals, groups, or nations results from compatible or incompatible perceptions and values.

This chapter deals with several theories of human effectiveness found to have relevance to the industrial organization. They are based at least in part on attempts by behavioral scientists to observe, measure, and interpret human behavior. That several theories exist to explain the same phenomena indicates that the observation, measurement, and interpretation processes have not been completely objective. However, most of the theories discussed in this chapter are based on common research results and other widely accepted theories to the extent that their commonality outweighs their differences.

COMMONALITY OF THEORIES

Figure 1-1 portrays twelve theories of human effectiveness, selected more to reflect variety than to be comprehensive. Each of these theories is presented on a linear scale, the left end representing conditions conducive to ineffectiveness, and the right end conditions for

	INEFFECTIVENESS			EFFECTIVENESS	
ROBERT BLAKE	1, 1 Neutrality and Indecision	MANAGERIAL GRID 1, 9 Inadequate concern for production 5, 5 Compromise, middle-of-the-road 9, 1 Inadequate concern for people		9, 9 Integration of Resources	MANAGERIAL STYLES
JAY HALL	1, 1 Decisions by default and precedent	DECISION-MAKING GRID 1, 9 Inadequate concern for quality decision 5, 5 Decision through bargaining 9, 1 Inadequate concern for commitment		9, 9 Adequate concern for commitment and quality decisions	
RENSIS LIKERT	SYSTEM 1 Exploitive authoritative	SYSTEM 2 Benevolent authoritative	SYSTEM 3 Consultative	SYSTEM 4 Participative group	
DOUGLAS McGREGOR	THEORY X Reductive assumptions		THEORY Y Developmental assumptions		
CHRIS ARGYRIS	AUTOCRATIC RELATIONSHIPS Conflict and conformity, Alienation		AUTHENTIC RELATIONSHIPS Interpersonal and technical competence, Commitment		MANAGERIAL STYLES & SYSTEMS
WARREN BENNIS	BUREAUCRACY Authoritarian, restrictive management structure		DEMOCRACY Goal-oriented, adaptive management structure		
FREDERICK HERZBERG	ENVIRONMENTAL COMFORT ← — — — —Hygiene seeking— — — — — — — — — — —		MEANINGFUL WORK — — — — — — — — — —Motivation seeking— — — — →		
JOHN PARÉ	BOSS POWER -- Direction and control by authority SYSTEM POWER -- Bureaucratic controls PEER POWER -- Social pressure of group		GOAL POWER -- Self-alignment with organizational goals		
ERICH FROMM	ESCAPE FROM FREEDOM Conformity, domination , destructiveness		FREEDOM Self-reliance, spontaneity, responsible behavior		STYLES & SYSTEMS
WILLIAM GLASSER	AVOIDANCE OF REALITY Maladjustment		COPING WITH REALITY Responsible behavior		CONSEQUENCES OF
ABRAHAM MASLOW	LOWER-NEED FIXATION Halted growth		SELF-ACTUALIZATION Realizing potential		
DAVID McCLELLAND	LOW nACH More interested in things like affiliation, security money, possessions		HIGH nACH Achievement its own primary reward, high challenges, moderate risks, independence		

FIG. 1-1   Theories of human effectiveness.

greater effectiveness. These scales do not reflect the full complexity of these theories or their application, nor are they intended to define the scope or primary focus of their developers' professional competence. Rather, they are displayed as an aid in comprehending the commonality, as well as the uniqueness, of what might otherwise appear as a confusing and contradictory proliferation of theories. The top four theories place the focus on managerial styles or assumptions, the middle four are generally described as combinations of managerial style and management systems, and the lower four are predominantly descriptors of the impact of managerial styles and systems. The first four theories have as much impact as the middle four on systems, for managerial styles and values inevitably find expression in system design and administration.

Though the terminology and scope of these theories and their mechanisms for limiting or achieving effectiveness may differ, they have the common purpose of defining conditions which inhibit or enhance the expression of human talent. Applied in the business setting, these theories define conditions for improved goal orientation and for the reduced or more constructive use of authority. However, it should be noted that a descriptor on any given scale is not necessarily vertically aligned with synonymous terms on other scales. For example, Likert's System 1 refers to a style of management through exploitive use of authority, whereas Maslow's "lower-need fixation" represents a consequence of System 1 management or the environmental restrictions included in Bennis's "bureaucracy." Blake's 9,1 management style is similar to Likert's System 1 or Paré's "boss power," but is positioned to the right of these, as Blake sees 1,1 as a condition of lesser effectiveness—something of a syndrome of disengagement or security seeking similar to that described in Fromm's *Escape from Freedom*.

Robert Blake and Jane Mouton[1] define organizational effectiveness in terms of two coordinates of a grid, numbered 1 to 9, showing the manager's concern for the human factor on the ordinate and his concern for production on the abscissa. The ideal 9,9 manager has strong and integrated concern for production and human needs. The 1,1 manager at the other extreme is disengaged from responsibility,

---

[1] Robert Blake and Jane Mouton, *Corporate Excellence through Grid Organizational Development*, Gulf Publishing Company, Houston, 1968.

and his behavior is typified by neutrality, conformity, and indecision. The 1,9 manager will subordinate organizational goals to human needs, while the 9,1 manager will drive for attainment of organization goals at the expense of human resources. The 5,5 manager compromises his position to balance the conflicting and fluctuating demands of commitment and authority.

Jay Hall,[2] with Vincent O'Leary and Martha Williams, describes group effectiveness as a function of the decision maker's concern for decision adequacy and his concern for commitment of others to the decision. The mix of the group leader's concern is plotted on a grid, the ordinate denoting concern with commitment and the abscissa concern with decision adequacy. Traditional decision making often presumes the pursuit of high commitment to be incompatible with decision excellence, requiring bargaining and compromise. Capitulation may take the form of a traditional 5,5 majority decision, a 1,9 good-neighbor decision, a 9,1 leader-knows-best decision or, at its worst, a 1,1 acquiescence to a default decision. The ideal 9,9 decision maker assumes that better decisions can be reached if all resources available in the group are utilized, and strives for both high commitment and best decision.

Rensis Likert[3] describes managerial style in terms of four systems. System 1, *exploitive authoritative,* refers to the use of authority and coercion with little concern for the needs of humans. System 1 found common expression in the management prerogative era of the nineteenth century, and lingers on as the dominant style of some managers today. System 2, *benevolent authoritative,* found accelerated acceptance with the Hawthorne studies which revealed, among other things, that people responded well to attention and interest in their welfare. Early human relations training efforts put a veneer over System 1, resulting in System 2 with its paternalism and increased benefits. System 3, *consultative,* evolved gradually as managers learned that people were more likely to support what they helped create. Though participation sometimes emerged as manipulation, and management retained its prerogative of accepting or rejecting suggestions, at least people had increased opportunity to be heard. System 4,

---

[2] Jay Hall, Vincent O'Leary, and Martha Williams, "The Decision-making Grid: A Model of Decision-making Styles," *California Management Review,* Winter, 1964.

[3] Rensis Likert, *The Human Organization,* McGraw-Hill Book Company, New York, 1967.

participative group, refers to an ideal model in which the influen
talent or competence, rather than the influence of authority, pro
the basis for achieving organizational goals. System 4 is base
assumptions that people's initiative, creativity, and responsibility find
constructive expression if they have access to information and the opportunity to solve problems and set goals.

Douglas McGregor's[4] classic theory holds that a manager's style of
managing reflects his assumptions about people. The *theory X,* or
reductive, manager assumes that people need authority and coercion
to motivate them, that satisfactory performance can be assured only
through ordering and forbidding. He assumes that most people avoid
work, shun responsibility, require definition of job goals, must be
subjected to close control, and will misuse freedom. They should be
rewarded for their successes and punished for their mistakes. The
theory Y, or developmental, manager assumes that people prefer to
discipline themselves through self-direction and self-control. He
assumes that people respond better to challenges than to authority,
that people seek responsibility, and that under the right conditions
they can enjoy work. He assumes that high expectations, coupled with
goalsetting opportunity by job incumbents, will result in higher goals
and greater achievements. He assumes that freedom to exercise
independence and to learn from mistakes are necessary conditions
for responsible behavior and growth.

Chris Argyris[5] has defined *interpersonal* and *technical competence,* as
well as *internal commitment,* as the key ingredients of organizational
effectiveness. Technical and interpersonal competence are fostered
by authentic relationships, high but realistic expectations, meaningful
work, freedom to act, accountability, and goal-oriented team action.
These conditions, in turn, can be significantly influenced by organizational relationships and administrative control systems.

Warren Bennis[6] defines conditions for human effectiveness in
terms of the organization's governing systems. *Bureaucracy* tends to
quash initiative through its enmeshing network of complex, inflexible

[4] Douglas McGregor, *The Professional Manager,* McGraw-Hill Book Company, New
York, 1967.
[5] Chris Argyris, *Integrating the Individual and the Organization,* John Wiley & Sons, Inc.,
New York, 1964; Chris Argyris, *Organization and Innovation,* Richard D. Irwin, Inc.,
Homewood, Ill., 1965.
[6] Warren Bennis, *Changing Organizations,* McGraw-Hill Book Company, New York,
1966.

and restrictive rules and systems. *Democracy* is inevitable for the successful organization, as it enables people to give expression to their talents in defining and achieving synergistic organizational-personal goals in a climate of goal-oriented supervision and adaptive and flexible systems.

Frederick Herzberg[7] holds that man's lower-order needs and higher-order needs do not operate on a single continuum. The satisfaction of man's *hygiene,* or lower-order needs, has only fleeting motivational value and even then only up to a level of diminishing return. But man's motivational, or self-actualization, needs operate somewhat independently and have the potential for motivating a person beyond the level attainable by hygiene satisfiers. Meaningless work which offers limited opportunity for the expression of talent may result in hygiene seeking; on the other hand, meaningful work which offers opportunity for growth, advancement, responsibility, achievement, and recognition inspires motivation and tends to desensitize persons to their hygiene needs.

John Paré[8] shows source of power to be a key factor in limiting or enhancing human effectiveness. *Boss power* refers to the use of authority presumed to be associated with level or status in the organization, traditionally an expression of "management's prerogative." *System power* is expressed through controls imposed by management systems and procedures and, at its worst, represents networks of bureaucratic restrictions. *Peer power* is the influence of associates springing largely from affiliation needs which may emphasize the goals and needs of the group over the welfare of the organization. *Goal power* refers to the attraction of meaningful goals which offer opportunity for simultaneously satisfying individual and organizational needs.

Erich Fromm[9] describes man's effectiveness in terms of his ability to cope with freedom. If an individual during maturation is granted freedom, respect, and responsibility commensurate with his ability to handle it, he can emerge as a self-reliant, spontaneous, and responsible individual. If the severing of the apron string is coordinated with his naturally unfolding growth and independence needs, he is likely

[7] Frederick Herzberg, *Work and the Nature of Man,* The World Publishing Company, Cleveland, 1966.

[8] John Paré, "What's your Power Structure?" *Canadian Business,* April, 1968.

[9] Erich Fromm, *Escape from Freedom,* Holt, Rinehart and Winston, Inc., New York, 1941.

to attain autonomy and freedom. But the individual who has been conditioned into dependency relationships and has learned to associate security and love with the use of authority, finds freedom frightening after leaving home and seeks substitute apron strings. His inability to cope constructively with authority and autonomy attracts him to patterns of conformity, manipulation, and destructiveness.

William Glasser's[10] reality therapy defines human effectiveness as a function of ability to get involved with others in responsible relationships and through this involvement to learn to cope effectively with reality. Persons in an environment where their talents can be used and where they are accountable for their conduct tend to develop patterns of responsible behavior. Maladjustment is a manifestation of escape from reality brought about by irresponsible social, authority, and work relationships. Unlike traditional psychoanalytic theory, reality therapy does not require the probing of the subconscious past; rather, it helps the individual face reality and accept responsibility for satisfying his needs through responsible role relationships that do not deprive others of need fulfillment.

Abraham Maslow[11] defines human effectiveness as a function of matching man's opportunities with the appropriate position on his *hierarchy of needs,* enabling him to progress upward. Primeval man, for example, was concerned with the lower-order needs of survival, reproduction, finding food and shelter, and escaping hazards of his environment. As he was able to satisfy these physical needs, his status and social needs assumed relatively greater importance. In modern societies of increasing affluence, he is increasingly concerned with prepotent higher-order needs for growth, achievement, responsibility, and recognition. Thwarted self-actualization needs result in lower-need fixation and halted growth, but opportunity to utilize talents enables a person to realize his potential mentally, emotionally and aesthetically.

David McClelland[12] has identified achievement motivation as a primary expression of human effectiveness. People who have a high

[10] William Glasser, *Reality Therapy,* Harper & Row, Publishers, Incorporated, New York, 1965.

[11] Abraham H. Maslow, *Toward a Psychology of Being,* 2d ed., D. Van Nostrand Company, Inc., New York, 1968.

[12] David McClelland, *The Achieving Society,* D. Van Nostrand Company, Inc., New York, 1961.

need for achievement (n Ach) thrive on freedom to pursue challenging goals involving moderate risks, their primary reward being a job well done. People with low n Ach are more interested in other things such as peer acceptance, security, money, and material possessions, and are more inclined to avoid all risks or undertake unjustifiably high risks. Though n Ach varies among individuals, it is situational in that a person's n Ach may differ with his various roles. Also, n Ach can be developed and is often a function of cultural norms; the people of North America and northern Europe, for example, historically tending to have higher n Ach than people in some of the Middle Eastern countries.

TRANSLATION OF THEORIES

Theories are springboards to action and change. However, theories rarely lead to changed behavior until deliberate and intensive efforts are made to apply them. The intellectual understanding of management theory has about the same impact on a manager's supervisory style that the intellectual study of snow skiing has on teaching him how to ski. In either case, his competence is developed primarily through application—through the actual practice of supervision or by actually skiing. If he is satisfied with his style of supervising or skiing, he will expend little effort in learning and applying theories for the purpose of changing his styles.

However, if he is dissatisfied with his performance to the point that his desire to improve exceeds his reluctance to accept assistance, he may approach the study of theory with a readiness to change. A theory will be useful to him if he can translate it into remedial action that will reward his efforts. It may begin acquiring relevance in the classroom and follow several patterns.

Some theories find immediate relevance when introduced in response to appeals for help in solving pressing problems, such as an anticipated union organization drive, or increased personnel turnover or absenteeism. Theory becomes relevant in the classroom when actual problems are brought in for analysis and problem solving. This approach is followed in the Texas Instruments Motivation Seminar described on pages 16 to 18. Some theories acquire meaning when they become the instruments, first, for identifying and diagnosing problems, and then for prescribing remedial actions. This approach is illustrated in the description of Likert's four systems, Blake's managerial grid, and Paré's power structures on pages 20 to 23.

The Translation Process

The translation of theory is accomplished, for example, when the application of a management theory leads to desired changes in managerial behavior. The application of theory generally requires a four-step process:

1. Awareness
2. Understanding
3. Commitment to change
4. New habits

STEP 1: *Awareness* may result from a convincing speech, reading a book, viewing an educational film, attending a public seminar, or simply shop talk. This first step may occur for a manager when he gains at least a superficial insight into a new theory and the implied deficiency in his present style of managing.

STEP 2: *Understanding* may result from activity precipitated by his awareness of the possible need to change. He may read numerous books and articles on the theory and selectively choose training programs and attend lectures on the subject. This step may be thought of as an intellectual conditioning process. He may become an articulate spokesman for his newly acquired insight, but his managerial style may continue to follow old habit patterns.

STEP 3: *Commitment to change* occurs when he becomes aware of the discrepancy between his newly adopted theory and his everyday behavior, but only if he believes he will benefit personally through changing his style of management. Initial attempts are often discouraging and, if not reinforced by some type of rewarding feedback, may gradually be discontinued. Commitment and reinforcement must be strong and continuous to overcome established habit patterns. Moreover, his changed behavior is often viewed with suspicion by persons whose opinions about him have been crystallized by his previous style.

STEP 4: *New habits* are established when sustained deliberate applications of the new theory finally result in attitude changes and automatic and natural expressions of the desired changes in style of management. Attainment of the new habit-formation stage is a long and difficult process requiring perhaps 5 to 10 years of sustained reinforcement from steps 2 and 3. Some individuals never progress beyond step 2, particularly when others in the organization upon whom they depend for continuing opportunity do not encourage them through their language of action and words.

The application of management theory in a business organization generally begins with a step 2 intellectual conditioning experience to prepare managers for the step 3 translation process. The motivation seminar in Texas Instruments, described on pages 16 to 18, was based on an amalgamation of several theories, and it illustrates the nature and role of an intellectual conditioning process. Dubbed the "motivation-maintenance theory," it defines media in the typical industrial organization through which the needs of people at work are satisfied, as illustrated in Figure 1-2. The TI motivation-maintenance theory is presented in the following pages as a specimen intellectual message.

A Specimen Intellectual Message

Maintenance needs are synonymous with Maslow's lower-order needs or Herzberg's hygiene needs, and the term "maintenance" is used to denote the fact that people, like buildings and machines, must be

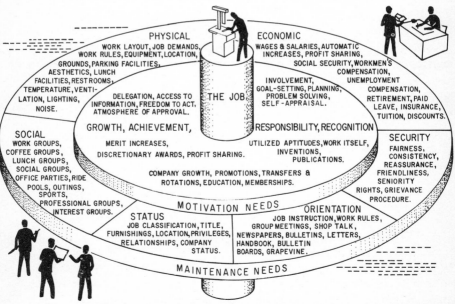

FIG. 1-2   Employee needs—maintenance and motivational. (M. Scott Myers, Who Are Your Motivated Workers? *Harvard Business Review,* **Jan.–Feb. 1964, p. 86.)**

maintained. Motivation needs, synonymous with Maslow's higher-order self-actualization needs, are satisfied when man is developing his potential through the pursuit of meaningful goals.

Maintenance Needs   The maintenance needs of people at work are quite similar whether the individual is a machine operator, as illustrated in the diagram, or the president, the vice-president, the middle manager, the foreman, the technician, the secretary, or the floor sweeper. Though the maintenance of people is not the key to motivating them in the business organization, it is usually a prerequisite for motivation. The same needs apply to people outside the industrial organization, such as housewives, policemen, clergymen, schoolteachers, and students. All require the satisfaction of their maintenance needs, defined here in terms of economic, security, orientation, status, social, and physical factors.

- *Economic* maintenance needs involve wages, salaries, and supplemental benefits received almost automatically by virtue of simply being on the job. Economic maintenance needs do not include forms of compensation stemming from meritorious performance, mentioned later as reinforcements of motivation.
- *Security* maintenance needs refer to feelings of people arising primarily from their perception of their supervisor as an impartial, consistent, reassuring, friendly type of person, and from the knowledge that they are protected by a just system in the job situation.
- *Orientation* maintenance needs require the knowledge of the company and the job. This information is supplied by the supervisor, the printed media, such as newspapers and bulletins, or through the informal "grapevine" which exists in every organization.
- *Status* maintenance needs are generally satisfied through job classifications, titles, furnishings, privileges, relationships, and the company image or product image. The process of *acquiring* status is related to motivation factors of growth and achievement discussed later, but the possession of status or symbols of it is largely maintenance.
- *Social* maintenance needs are satisfied through formal or informal group activities in work groups, luncheon groups, coffee groups, ride pools, or after-hours recreational activities.
- *Physical* maintenance needs are satisfied by the work layout,

parking facilities, air conditioning, lighting, rest rooms, eating facilities, noise levels, and other physical factors.

When lower-order needs are maintained at adequate levels, dissatisfactions stemming from them are minimized. However, the maintenance factors in these six categories have only fleeting value as motivators. For example, when a plant manager air conditioned one of his buildings that had not previously been air conditioned, the enthusiastic response during the first week seemed like motivation. However, enthusiasm soon tapered off to a level that could only be called the absence of dissatisfaction with air conditioning. But when the air conditioning system failed, the response was immediate dissatisfaction, vociferous complaints, and lowered production. And when the system was repaired, building occupants were not motivated, they were merely returned to the level of absence of dissatisfaction. Their typical comments to the repairmen were: "What took you so long?" and "Why did you let the air conditioning go out?" Once employees have built air conditioning into their expectations, their feelings toward it can only go downward. Hence, maintenance factors are characterized by the fact that they inspire little positive sentiment when added, but incite strong negative reaction when removed.

Maintenance factors are peripheral to the job, as they are more directly related to the environment than to work itself. For the most part they are group-administered, usually by staff personnel, and their success usually depends upon their being applied uniformly and equitably.

Managers often fail to understand the ingratitude of employees toward maintenance factors such as the Christmas turkey, free coffee, and other expressions of well-intentioned paternalism. They are particularly disillusioned when these "gifts" become the subject of collective bargaining, and become perpetuated as "rights of labor."

Since the turn of the century, supplemental benefits have increased in cost from less than 10 percent of the payroll budget to more than 30 percent. The more supplemental benefits are added as maintenance factors, the higher becomes their potential for dissatisfaction. However, it would be an oversimplification to conclude that maintenance factors are only increasing dissatisfaction, or that they are the primary sources of dissatisfaction.

Maintenance factors serve a necessary function that can be appreciated only in historical perspective. In the early decades of the twentieth century, the working man lived in a world of management prerogatives of arbitrary "hire and fire." He lived and worked in sub-standard conditions and received substandard wages. But over the years two primary influences have brought about the "affluent society"[13]: (1) the intervention of labor unions, which forced the sharing of company wealth, and (2) the mass-production technology, which prices automobiles, washing machines, refrigerators, and other consumer products within the reach of increasingly higher percent-ages of the population.

Maintenance factors embrace the wages, hours, and working condi-tions which have been the focus of collective bargaining for many years. The emphasis on maintenance factors by unions raises a ques-tion regarding the future rule of labor unions and their ability to survive through a continuing strategy based on improving wages, hours, and working conditions. Life in an affluent society where main-tenance needs are satisfied would seem to preclude the need for unions. Because people's needs change, moving upward as lower needs are satisfied, employees in increasing numbers are failing to ex-perience the satisfaction previously derived from improved mainte-nance factors, and are aimlessly seeking, with mingled hope and despair, something more meaningful than comfortable working con-ditions and routinized work. The union's role has gradually, subtly, and inadvertently shifted from "people's defender" to a medium for displacing the aggression stemming from frustrations which it helped create.

Motivation Needs   The only constructive outlet for these frustrations in the business organization is upward through Maslow's hierarchy of needs to opportunities for satisfying self-actualization or motivation needs in terms of such factors as growth, achievement, responsibility, and recognition, illustrated in the inner circle of Figure 1-2.

- *Growth,* in this context, refers to mental growth. Though physi-cal growth generally levels off before age twenty, mental growth may continue throughout the life span of the individ-ual. Factors associated with the continuing growth or obsoles-cence of managers detailed on pages 105 to 109. One of the most effective antidotes to mental stagnation and vocational ob-solescence is a challenging job, as described on pages 62 to 70.

- *Achievement* refers to the need for achievement (*n* Ach) that McClelland has shown to be a key motive when it can find

[13] J. K. Galbraith, *The Affluent Society,* Houghton Mifflin Company, Boston, 1958.

expression. Individuals differ from each other in terms of their need for achievement, and a given individual's level of achievement motivation will vary with his opportunity to find expression for it. When jobs offer little opportunity for satisfying achievement needs, high n Ach people seek outlets for their achievement needs within or outside the organization. Jobs rich in opportunity for growth and achievement attract and retain high achievers. Low n Ach people in such an environment may develop n Ach through the multiple influences of a challenging role, peer pressure, and image emulation. By the same token, jobs lacking in challenge tend to attract and retain low achievers whose needs are satisfied largely through the maintenance factors such as security, benefits, affiliation, and comfortable surroundings.

■   The term *responsibility* refers to a sense of commitment to a worthwhile job. It has long been recognized that a sense of responsibility is a function of level in the organization—people high in management have a proportionally higher sense of responsibility than people at lower levels. A study of factors relating to motivation of managers at Texas Instruments[14] demonstrated this relationship, but it also revealed that level of motivation was more strongly related to style of supervision than it was to level in the organization. Figure 1-3 shows the relationship of level of motivation to level of management and boss's style of supervision. Level of motivation was based on the extent to which 1,344 managers rated their jobs in terms of factors such as challenge, interest, utilization of talent, freedom to act, sense of achievement, and personal growth. Upper management consisted of the president and two levels below him, lower management of first- and second-level supervision, and middle management the levels in between. Boss's style was measured in terms of descriptions provided by subordinates— "developmental" and "reductive" being synonymous with McGregor's theory Y and theory X, respectively, and "traditional" representing a middle ground. Hence, a person's sense of commitment or responsibility is strongly a function of his boss's style of supervision.

[14] M. Scott Myers, "Conditions for Manager Motivation," *Harvard Business Review*, January–February, 1966.

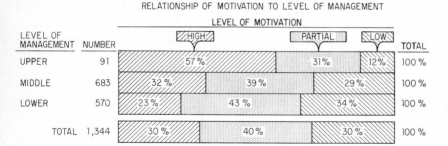

RELATIONSHIP OF MOTIVATION TO LEVEL OF MANAGEMENT

LEVEL OF MOTIVATION

LEVEL OF MANAGEMENT	NUMBER	HIGH	PARTIAL	LOW	TOTAL
UPPER	91	57%	31%	12%	100%
MIDDLE	683	32%	39%	29%	100%
LOWER	570	23%	43%	34%	100%
TOTAL	1,344	30%	40%	30%	100%

RELATIONSHIP OF MOTIVATION TO BOSS'S STYLE

BOSS'S STYLE

LEVEL OF MOTIVATION	NUMBER	DEVELOPMENTAL	TRADITIONAL	REDUCTIVE	TOTAL
HIGH	403	52%	40%	8%	100%
PARTIAL	538	30%	48%	22%	100%
LOW	403	8% 29%	63%		100%
TOTAL	1,344	30%	40%	30%	100%

FIG. 1-3   Motivation related to organizational level and style of supervision.

- *Recognition,* as a motivation need, refers to earned recognition stemming from meritorious performance. Unearned recognition of friendliness, defined as a condition of security in the outer circle, is needed for keeping communication channels open so that when vital issues arise, they may be surfaced and dealt with. But, within the inner circle, recognition as positive feedback for a job well done is a reinforcement of motivated behavior. Recognition at its best does not depend on the value judgments of an authority figure to translate achievements into praise, advancements, respect, awards, pay increases, and other rewards. Recognition dispensed by value judgment places unjustified faith in the objectivity, reliability, sensitivity, attentiveness, and competence of the judge, and tends to foster dependency relationships.

  Ideally, recognition should not depend on an intermediary, but should be a natural expression of feedback from achievement itself. When the astronauts landed on the moon, or when Jonas Salk discovered polio vaccine, or when Babe Ruth batted a home run (or when Casey struck out!), they didn't need a supervisor to give them recognition. They received feedback naturally and spontaneously, and the quality of this feedback was not distorted by the interpretation of an intermediary. Hence, recognition at its best is primarily an expression of direct feedback.

Though achievement and responsibility may be their own rewards, they too are reinforced when someone upon whom the individual depends for continuing opportunity recognizes him for his achievements. As long as the supervisor's authority is the basis for continuing opportunity and his judgment is the basis for pay and status changes, his feelings are a necessary part of the feedback.

The Need for Equilibrium   The relative importance of the four motivation needs and of the six maintenance needs is situational, as can easily be seen in an everyday situation. For example, a given maintenance need, such as "physical," may loom as the most important if it is the main source of current dissatisfaction. But once the air-conditioning or noise-level problem, or whatever is the focus of concern, is solved, other factors may assume greater importance. If product obsolescence and organizational stagnation stymie growth opportunity, growth needs assume greater importance. However, thwarted growth needs are often misleadingly displaced and expressed as amplified concern for maintenance factors. Increasingly, the real problems of people at work are lack of inner-circle opportunities, though outer-circle factors linger as the issue of conflict, as noted on pages 217 and 218. Both maintenance and motivational needs must be satisfied, not so that one can replace the other but rather to provide better balance between the two.

People in upper levels of management have relatively more opportunity to satisfy inner-circle needs, but they devote much of their effort in coping with "labor" problems stemming from the inability of people at lower levels to get into the inner circle. Management's mission, then, must be to get people into the inner circle, not for reasons of altruism or as missionaries for participation, but rather as a sound business strategy to provide outlets for human talent in the pursuit of organizational goals.

The Texas Instruments Motivation Seminar

The preceding intellectual message is the foundation for the Texas Instruments motivation seminar. Though the scope, content, and duration of the seminar vary with the trainer and operation, the basic outline includes six 2-hour sessions:

1. State objectives. The role of theory; review research.
2. Development of a theory; relationship to other theories.
3. Self-examination. Application of theory to filmed problem.
4. Texas Instruments management philosophy as foundation for motivation. Home assignment.
5. Application of theory to actual problems.
6. Application of theory to actual problems. Self-evaluation.

The seminar is conducted with peer groups of eight to twelve supervisors, usually from a common operation. It is desirable to mix the mainstream and staff support personnel in the seminar to reinforce the total team concept and to overcome the functional isolation sometimes encountered. Participation in the seminar is largely voluntary, but is encouraged by the fact that the president and vice-presidents initiated the program by their participation and support.

In the first session the objectives of the seminar are defined:

1. To develop an understanding of a useful theory of management.
2. To stimulate participants to examine their supervisory jobs in terms of opportunities to apply principles and techniques of motivation theory.
3. To develop attitudes and skills necessary for day-to-day application of motivation theory.

Also during the first session each participant is asked to discuss theories or concepts he found useful in supervision. The universal application of theory, consciously or subconsciously, is established. Texas Instruments motivation research is described and illustrative data are gathered from participants and interpreted in terms of motivation-maintenance theory.

Session 2 includes lecture and discussion to give participants an understanding of the intellectual message presented on pages 10 to 16. Discussion of the relationship between motivation-maintenance theory and other theories such as those presented in Figure 1-1 is optionally included.

Session 3 begins with a question-and-answer period followed by a multiple-choice test of knowledge of motivation-maintenance theory. Papers are self-scored from answers furnished orally by the conference leader, and incorrect responses are discussed and clarified. A 10-minute filmed problem in delegation is presented and analyzed by the participants.

Session 4 begins with a lecture-discussion on Texas Instruments' management philosophy, an analysis of organizational climate factors, and examples of the intended use and the undesired abuse of management systems. Participants are given a home assignment to prepare a list of previous, current, or anticipated problems in motivation and to categorize them by motivation-maintenance criteria.

Session 5 begins with a blackboard listing of motivation problems compiled by the participants. Each participant elaborates on his problem and presents his motivation-maintenance diagnosis of it. Participants as a total group, or in subgroups, analyze problems or groups of problems.

Session 6 is usually a continuation of problem analysis and is concluded with a self-evaluation in terms of McGregor's theory X and theory Y assumptions, as illustrated in Figure 2-2. Session 6 is often extended into additional application sessions at the option of the participants.

Further Examples of Theory Translation

The translation of theory ideally has the potential for influencing the person to be changed in four ways; first, to discover and accept the fact that he has a problem; second, to provide insights and procedures for diagnosing the problem; third, to provide a frame of reference and a systematic approach for implementing remedial actions; and finally, to enable him to measure his progress. Innovative approaches for translating theory are unlimited, and the Texas Instruments motivation seminar and the four examples below serve simply to illustrate five separate and potentially successful translation processes.

Analysis of Assumptions and Styles of Management   Many training programs have based management development efforts on the concepts of McGregor's theory X and theory Y summarized in Figure 2-1 on page 29. Figures 1-4 and 1-5 are work sheets to enable individuals to define their own assumptions about people and to describe their supervisor's style of managing. In completing the statements about his assumptions, the supervisor is able to determine where he falls on the theory X–theory Y continuum. The system is limited, of course, by its brevity and by the deliberate or subconscious desire of the individual to provide the "correct" answers rather than the ones that describe his actual assumptions. The supervisory style work sheet,

Statements below, arranged in pairs, represent assumptions about people. Assign a weight from 0 to 10 to each statement to show the relative strength of your belief in the statements in each pair. The points assigned for each pair must in each case total 10.

1 –   It's only human nature for people to do as little work as they can get away with.
 –   When people avoid work, it's usually because their work has been deprived of its meaning.   _____
           10

2 –   If employees have access to any information they want, they tend to have better attitudes and behave more responsibly.
 –   If employees have access to more information than they need to do their immediate tasks, they will usually misuse it.   _____
           10

3 –   One problem in asking for the ideas of employees is that their perspective is too limited for their suggestions to be of much practical value.
 –   Asking employees for their ideas broadens their perspective and results in the development of useful suggestions.   _____
           10

4 –   If people don't use much imagination and ingenuity on the job, it's probably because relatively few people have much of either.
 –   Most people are imaginative and creative but may not show it because of limitations imposed by supervision and the job.   _____
           10

5 –   People tend to raise their standards if they are accountable for their own behavior and for correcting their own mistakes.
 –   People tend to lower their standards if they are not punished for their misbehavior and mistakes.   _____
           10

6 –   It's better to give people both good and bad news because most employees want the whole story, no matter how painful it is.
 –   It's better to withhold unfavorable news about business because most employees really want to hear only the good news.   _____
           10

7 –   Because a supervisor is entitled to more respect than those below him in the organization, it weakens his prestige to admit that a subordinate was right and he was wrong.
 –   Because people at all levels are entitled to equal respect, a supervisor's prestige is increased when he supports this principle by admitting that a subordinate was right and he was wrong.   _____
           10

8 –   If you give people enough money, they are less likely to be concerned with such intangibles as responsibility and recognition.
 –   If you give people interesting and challenging work, they are less likely to complain about such things as pay and supplemental benefits.   _____
           10

9 –   If people are allowed to set their own goals and standards of performance, they tend to set them higher than the boss would.
 –   If people are allowed to set their own goals and standards of performance, they tend to set them lower than the boss would.   _____
           10

10 –   The more knowledge and freedom a person has regarding his job, the more controls are needed to keep him in line.
 –   The more knowledge and freedom a person has regarding his job, the fewer controls are needed to insure satisfactory job performance.   _____
           10

FIG. 1-4 My assumptions.

particularly if completed by his subordinates, represents a validity check on his own self-defined assumptions. Use of these two work sheets helps illustrate the distinction between, as well as the interdependence of, values and behavior. When they are used in conjunction with problem analysis, such as sessions 5 and 6 in the Texas Instruments motivation seminar, managers develop an understanding of their need not only to change their supervisory practices, but

Statements below, arranged in pairs, represent supervisory style. Assign a weight from 0 to 10 to each statement to show the relative accuracy of the statements in each pair for describing your supervisor's style. The points assigned for each pair must in each case total 10.

1 - Easy to talk to, even when under pressure.
  - You have to pick carefully the time when you talk to him.
                                                                          _____
                                                                            10

2 - May ask for ideas, but usually his mind is already made up.
  - Tries to see the merit in your ideas even if they conflict with his.
                                                                          _____
                                                                            10

3 - Tries to help his people understand company objectives.
  - Lets his people figure out for themselves how company objectives apply to them.
                                                                          _____
                                                                            10

4 - Tries to give his people access to all the information they want.
  - Gives his people the information he thinks they need.
                                                                          _____
                                                                            10

5 - Tends to set his people's job goals and tell them how to achieve them.
  - Involves his people in solving problems and setting job goals.
                                                                          _____
                                                                            10

6 - Tends to discourage his people from trying new approaches.
  - Tries to encourage people to reach out in new directions.
                                                                          _____
                                                                            10

7 - Takes your mistakes in stride, so long as you learn from them.
  - Allows little room for mistakes, especially those that might embarrass him.
                                                                          _____
                                                                            10

8 - Tries mainly to correct mistakes and figure out how they can be prevented in the future.
  - When something goes wrong, tries primarily to find out who caused it.
                                                                          _____
                                                                            10

9 - His expectations of subordinates tend to fluctuate.
  - Consistent, high expectations of subordinates.
                                                                          _____
                                                                            10

10 - Expects superior performance and gives credit when you do it.
  - Expects you to do an adequate job, doesn't say much unless something goes wrong.
                                                                          _____
                                                                            10

FIG. 1-5 My supervisor's style.

more importantly, to embark on the long-range process of acquiring additional insights and changed values and habits.

Profile of Organizational Characteristics   Rensis Likert's four systems are translated into meaningful exercises by a profiling process illustrated in abbreviated form in Figure 1-6. Individuals or groups may collaborate in completing this questionnaire by consensus or averages, diagnosing the organization in terms of leadership, motivation, communication, decisions, goals, and control processes. Typically a group will profile the actual and ideal pattern for their organization. The difference between the actual and the ideal represents the challenge or goal to be undertaken within the organization through the appropriate mix of individuals, levels, and functions. Participation in the problem-solving task forces can result in the development of remedial strategies and commitment to their implementation. The comparison of current conditions against previous profiles provides the system user with feedback on the success of his remedial actions.

Blake's Managerial Grid Blake and Mouton's two-factor grid, illustrated in Figure 1-7, is a basis for individuals and groups to diagnose their own managerial styles and the styles of others in terms of

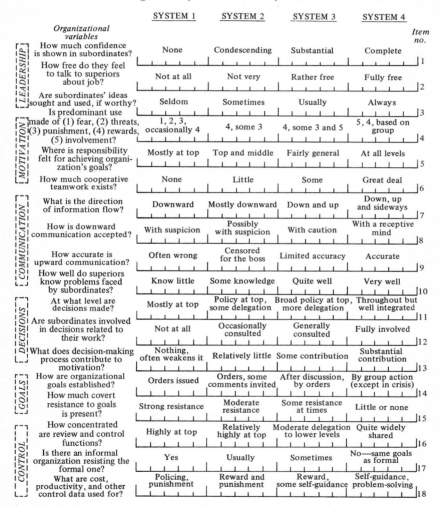

Organizational variables	SYSTEM 1	SYSTEM 2	SYSTEM 3	SYSTEM 4	Item no.
LEADERSHIP — How much confidence is shown in subordinates?	None	Condescending	Substantial	Complete	1
How free do they feel to talk to superiors about job?	Not at all	Not very	Rather free	Fully free	2
Are subordinates' ideas sought and used, if worthy?	Seldom	Sometimes	Usually	Always	3
MOTIVATION — Is predominant use made of (1) fear, (2) threats, (3) punishment, (4) rewards, (5) involvement?	1, 2, 3, occasionally 4	4, some 3	4, some 3 and 5	5, 4, based on group	4
Where is responsibility felt for achieving organization's goals?	Mostly at top	Top and middle	Fairly general	At all levels	5
How much cooperative teamwork exists?	None	Little	Some	Great deal	6
COMMUNICATION — What is the direction of information flow?	Downward	Mostly downward	Down and up	Down, up and sideways	7
How is downward communication accepted?	With suspicion	Possibly with suspicion	With caution	With a receptive mind	8
How accurate is upward communication?	Often wrong	Censored for the boss	Limited accuracy	Accurate	9
How well do superiors know problems faced by subordinates?	Know little	Some knowledge	Quite well	Very well	10
DECISIONS — At what level are decisions made?	Mostly at top	Policy at top, some delegation	Broad policy at top, more delegation	Throughout but well integrated	11
Are subordinates involved in decisions related to their work?	Not at all	Occasionally consulted	Generally consulted	Fully involved	12
What does decision-making process contribute to motivation?	Nothing, often weakens it	Relatively little	Some contribution	Substantial contribution	13
GOALS — How are organizational goals established?	Orders issued	Orders, some comments invited	After discussion, by orders	By group action (except in crisis)	14
How much covert resistance to goals is present?	Strong resistance	Moderate resistance	Some resistance at times	Little or none	15
CONTROL — How concentrated are review and control functions?	Highly at top	Relatively highly at top	Moderate delegation to lower levels	Quite widely shared	16
Is there an informal organization resisting the formal one?	Yes	Usually	Sometimes	No----same goals as formal	17
What are cost, productivity, and other control data used for?	Policing, punishment	Reward and punishment	Reward, some self-guidance	Self-guidance, problem-solving	18

FIG. 1-6 Profile of organizational characteristics.

concern for production and people. By completing questionnaires in which they describe actual behavior and define ideal styles, they become focused on the mission of developing 9,9 managerial style and strategies for the organization. The marketing of the managerial grid illustrates the potential that can be exploited for any sound theory when the application of a theory is backed by strong entrepreneurial interests. Blake and his associates have written five textbooks providing theoretical and testimonial evidence of the usefulness of the grid and, at the writing of this book, the grid marketing brochures for a one-year period included schedules for public seminars at sixty-three locations—twenty-seven within the United States and thirty-six elsewhere throughout the world.

Power Structure Seminar   John Paré has developed a profiling system to enable individuals and groups to diagnose the power structure

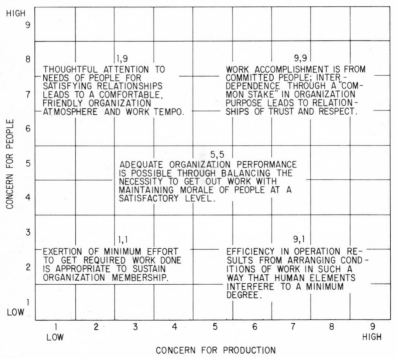

FIG. 1-7   The managerial grid. (R. R. Blake and J. S. Mouton, *The Managerial Grid,* **Gulf Publishing Company, Houston, 1964, p. 10.)**

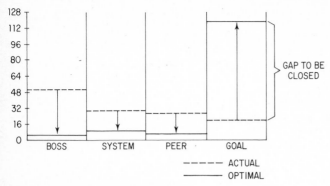

FIG. 1-8   Power structure profile sheet.

within retail store operations in terms of the four sources of power reflected in Figure 1-8. After diagnosing the actual structure and concurring on optimal structure, the group then becomes involved in formulating strategies for overcoming the gap between actual and optimal. The power structure seminar has been highly successful in increasing organizational effectiveness in department stores, and its application illustrates a phenomenon noted in the discussion of management systems on pages 126 and 127. People's attitudes and perceptions are a primary cause of a system's successes and failures, and the success of the power structure seminar in replacing other theory applications is probably as much a function of the attitudes of the users as it is of the intrinsic characteristics of the system itself.

chapter two

Conditions for Human Effectiveness

This chapter attempts to integrate three strategies commonly used as the focus for organizational development: human relations, management by objectives, and the systems approach. Human relations gained emphasis when experiments in the 1920s showed that the depersonalizing processes of the Industrial Revolution needed an antidote. However, neither organizational effectiveness nor human relationships can be maximized in the absence of meaningful goals for achieving them. The Industrial Revolution, with its emphasis on the scientific method, and, more recently, management systems specialists have attempted to organize material and humans, but neither has had sufficient regard for the needs of the humans who must make the systems work. Proponents of management by objectives, while recognizing the need for aligning people's goals and their systems with organizational goals, have not placed sufficient emphasis on this strategy at the lower levels of the organization.

Human relations, management by objectives, and the systems approach collectively have the potential for overcoming the shortcomings of any one of these strategies. Labeled herein as interpersonal competence, meaningful goals, and helpful systems, these three conditions are shown to be interdependent and essential for organizational effectiveness at all levels. And because all management is the management of human effort, the purpose of the combined strategies is human effectiveness.

INTERPERSONAL COMPETENCE

Interpersonal competence in industry refers to ideal relationships among people at work, united in the pursuit of compatible personal and organizational goals. Interpersonal competence is generally a function of two factors: managerial style and the systems framework of the organization. Generally speaking, both managerial style and management systems reflect the values of managers and, hence, the philosophy of the organization. Interpersonal competence is discussed here in terms of the informal relationships among members of the organization and in terms of the influence of managerial assumptions, particularly those assumptions that find expression in the reductive or constructive use of authority.

The formal systems in business and industry reflect the values of the people who developed the systems and who administer them. The organization culture which arises in support of, in spite of, or in reaction to the formal structure of industry may be termed the informal organization of industry. It is not reflected on organization charts, nor is it always acknowledged by management. But nonetheless, it is the medium through which interpersonal competence or conflict finds expression.

The Informal Organization of Industry

Organizational relationships are usually defined formally through organization charts and job descriptions. Though formal relationships are the basis for many informal relationships, many social and technical (sociotechnical) relationships form quite independently of the formal organization. People may form social or "primary"[1] groups because they do the same kind of work, are of similar ethnic or regional origin, have similar interests, are the same age or sex, or have similar seniority in the firm. However, more often they come together

[1] J. A. C. Brown, *The Social Psychology of Industry*, Penguin Books, Inc., Baltimore, 1965, pp. 124–256.

simply because they are near each other in the work area. The structure of a primary group is not stable, but changes in a fluid process as membership, job relationships, and work assignments change and events occur that alter the roles of individuals within the group. Primary groups based on work-station relationships may be preempted by other primary-group memberships in other role relationships such as in ride pools, the coffee bar or lunch room, and bowling teams. However, these other groups do not detract from the work-group membership and, in fact, may even be a source of its enrichment.

Large organizations are composed of small informal groups held together by the process of face-to-face communication. A primary group will sometimes develop its own jargon, which tends to create group solidarity and serves as a means of identifying group membership. These small primary groups vary in size, but average six to ten people. Because problems of communication increase with the size of the group, a group tends to break up or subdivide after it has reached a certain critical size.

When a person enters a job with the intention of permanent employment, he will naturally strive to succeed and develop primary-group relationships. Interpersonal competence through primary groups is most likely to exist in skilled trades where turnover is low, where the plant is located in a relatively small and stable community, and where the work force is stable and not subject to fluctuations of seasonal employment, temporary help, layoffs, or high turnover for whatever reason.

The primary group is the medium through which individuals acquire their attitudes, values, and goals. It is also a fundamental source of discipline and social control. Members of primary or natural work groups expect a fair share of the group's work from each other, and will rally against the member who benefits at the expense of another. Because the informal working group is the main source of social control, attempts to change human behavior should be made through the medium of the group rather than through the individual. The supervisor should try to exercise legitimate influence through such groups and should avoid breaking them up.

John Paul Jones[2] has enumerated five conditions, summarized

---

[2] John Paul Jones, *The Ties that Bind*, National Association of Manufacturers, New York, pp. 21–23, 1967.

below, which exist in an effective primary group or team:

1. *Mutual trust.* Mutual trust takes a long time to build and can be destroyed quickly. It is established in a team when every member feels free to express his opinion, say how he feels about issues and ask questions which may display his ignorance and disagree with any position, without concern for retaliation, ridicule or negative consequences.

2. *Mutual support.* Mutual support results from group members having genuine concern for each other's job welfare, growth and personal success. If mutual support is established in a team, a member need not waste time and energy protecting himself or his function from anyone else. All will give and receive help to and from each other in accomplishing whatever object the team is working on.

3. *Genuine communication.* Communication has two dimensions: the quality of openness and authenticity of the member who is speaking, and the quality of non-evaluative listening by other members. Open authentic communication takes place when mutual trust and support are so well established that no member feels he has to be guarded or cautious about what he says. It also means that members of a good team won't "play games" with each other, such as by asking "trap" questions or suggesting wrong answers to test another member's integrity. Non-evaluative listening simply means listening with "bias-filters" removed to what the other person is trying to communicate. Most persons listen through an evaluative screen and tend to hear only those aspects of a communication which do not threaten status, roles and convictions.

4. *Accepting conflicts as normal and working them through.* Individuals differ uniquely from one another and will not agree on many things. An unproductive heritage left by the old school of "human relations" is the notion that people should strive for harmony at all costs. A good team (where mutual trust, mutual support and genuine communication are well established) accepts conflict as normal, natural and as an asset, since it is from conflict that most growth and innovation are derived. It is also worth noting that conflict resolution is a group process, and the notion that a manager can resolve a conflict between or among subordinates is a myth.

5. *Mutual respect for individual differences.* There are decisions which, in a goal-oriented team, must be team decisions because they require the commitment of most or all of the resources of the team and cannot be implemented without this commitment. However, a good team will not demand unnecessary conformity of its members. It is easy for a group to drift into the practice of making decisions for or forcing decisions on an individual where clearly, for his own growth and for the good of the organization, he should make the decision. The individual member should be free to ask advice from other members who, in turn, will recognize that he is not obligated to take the advice. A good team delegates within itself. In a well established team, with high mutual trust and support, the leader, or any member, will be able to make a decision which commits the

team. In such a team, only important issues need to be "worked through," and there is much delegation from leader to members, from members to members and even from members to leader.

The leader of a primary group is not only a member of his own working unit; he also joins with other primary-group leaders to form a higher-echelon group whose members act as "linking pins"[3] in maintaining contact among the primary groups. This overlapping membership is necessary to make an organic whole of a larger complex organization—sometimes referred to as the secondary group. Attitudes of individuals toward the secondary group are usually determined by the extent to which its goals coincide, or conflict, with the goals of their own primary group. When all the primary groups within a secondary group direct their efforts toward a common goal, organizational cohesiveness is maximized.

A crowd or mob is different from the primary or secondary group. Members of a mob are usually not acting through primary- or secondary-group memberships, typically have no established interpersonal relationships, and do not subordinate their impulses to a functional task. Each member remains virtually anonymous and lost in the mass. The effect of the crowd on its members is largely contagious, and normally quiet and thoughtful citizens may cast aside inhibitions connected with their family, their neighbors, the law, and their work, and participate in thoughtless violence.

Supervisory behavior is a key factor at all levels of the organization in permitting the natural formation of primary groups out of what might otherwise be a mob or anonymous individuals lost in the mass. Moreover, leadership style determines whether primary groups are united in support of, or in rebellion against, the formal organization.

A supervisor's behavior at any level is a function of his own values and his fulfillment of role expectations dictated by systems and people above him in the organization. Hence, the values of top management are the key determinant of organizational climate as created by supervisory behavior and management systems. As noted earlier, Douglas McGregor explained managerial style as a function of the manager's assumptions about people.[4] He defined assumptions in terms of their

[3] Rensis Likert, *The Human Organization*, McGraw-Hill Book Company, New York, 1967, p. 50.

[4] Douglas McGregor, *The Human Side of Enterprise*, McGraw-Hill Book Company, New York, 1960.

Theory X assumptions	Theory Y assumptions
People by nature:	People by nature:
1. Lack integrity.	1. Have integrity.
2. Are fundamentally lazy and desire to work as little as possible.	2. Work hard toward objectives to which they are committed.
3. Avoid responsibility.	3. Assume responsibility within these commitments.
4. Are not interested in achievement.	4. Desire to achieve.
5. Are incapable of directing their own behavior.	5. Are capable of directing their own behavior.
6. Are indifferent to organizational needs.	6. Want their organization to succeed.
7. Prefer to be directed by others.	7. Are not passive and submissive.
8. Avoid making decisions whenever possible.	8. Will make decisions within their commitments.
9. Are not very bright.	9. Are not stupid.

FIG. 2-1 Supervisory assumptions.

position on a theory X–theory Y *continuum,* as summarized by John Paul Jones[5] in Figure 2-1.

Supervisory Assumptions

The goal-oriented, developmental (theory Y) supervisor embraces a set of values which reflects confidence in, and respect for, his fellow man. Though he recognizes that not all persons have earned respect and confidence, he assumes that they are capable of doing so and presumes that an individual is competent and has integrity until he learns otherwise.

He recognizes that many people find work unpleasant, but tends to see this as more of an indictment of job design or supervision than of the inherent characteristics of the job incumbent. He believes that people are not naturally lazy, but seem so when work has been

[5] Jones, *op cit.,* p. 15.

deprived of its meaning. He assumes that most people are imaginative and creative, and that if they fail to display these traits, it is largely a result of constraints imposed by supervision or apathy stemming from the absence of challenge. He believes that freedom and responsibility go hand in hand and that the more information he shares with people, the more they will tend to think and behave responsibly. He has consistently high expectations of others and assumes that, with access to information and freedom to pursue goals, they will set and achieve high goals without continuing intervention.[6] In his view, it is better to give people both good and bad news, believing most people capable of accepting the whole story, no matter how painful it is. He assumes that mistakes are inevitable and should provide a basis for learning, as punishment tends primarily to evoke defensiveness. Though he recognizes the importance of money and believes that it should be distributed according to merit, he assumes that most people are more strongly motivated by interesting and challenging work.

The authority-oriented, reductive (theory X) supervisor, in contrast, tends to quash initiative or evoke defensiveness through behavior reflecting lack of confidence in and respect for others. Though his assumptions cannot be neatly catalogued as a pure syndrome, the following characteristics usually cluster together. He assumes it only natural for people to do as little work as possible, and believes close supervision and a little fear are needed to prevent them from lowering their standards or to push them toward higher goals. In his opinion, few people have much imagination and ingenuity, and their perspective is too limited to expect them to provide realistic suggestions. Moreover, he interprets his role as "superior" literally, assumes that it entitles him to respect, and believes his prestige would be weakened if he asked for suggestions or admitted to the superiority of a subordinate's ideas. He assumes that people are not usually responsible, are not to be trusted with information, and are not capable of accepting unpleasant news. The more knowledge and freedom people have regarding their job, the more controls are assumed to be needed to keep them in line because, "if you give them an inch, they'll take a mile." Though he readily admits that people like responsibility, recognition, and other forms of "mollycoddling," he feels that they

---

[6] For further elaboration on the role of a manager's expectations, see J. Sterling Livingston, "Pygmalion in management," *Harvard Business Review*, pp. 81–89, July-August, 1969.

are bound to gripe about something, and the only real way to motivate them and keep them happy is to give them enough money. He is usually unable to differentiate between happiness and motivation.

Supervisory Style

The supervisory style of the goal-oriented manager is characterized by balanced concern for the needs of the organization and its members. His behavior reflects confidence in, and respect for, others. He takes time out, even during busy schedules, to listen, and will attempt to see the merit of ideas which conflict with his own. He solves problems by sharing company information with people under his supervision and by involving them in solving problems and setting goals. He encourages people to reach out in new directions, taking mistakes in stride, and tries mainly to discover how they can be avoided in the future. He expects and acknowledges superior performance.

Authoritarian assumptions more often find expression in a style of management which reflects high concern for the organization or self, but little concern or respect for its members. He sets job goals for his subordinates (or abandons the subordinates, leaving them without the information that would enable them to set their own goals), doles out information, discourages them from deviating from specified procedures, expects adequate performance, and says little unless something goes wrong. In paying lip service to new theory, he may ask for ideas, but his mind is usually already made up, and when confronted with conflict, he may try to suppress it or may capitulate by attempting to appease the troublemakers. There is little room for mistakes in his organization, especially mistakes that might embarrass him. When something goes wrong, he tries primarily to find out who caused it, and he sees to it that the culprit is punished.

Trends in organization development are leading away from authority orientation as a foundation for human effectiveness. Few thoughtful managers today would deliberately defend the traditional application of authority. Most managers have assisted in the preparation of formal statements of philosophy to idealize their organization as democratically goal-oriented, and they may have conscientiously committed themselves to this principle through both written and spoken words. However, in many ways, both subtle and flagrant, as a result of habit, tradition, policy, systems, insensitivity, and introspective myopia, some managers create and perpetuate an orientation to the power of authority.

The Reductive Use of Authority

The most overt forms of authority orientation are reflected in "superior-subordinate" relationships which imply "ownership" of subordinates by the supervisor. The supervisor demands rather than requests actions from his subordinates, and will, for example, without apparent consideration for their convenience, summon them to his office or otherwise interrupt their activity. He phones orders to underlings without inquiring about their availability, or simply barks to the subordinate's secretary, for example, "Tell Bill to come to my office." Though he may drive his points home in meetings by shouting and pounding the conference table, he makes it generally understood that subordinates will not respond with shouting and table pounding. He preempts conference rooms reserved by subordinates, calls subordinates out of training programs, bypasses a subordinate's secretary, interrupts subordinates' staff meetings, preempts social relationships and commitments, conscripts a subordinate's secretary for personal use or to lend to some higher-up, or criticizes a subordinate's mode of dress or hair style, reminding him with an authority-laden smile that, "There are no sideburns at the top, Dave."

Tradition has bestowed rank with privileges so commonplace that they find unquestioned acceptance, usually without conscious awareness of their original and lingering significance. Class distinctions are created or reinforced through authority-based privileges and symbols such as exclusive dining and parking facilities, office size and furnishings, distinctive identification badges, and mode of attire. Special coffee service, exemption from parking rules, disregard of time signal bells, nonobservance of lunch and coffee schedules, and circumvention of job-posting procedures are examples of common privileges of rank, unthinkingly or flagrantly perpetuated by managers long after they have declared themselves officially against authority orientation. Symbols associated with these privileges tend to increase social distance and inhibit communication, thus creating and exaggerating cleavages between groups at various levels of the organization.

The authority-oriented supervisor rarely stands on convictions born of professional competence but, rather, devotes much of his energy to aligning himself with the power structure of the organization. If a project managed by a subordinate is viewed favorably by upper management, he becomes identified with it and gradually and subtly reverses the delegation process until he is pulled into the limelight and becomes the official spokesman for the project. The subordinate, characteristically led on with expectations of presenting a proposal personally, completes the necessary research and development work, only to have the boss whisk it away to an unknown fate. If the project loses favor in the eyes of upper management, the boss quickly divests himself of it by redelegating it.

The "chain of command" is the authoritarian's primary basis for both official and unofficial relationships. He expects all information to flow upward or downward through him or other "official channels." A subordinate who wishes to contact a member at his boss's level or above, for example, to be guest speaker at a graduation banquet, soon learns that the transaction must be performed by the boss. However, the subordinate is free to contact those at his own level or below. The authority-oriented person tends to choose persons at his own level or above for luncheon dates or social activities, though he would find it acceptable to accompany a *group* of his subordinates to lunch. For him, social stratification within, and even outside, the organization is determined largely by position in the official hierarchy.

If one of the authoritarian's subordinates loses favor with a higher-up, for whatever reason, his own perception of the subordinate is altered, and he readily turns and "takes the second bite" at the heels of the subordinate. He may salve his conscience by uttering feeble demurrals, damning the subordinate with faint praise, but will ultimately acquiesce and obediently perform the painful ceremony of admonishment, transfer, demotion, or termination with the courage displayed by all official ax men.

Occasionally, goal-oriented work groups form within the authoritarian's organization, made up of individuals whose professional competence immunizes them against his arbitrary use of power. He holds them in awe because he respects power of any kind, and as long as they incur top management favor and support, he does not stand in their way. However, his relationship to them is not usually one of goal-oriented reciprocity. For the authoritarian, solidarity or equality is an uncomfortable experience. Hence, he tends to abandon them or disengage himself from involvement in their efforts. If the group finally disbands and leaves his organization in reaction to his style of leadership, and he is faced with the mission of restaffing the vacated positions, he vows he will never again let another "power base" develop within his organization!

Slightly more subtle are the cat-and-mouse tactics employed by the boss to remind underlings that their security and freedom exist only through his magnanimity. The arbitrary withholding and dispensing of information according to whim, the last-moment scheduling or cancelling of meetings, the delaying and extending of staff meetings, the extraction of "reasons" for personal leave, the selective distribution of homemade Christmas cakes to his favorites, and the dog-in-the-manger authorization to use company-financed club facilities are examples of more subtle misuse of authority.

When the authoritarian supervisor chairs a staff meeting, for example, to solve a problem or to evaluate a proposal, his subordinates develop an infallible method for taking the "right" position on any issue: they learn to read his facial expression! They sit in silence until the chief speaks and then converge on an elaboration of his viewpoint. So firmly established become these cue-reading patterns that subordinates, as well as the boss, are often deceived into interpreting conformity as consensus.

The boss's authority is often adopted by his secretary through a process of authority by association. His secretary's "requests" for information frequently come through as orders to subordinates and their secretaries. Exempted from timekeeping regulations, rotational relief assignments, and many standard ground rules, she gradually activates a conditioning process which increases subordinate acquiescence and alienation, and also increases her secretarial imperiousness. Attempts to give feedback to the boss regarding his secretary's "little-dictator" syndrome characteristically evoke a defensiveness that effectively shuts off future feedback attempts.

Perhaps the most discouraging aspect of the misuse of authority is the supervisor's insensitivity to his syndrome. It should be noted that authority orientation is not usually an expression of intentional or deliberate malice. It is usually a form of pathology, perhaps a result of years of adapting to authoritarianism in the home, schools, the church, the armed forces, and previous jobs. The intelligent authoritarian typically experiences occasional flashes of insight and brief periods of remorse. In fact, a true authoritarian is also a masochist who pathologically enjoys punishment or criticism—as long as it comes from a respected authority and represents an opportunity for atonement from which he can recover. When he becomes aware of alienation in his group, he may attempt to win goodwill through the paternalistic generosity of an office party, a home barbecue, a Christmas turkey, or other irrelevant tactics. Paternalism, of course, only increases social distance. His attempts to change are sincere, but most such attempts are superficial veneers which fail to conceal the real personality that he exposes through his day-by-day language of action.

Finally, it must be noted that the authority-oriented supervisor should not bear the full brunt of his ineptness. The managers above him, who appointed him and reinforced his behavior through rewards, authoritarian systems, and their own leadership styles are the primary problem. If he *can* change, he certainly will not do it until he gets different cues from above, as his behavior largely reflects his attempts, usually subconscious, to build himself in their image.

Figure 2-2 shows how 1,344 managers were described by highly motivated and poorly motivated subordinates.[7] Highly motivated managers use descriptors characterizing goal-oriented supervisors, defined on page 31. Poorly motivated managers were almost evenly balanced in describing their boss as authority-oriented or goal-oriented, with some emphasis on reductive descriptors. These results suggest that interpersonal competence, as defined in these terms, is a requisite for high motivation, but that interpersonal competence alone does not ensure it. Other requirements for high motivation are meaningful goals and helpful systems, as portrayed in Figure 2-8 and discussed in the following pages.

MEANINGFUL GOALS

Everyone has goals. Some goals are set by the individuals pursuing them, some are set with the participation of others, some are set exclusively by others. Generally speaking, individuals most actively pursue the goals they set themselves. When too many of a person's goals are set by others, he reacts individually or collectively to set goals to circumvent, violate, or change these goals. These goals of avoid-

[7] M. Scott Myers, "Conditions for Manager Motivation," *Harvard Business Review,* p. 63, January–February, 1966.

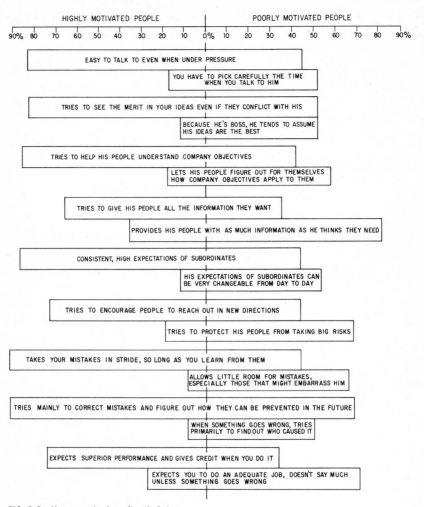

FIG. 2-2 How people describe their bosses.

ance and rebellion then become personal goals. Therein lies the crux of the problem of goal setting in industry.

The higher a person's position in the organization, the more degrees of freedom he has to set goals. If the man at the top defines his goals with the genuine involvement of the people below him, his goals are also their goals.

But if goal setting is a "top management" function to be "sold" downward through the use of persuasion, authority, bribery, and manipulation, his people respond with words and actions that say, "those are not my goals, they are management's goals." If "management" is seen as his enemy, the individual fights back in subtle or overt ways, often ingeniously, sometimes subconsciously, to thwart management goals; if management is perceived as benevolent and friendly, he may curb his inner frustrations, turn out a fair day's work, and appreciate their well-intended praise and rewards. But most of the time he thinks and talks about his own goals—which he finds off the job.

Some Dynamics of Goal Setting

Goals are related to satisfaction according to this equation:

$$\text{Satisfaction} = \frac{\text{achievements}}{\text{goals}}$$

Goals nearly always exceed achievements, and hence, satisfaction increases as achievements approach goals. But in reality, this satisfaction is illusory and fleeting because, as an individual's achievements approach a particular goal, he begins raising his goals or directing them elsewhere. For example, a person's goal to limit his smoking to three cigarettes per day, when achieved, may be adjusted to a goal to stop smoking altogether. When he is hungry, his immediate goal is to eat. Having satisfied that goal, he redirects his aspiration, say to reading a book or completing some office homework.

The equation also has long-range application. For example, a high school graduate's goal may be a bachelor's degree in electrical engineering. When he gains the satisfaction of attaining this goal (usually before graduation day), he sets a new goal—perhaps to get a job as an engineer in a certain company, or to pursue an advanced degree. While working toward these long-range goals, he has, of course, set and achieved (or set, failed to achieve, and readjusted) many short-range goals such as pledging a particular fraternity, earning an A in calculus, getting a passing D in history, taking a particular girl to the spring dance, winning a tennis match, and learning to parallel on snow skis.

Victor Vroom[8] defines the attractiveness of a particular goal as a function of the net desirability of any number of consequences of its attainment. Further, the level of motivation with which an individual pursues a goal is a function of the net value of the anticipated

[8] V. H. Vroom, *Work and Motivation,* John Wiley & Sons, Inc., New York, 1964.

consequences of having achieved the goal. Thus, a high school graduate may volunteer for an undesirable military assignment to earn educational assistance to get a college education which he values more
than he dislikes the military assignment. While performing his unin-
spiring military duties, he may unexpectedly discover an opportunity
to apply for a military-sponsored educational assignment which is relevant to his professional interests and which will also grant him
college credits. He pursues the assignment with newly kindled enthusiasm, for now the presumed negative value of the military assignment itself has the potential of leading to a positive outcome to be
coupled with the positive value of his long-range college plan.

Goal-setting problems often arise from supervisory assumptions
that people have little interest in organizational goals. This view stems
largely from the fact that many supervisors, not understanding the
characteristics of meaningful goals, assign only tasks or duties to
people. Tasks and duties must be performed, of course, to achieve the
supervisor's goals, but the supervisor often has little success in getting
others to perform tasks and duties with the enthusiasm he feels
toward his goals. The corrective mission, in this case, becomes one of
helping the supervisor understand the need for a framework or hierarchy of goals within the organization that is meaningful at any level.
Tasks and duties take on meaning when those who perform them can
relate them to a meaningful chunk of a hierarchy of goals and see the
relationship between their efforts and the attainment of these goals.
Job efforts have maximum meaning when they include the planning
and measurement of achievements in accordance with the plan-do-
control concept described on pages 69 and 70.

Finding a Goal-setting Arena

Most people ultimately find the arena in life in which they can
achieve goals, usually by trial-and-error processes. The new college
graduate entering industry usually finds ever-blossoming opportunities for setting and achieving increasingly higher goals. Since his
college degree opens most doors, his success in the company is largely
a function of his ambition and talent. His economic maintenance
needs are routinely met through his expanding compensation
package and are not his primary concern as long as his broadening
professional role in the organization provides growth, responsibility,
and recognition for the achievement of challenging goals. Indeed, he

may become so engrossed in self-actualizing experiences on the job that he gradually, voluntarily, and sometimes unconsciously, disengages himself from outside interests to devote ever-increasing amounts of time and energy to the job, which is *his* arena for goal setting and achievement.

But his former high school classmate who entered industry without a college degree usually finds the industrial work place only temporarily rewarding. Having escaped parental control and satisfied his immediate maintenance needs, he casts about impatiently for new opportunities, only to find them reserved for the newcomer with a degree, who is often younger and less experienced than he. His alternatives are few, difficult, and not often satisfying. He can do double duty and acquire the requisite academic credentials by attending classes after working hours, he can earn advancement through sheer talent, initiative, and perseverance, or he can abandon the organization—physically or mentally.

Most who enter industry without benefit of a college degree stay on the work force physically, job-hopping occasionally, preoccupied during duty hours with wages, hours, and working conditions, finding and gradually accepting their identity through their work roles and memberships in peer groups. But their compliant performance of simplified tasks is undemanding of their talents, and their interests and energies are channeled outward to *their* arena for self-actualization—off the job.

Off the job, the individual may satisfy growth needs through travel, reading, Toastmasters, stamp collecting, bird watching, ham radio, technical group memberships, and miscellaneous intellectual pursuits. Achievement opportunities abound in a variety of activities, such as bowling, fishing, hunting, skiing, flying, sailing, painting, stock speculation, photography, mountain climbing, linguistics, ceramics, and home workshop projects. Vicarious achievement is experienced through spectator sports, movies, television, and reading. He may experience a sense of responsibility as a scoutmaster or Sunday school teacher, and through school board membership, public office, PTA leadership, and participation in social action groups. Recognition needs may be satisfied through many of the foregoing, plus activities such as little theater, ballroom dancing, public speaking, competitive sports, and social group membership. While his contemporary with a degree is gradually channeling more of his energy into the pursuit of organizational goals, the employee without a degree is more often disengaging himself from organizational commitment and finding expression for his talents in the pursuit of meaningful goals off the job.

Hence, the manager and the worker go separate ways in pursuit of goals. The problem is circular and self-perpetuating. The manager finds he must do extra duty to make up for the lack of commitment to goals at the lower levels. But people at the lower level pursue goals outside the organization because managers have reserved the more interesting aspects of their jobs for themselves.

The Consequences of Overcommitment

It is not uncommon to encounter overcommitment to the job at the higher management levels—overcommitment in the sense that the individual is deprived of a well-rounded life of responsible citizenship. The avid corporate goal setter rarely has enough energy and time left over from his company duties to attend to his personal and professional growth, his family and community responsibilities. The more engaged he becomes in the pursuit of meaningful goals on the job, the more tunnel-visioned he becomes and the more disengaged he becomes from involvement with the members of his family, and hence, the less opportunity he has to experience goal setting within family and community units. Moreover, his family's familiarity with his vocational role is usually so fragmentary that it offers little opportunity for them to experience his achievements vicariously.

Members of the corporate goal setter's family often have life roles similar in many respects to the work roles of lower-level workers in his organization. Like the traditional hourly paid worker, they do not share his higher-order corporate goals as a foundation for their goal setting. It would be unrealistic, of course, for them to expect to share his job goals unless they were also members of his organization. Of course, however, each family, like each organization, does have unique goals which need the involvement, support, and commitment of all members of the family unit, including the person who earns the income to pay the bills. But checkbook benevolence is not an adequate substitute for personal participation. Many business organizations, however, seem to thrive, at least temporarily, at the expense of a community whose wives and children display symptoms of ennui and neuroses as a result of absentee husbands and fathers, overcommitted to corporate goals.

The Consequences of Undercommitment

The other population, comprised primarily of the hourly, nonexempt workers may have just as much imbalance in their lives. Their goal-setting efforts within the organization, because of their alienation, are often unofficial and aimed at counteracting limitations imposed by corporate goal setters. Because they have little opportunity to apply their talents in influencing company goals or in managing challenging jobs which support them, their talents find expression at work in pursuit of goals associated with wages, hours, and working conditions, which tradition and labor legislation have placed within their realm of jurisdiction. Higher wages, paid leave, broadened insurance, liberal retirement benefits, and shorter hours are only intermediate goals, of course, as they provide the means to achieve the goals which are attractive to the workers off the job. In addition, of course, the attainment of economic goals affords the satisfaction and excitement of thwarting management authority and, thus, gaining temporary respite from a monotonous existence.

In the absence of challenging jobs, workers' goals become associated with a wide spectrum of maintenance factors extrinsic to work itself. The workers seem to have capricious and vacillating interests in issues peripheral to the job, such as improving the grievance procedure, revising work rules, changing the content of the company newspaper, using the bulletin boards, getting better-sounding job titles, changing the cafeteria menu, getting the new typewriter or the chair at the end of the assembly line, avoiding the noisy work area, being located near the lunch facilities and rest rooms, and having convenient parking facilities. Goals often relate to social needs such as gaining acceptance and status within work groups, meeting friends at the coffee bar, joining a particular group at lunch time, organizing office parties, finding a congenial ride pool, planning recreational outings, and participating in special-interest-group activities.

Most nonproductive or unofficial work-place preoccupations serve primarily to make time at work more bearable or to reinforce off-the-job pursuits. As noted earlier, workers' after-hours goals involve them in sports and outings, professional societies, community projects, civic undertakings, social affairs, and family activities. Efforts directed toward these off-the-job activities sometimes seem wasteful to the corporate goal-setter. But off-the-job activities have greater potential than company activities for involving the family and, hence, for contributing to family cohesiveness and community stability. Thus, wage earners, because of their freedom from the organization, as well as their greater numbers, have a disproportionately greater influence on the values and behavior patterns of a culture.

Unfortunately, ability to meet responsible citizenship roles is inversely related to the time available to do so. When the growth and responsibility needs of people are thwarted on the job, as is often the case with wage earners, they become culturally conditioned to irresponsible maintenance-seeking habits and attitudes which handicap them for effective leadership roles in their families and community. In contrast, the corporate goal setter, whose leadership talents are often being challenged and developed through his involvement in responsible roles on the job, has the least time to utilize this competence in the family and community. Ideally then, a balance should be sought in which more of the corporate goal setter's leadership can be devoted to the community and family, and more of the wage earner's leadership talents can be developed through responsible goal-oriented job activities.

Requirements for Meaningful Goals

Meaningful goals can give meaning to almost any type of activity, on or off the job. Ideally, of course, work itself is intrinsically interesting. However, even distasteful, enervating, and humdrum activities are usually tolerated as long as they lead to meaningful goals. Otherwise, diapers would not be changed, dishes would not be washed, and lawns would not be mowed. Factors which give meaning to goals and, thus, inspire people to achieve them, may be defined in terms of the characteristics of goals themselves, and the impact that the pursuit or attainment of goals has on the goal setter.

Goals which have maximum motivational value are
1. Influenced by the goal-setter
2. Visible
3. Desirable
4. Challenging
5. Attainable

and they lead to the satisfaction of needs for
6. Growth
7. Achievement
8. Responsibility

9. Recognition
10. Affiliation
11. Security

"Company success" can be a motivational goal in satisfying the above conditions, but only in terms of criteria meaningful to each job holder. To the president, it might be return on investment, share of the served available market, or profit before taxes. To a brand manager, company success may be capturing a greater share of the market from competitive brands. An engineer's goal might be a technological breakthrough needed to solve a product performance problem. Members of an assembly line contribute to company success when they are producing units to meet quantity and quality goals which they, themselves, have set. To the extent that each of these goal setters identifies his goal with company success, and his goal meets the criteria enumerated above, it can be said that "company success" is a meaningful goal.

Consider, for contrast, goal setting through the task-force approach, as described on pages 49 and 50, versus traditional supervisory goal setting. In the task-force process, the supervisor convened the operators in a conference room, shared cost information with them, explained the company commitment to meet a goal established by the competitive bidding process, and asked for their ideas. Suggestions obtained from the operators through this conference approach led to process improvements, greater cooperation and commitment, and the attainment of goals which surpassed the competitive bid requirements.

Prior to the group problem-solving–goal-setting process, the operators had been assigned to work stations on a line balanced by engineers, and had been given job instruction by supervisory and engineering personnel. Attempts to improve the line through "better engineering" and to "motivate" the girls by persuasion and enforcement of standards did not evoke the desired performance ultimately achieved through the group process. Analysis of these two processes in terms of eleven criteria of meaningful goals, presented in Figure 2-3, shows the task force to excel the traditional approach on every point.

The eleven criteria of meaningful goals are not presented as an exhaustive list of factors which can give meaning to goals but, rather, as ideal characteristics and consequences of work itself. The relative importance of factors varies among individuals and may fluctuate for any given individual. Moreover, even meaningless work satisfies needs for money and other goals which may be extrinsic to the job. Most of the characteristics in Figure 2-3 can be, and often are, satisfied by off-the-job goals. In addition, it must be recognized that some goals are desirable simply because they represent stepping-stones to other goals.

Characteristics of meaningful goals	Task force goal-setting	Supervisory goal-setting
1 – Influenced by goal-setter	Operators participate with supervisor and others to help set goals based on analysis of problems.	Operators receive goals from supervisor, usually in terms of engineered standards.
2 – Visible	Operators see goals as customer goals in terms of quantity, quality and delivery dates.	Operators see performance goals in terms of standards established by "management."
3 – Desirable	Achievement of goals desirable for meeting personal commitments and to earn merit pay.	Achievement of goals desirable to earn merit pay and to avoid punishment.
4 – Challenging	Both mental and physical challenges to raise and achieve self-established goals.	Physical challenge to meet quantity and quality goals, and sometimes mental challenge to "beat the system."
5 – Attainable	Attainability determined by group problem-solving, consensus, and co-operation.	Goals usually established at levels where a majority can meet standard.
6 – Growth	Operators broaden perspective, develop problem-solving skills and mature attitudes.	Little on-the-job learning opportunity beyond immediate job skills.
7 – Achievement	Achievement motive recurrently stimulated and satisfied by goal-setting.	Achievement motive satisfied by attaining and exceeding standards, or by thwarting system.
8 – Responsibility	Responsibility for the project results naturally from voluntary commitment to goals.	Responsible for following instructions and being loyal to the supervisor and the company.
9 – Recognition	Recognition from within and outside the group for attainment of goals, and from prestige of group membership.	Praise from supervision for high performance, and acceptance from peers for supporting unofficial goals.
10 – Affiliation	Joint stake effort increases interpersonal competence and group cohesiveness.	Social needs satisfied through informal cliques.
11 – Security	Feelings of self-confidence fostered by knowledge and freedom.	Feelings of insecurity fostered by unpredictability of the job situation.

FIG. 2-3   A comparison of goal-setting techniques on the assembly line.

Goal-setting Opportunities in Industry

Two kinds of goal-setting opportunities exist within the organization. One of these is within the context of the work itself for which the individual was employed, and the other is in managing support systems normally administered by staff people.

Goal setting within the job situation finds natural expression in vertically enriched jobs, defined on page 63 and illustrated throughout this book. For example, problem solving–goal setting, defined on pages 81 to 87, enables members of work groups, individually and collectively, to set goals within the charter of departmental goals established by market surveys, competitive bidding, and strategic planning. The goal-setting performance review process defined on pages 164 to 169 offers opportunity for individuals to assist in establishing their short- and long-range goals, and in evaluating their own achievements. Work simplification, defined on page 191, permits goal setting as an individual or group process and, properly administered, affords many goal-setting opportunities without unnecessary intervention of supervision. In addition to these formalized processes, of course, effective supervisors routinely foster goal-setting behavior through an informal day-to-day practice of sharing information and problems with the people who are responsible for implementing the solutions.

Supplemental benefits and personnel services are administered through management systems serving employees who are in a real sense the customers or users of the system. The goals of these systems, such as group insurance, retirement, profit sharing, job posting, company newspapers, grievance procedures, and eating facilities, are usually established by top management. All these systems offer opportunity for the involvement of the users at the lower levels of the organization, as illustrated in the administration of the group insurance program on pages 176 to 180, the attitude measurement program on pages 203 to 212, and the job-posting system on pages 121 to 125.

Involvement of representative panels of users in the goal-setting process of these company programs results in the application of more talent, in the development of better systems, and in better understanding and acceptance by the users. Though the involvement of employees in planning and control functions results in what might be traditionally perceived as "nonproductive" time away from their jobs, it is often noted in practice that management systems, master-minded by top management goal setters, often evoke more resentment and hence more nonproductive efforts than systems designed through the involvement of the users.

Entrepreneurial behavior by managers is often deplored on the assumption that it results in the quashing of spirit at the lower levels of the organization. The indictment should not be made against entrepreneurial behavior, per se, but rather against reserving it only for top management. As Charles Hughes[9] points out, ideally every employee should be able to think of himself as an entrepreneur, not working for a company, but working for himself within a company, providing his services and talents in exchange for compensation and other benefits, much in the same way that a service station owner provides products and services in exchange for compensation. The difference in commitment between a service station owner-operator and a hired service station operator need not reflect the extreme contrast often in evidence. Given an opportunity to utilize his talents, a stake in the success of the enterprise, and accountability for his behavior, the hired operator could think and act like an entrepreneur.

HELPFUL SYSTEMS

When the tiny Lilliputians discovered the giant Gulliver[10] asleep on their shores, they staked him to the ground, as shown in Figure 2-4, so that when he awakened he could not move. They were acting on the assumption that anyone so large and powerful was probably dangerous. His roar of protest evoked a panicky retreat and a retaliation with tiny arrows and spears. His initial entreaties for release and offers of friendly assistance were rebuffed with suspicion, and he was transported at great expense and trouble to the Emperor. As the Lilliputians gradually became accustomed to his presence, and as he learned their language and won their trust through dialogue and helpful acts, they cautiously began freeing him. He earned their confidence, respect, and goodwill by adhering to their laws, by assisting them in their agricultural and construction activities, and by defending their shores against invaders. He was granted freedom

---

[9] Charles L. Hughes, *Goal Setting: Key to Individual and Organizational Effectiveness*, American Management Association, New York, 1965.

[10] Jonathan Swift, *Gulliver's Travels*, Macmillan & Company, New York, 1894, p. 5.

FIG. 2-4 The Lilliputians meet Gulliver. (Copyright 1894 by Macmillan & Co.)

within their specified guidelines, fed at a cost 1,700 times a Lilliputian's requirements, and given access to the Emperor.

More than 300 years later, Gulliver is reappearing in the form of giant and mysterious machines. Gulliver still talks to, and takes orders from, the Emperor of Lilliput, better known today as the "manager" in the factory. He still has a voracious appetite, and the Lilliputians sometimes feel dwarfed and frightened by him—particularly when they first see him. He is often seen as a source of oppression that takes the fun out of life at work. Many would prefer to see him staked down, and though they are assured by the Emperor that he is friendly and helpful, they must learn this from firsthand experience.

Why Play Is Fun

People's firsthand experience with recreational activities off the job provides examples of systems which could serve as models for improving systems on the job. The bowler in Figure 2-5 is attracted to the sport for a variety of reasons:

1. He has a visible goal.
2. He has a challenging but attainable goal.
3. He is working according to his own personally accepted standards.

FIG. 2-5 Why play is fun.

4. He receives immediate feedback.
5. He has opportunity to satisfy social needs.
6. He is an accepted member of a group.
7. He can earn recognition.

However, meaning could be taken away from the bowler's activity by doing to the bowling game what seems to have been done to many jobs in industry. Consider, for example, the consequences of the following modifications of the bowling game:

1. Eliminating the bowling pins so the bowler is merely rolling a ball down an empty alley.
2. Hiding the pins from the bowler by hanging a drape halfway down the alley to prevent feedback.
3. Under conditions of modification 1 or modification 2, having a "supervisor" give the bowler an opinion of how well he is doing—along with some "constructive criticism."
4. Changing the rules of the game and standards of performance without involving the bowler in the change process, or even telling him why the changes were made.
5. Preventing social interaction among bowlers or discouraging team effort.
6. Giving most of the credit and recognition to the supervisor for performance of the bowlers under his supervision.
7. Keeping bowlers on the job by threat of job security or by

paying them enough money to make the "time" in the bowling alley worth their while.

Bowling, under these conditions would, of course, lose its meaning, and bowlers would look for activities away from the bowling alley to satisfy the needs which were satisfied by the original bowling game.

When Work Is Fun

The characteristics of effective management systems, defined on pages 46 to 49, 117 to 129, and throughout this book, are examples of systems designed to satisfy the motivation and maintenance needs of people at work. These examples include the job-posting system described on pages 121 to 125 and 157 to 160, the performance review system on pages 164 to 169, the attitude survey on pages 203 to 212, work simplification on page 191, and problem solving–goal setting on pages 81 to 87.

The problem-solving–goal-setting approach satisfies many characteristics of a helpful system in that it not only leads to job enrichment but also is, in itself, a form of job enrichment. For example, assemblers confronted with the Company's problem of losing money on the production of radar units were given the opportunity to apply their talents in solving the problem. Their supervisor shared information with them regarding the duration of the contract, its dollar magnitude, delivery schedules, and the manufacturing costs stemming from overhead, materials, and labor. He asked them for their suggestions in reducing costs, particularly in regard to lowering the man-hours below the 100-hour breakeven point. Figure 2-6 shows the successive achievements of the group throughout the year. After a 2-hour meeting to compile, discuss, discard, and select ideas, the group set a goal of 86 hours. As shown by the chart, they surpassed their goal and achieved a 75-man-hour level. In subsequent meetings in which they expanded to include engineers, inspectors, and assemblers from other lines, they continued the goal-setting session until they reached a 41-hour level by year-end.

The problem-solving–goal-setting system has many of the characteristics of the natural bowling game, such as visible, challenging, and attainable goals; feedback; social and team involvement opportunity; and earned recognition.

In another application, when janitors and their supervisors became involved in a problem-solving–goal-setting process in order to "work

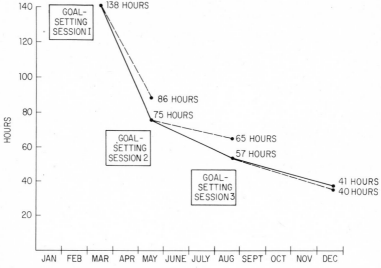

FIG. 2-6 Goal setting in radar assembly.

smarter, not harder," they first established the criteria of building maintenance and then took part in planning their own work. The results reflected in Figure 2-7 show improvements in terms of three criteria. The work force was reduced from 121 to 76, the reductions being achieved through job bidding and normal turnover. Quality of performance increased, and turnover dropped from 100 percent per quarter to 20 percent per quarter. Reduction in turnover illustrates the potential of even unattractive work for developing group cohesiveness and prestige through worthwhile and recognized achievements.

These models of helpful systems are drawn from the lower levels of the organization, primarily to show that processes traditionally applied only at higher levels can also apply at lower levels. Moreover, helpful systems at lower levels serve as models for the design of helpful systems at the top. By definition, an effective top-level system is one that interacts appropriately with members at all levels of the organization.

A Framework for Helpful Systems

The planning process which evolved in Texas Instruments illustrates a top-level problem-solving–goal-setting process which provides a framework for relevant problem solving–goal setting at all levels. Like all helpful systems, it is constantly evolving to serve the needs of its users.

Managers from worldwide operations convene annually to participate with peers and company officers in reviewing, modifying, and ratifying annual goals. Meeting in large working sessions of selectively varied memberships, each manager in a 10- to 30-minute period reviews his past year's targets and accomplishments, and outlines his plans for the year ahead. This presentation, involving more than 100 managers, serves four basic purposes:

- Communicates goals and achievements to all managers
- Appraises managerial effectiveness in planning and achieving organization goals
- Establishes compatible and challenging goals
- Develops managers through their involvement in the planning process

Planning presentations spring from a systematically interrelated hierarchy of goals known as the objective-strategy-tactics (OST) system. Objectives are formal statements of 10-year goals for business areas such as materials, exploration, and electronic components, or for intracompany staff functions such as personnel, facilities, and market-

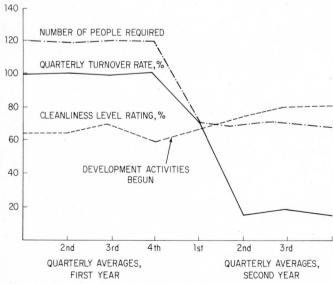

FIG. 2-7 Team improvement in building cleaning.

ing. Objectives are pursued through one or more supporting "strategies" which, in turn, are implemented through detailed 12- to 18-month "tactical action programs" (TAPs). TAPs are implemented ultimately through the goal-oriented systems at the lower levels of the organization; and of course, lower-level involvement provides a basis for TAPs development.   Strategies and TAPs are the basis for managing innovation in the various create-make-market and staff support groups. Each product-customer center defines its long-range mission through formal strategies and, with the participation of lower levels, recommends tactics and reports progress toward the strategy on standard TAP forms for top management approval and review. The ratified TAP thus becomes a meaningful official charter for implementation at all levels.

Reviews of selected strategies and TAPs are presented monthly to the office of the president or to the appropriate group or division vice-president by strategy and TAP managers who are, in most cases, several organizational levels below the president or reviewing officer. This presentation, directly to company officers, serves several vital purposes not usually satisfied in the large organization. First, it circumvents the traditional multilayer, upward-screening process and presents the president and other senior officers with firsthand progress reports on important projects. Second, it keeps the officers updated on developing technologies. Third, it gives the project head immediate feedback, undistorted by the traditional multilayer, downward-filtering process, and enables him to align his efforts more directly to the needs of the corporation. Needless to say, the recognition afforded by this process increases the incentive and opportunity for maximum effectiveness.

In short, the OST goal-setting model is a system for managing innovation at all levels in planning, implementing, and measuring goals within the framework of a meaningful whole. Moreover, the system itself is an innovative process for bypassing the traditional impediments to communication, decision making, and involvement which quash innovation and undermine the corporation's capability for competing successfully with smaller and more agile competitors.

Restrictive Systems

Many systems encountered by people at work do little to bring out the best in the workers; instead, the systems evoke anxiety, resentment, and "system-fighting" behavior. More restrictive than helpful, systems often require ingenuity, effort, and sometimes dishonesty to circumvent them. But pressures from supervision tend to quash nonconformity and encourage people to "follow instructions." Jobs are often designed to fit the lowest level of talent. The design of a keypunch operator's job, for example, is commonly guided by the directive, "assume that they can't think." Thus, creativity among keypunch operators is seldom rewarded and may actually provoke admonishments. System-controlled processes, such as the paced assembly line, though intended to increase efficiency, may do just the opposite. Man as an appendage to a machine must share its inefficiencies. The ore refinery, for example, geared to process 1,000 tons per day, enables the refinery operators to "stay busy" when the intake of raw material drops 50 percent. Also, some systems compete, to their mutual detriment. In the chemical industry, for example, engineering and operations may be inadvertently placed in conflict by inappropriate criteria of performance. Engineering may be rewarded for constructing processing plants at lower "per-square-foot" cost, even though a greater expenditure might result in greater efficiency by operations and, hence, greater return on investment to the company. Systems may also interfere simply because they are tradition-based, protocol-based, or authority-based. Rules sometimes remain in the rulebooks long after people have learned informal and efficient short cuts which disregard the official rules. Such a situation has double-edged potential for punishment, as people may be admonished for either "violating rules" or "slavish conformity." Finally, some systems perpetuate social stratification, such as those that prescribe rules according to status, typified by timekeeping procedures, compensation plans, paid leave, and other supplemental benefits.

A System for Human Effectiveness

The foregoing examples indicate that systems, to be helpful in sustaining the growth of the organization and its members, must incorporate meaningful goals and conditions of interpersonal competence as shown in Figure 2-8. Already defined and elaborated on pages 25 to 35 and 35 to 46, respectively, interpersonal competence refers to relationships based on theory Y assumptions, while meaningful goals satisfy the needs of both the organization and its members. It should

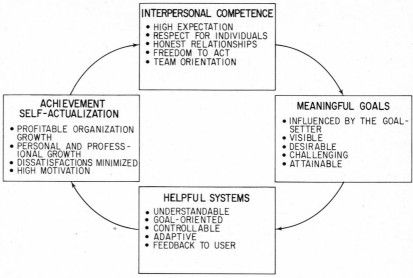

FIG. 2-8   A system for human effectiveness.

also be noted that systems are helpful when they meet the criteria of effective management systems defined on pages 125 and 126. The satisfaction of these three conditions leads to achievement and self-actualization in terms of criteria meaningful to both the organization and its members. This synergistic relationship tends to reinforce interpersonal competence and perpetuate the human effectiveness cycle. Thus, this diagram portrays a system for defining the characteristics of a helpful system. It is also a checklist to aid the manager in diagnosing administrative problems.

chapter three

Job Enrichment

HISTORICAL PERSPECTIVE[1]

The nature of work and the worker has evolved throughout the ages and can be traced as an evolutionary process from primeval times through the classical era, the Middle Ages, the Renaissance, the Industrial Revolution, and the twentieth century.

Preindustrial Man

Originally performed only as a means to survival, work has undergone several significant changes in history. According to Maslow's "hierarchy of needs" concept, when living is precarious, man devotes most of his attention to survival. Such was the case, of course, with the caveman, who was forced to devote most of his time to seeking food and shelter. For the caveman, work and living were one and the same, and work was indeed meaningful. His inability to predict or control his environment required him to react instead of to

---

[1] Adapted from an unpublished paper by Susan S. Myers, Southern Methodist University, Dallas, Tex., July, 1969.

think. Hence, efforts to control or cope with his environment through the use of crude weapons and fire resulted more from serendipity than from knowledge and logic. The continued and refined usage of happenstance discoveries rewarded the more innovative individuals with survival. The banding together for protection resulted in the development of social and status relationships.

Gradually moving up his need hierarchy, man in the medieval period found himself more formally concerned with social and status matters. However, tradition and environment had by then chained him to the role and the social order to which he was born. Limited by inherited role and social position, men born to families of artisans became artisans, and men born to royal families became kings, with virtually no mobility in between. But within the limits of his inherited sphere, the individual had freedom to express himself in his work and social life. In that respect, man in the medieval years was able to create, make, and market his own products, as long as he stayed within a particular product line and marketplace. At the same time, he enjoyed a certain amount of security and cohesiveness as a result of his membership in a particular guild, the church, and a circumscribed social order. Within his own sphere of influence, then, and in spite of being a captive in the feudal system, man was free to set his own standards and goals and to experience the rewards of achievement.

Emerging Capitalism

Events during the Middle Ages charted another course for man on which he could, for the first time in history, alter his own destiny. Skilled and motivated artisans reaped the benefits of quality workmanship, and competition developed between them and between other small businessmen, providing an example of social Darwinism or the concept of survival of the fittest. More successful artisans were able to hire less successful artisans to work for them, thus elevating their own social positions as a result of their increased wealth and status. Concomitant with the possibility of social mobility was the opportunity for geographical mobility and the opening of trade routes within and between Europe and the Orient. The horizons of the *nouveau riche* of the Renaissance were bright, but the future of the exploited working masses was grim. As they lost their ability to maintain their traditional memberships and relationships in guilds, they lost proprietary interest in their work, and their social, economic, and political status deteriorated.

The combination of competition, capital, and economic opportunity enabled the "fittest" of the artisans to survive and prosper, but at the expense of the weaker ones. The fittest became masters with entrepreneurial freedom and power to act and realize their personal ambitions. Members of the working class, on the other hand, enjoyed only enough freedom to choose to become silversmiths, cobblers, or blacksmiths; after that, their futures were largely determined for them by their employers. Work was then, as it is now, meaningful for members of "management," who could shape their jobs as they pleased, but for the workers, work was performed as directed. The situation was summarized by Erich Fromm, who states, " . . . as the number of journeymen under one master increased, the more capital was needed to become a master and the more guilds assumed a monopolistic and exclusive character, the less were the opportunities of journeymen. The deterioration of their economic and social position was shown by their growing dissatisfaction, the formation of organizations of their own, by strikes and even violent insurrections."[2]

Although dissatisfied workers discovered their strength in numbers, it was not enough influence to stem the inexorable development of the labor-management dichotomy in the late fifteenth century. Social and economic injustices of the times gradually brought the uniform theology of the period into question. The church member was taught that he had equal status with his fellow man in the eyes and love of God and that, though he shared the original sin with all, if he worked diligently to atone for his sins, he could be assured by his church of a place in heaven. The fact that the capitalists were reaping rewards at the expense of the working class suggested that the church represented the rich man's religion, and the workingman began developing an awareness of his own insignificance and powerlessness before the "official" church and the capitalists.

Birth of the Horatio Alger Philosophy

Thus the time was ripe for the Protestant theologies of Luther and Calvin. Both the working class and the middle class were ready to attack the authority and power of the wealthy and their church. Luther's followers believed that the way to heaven was through good work and success on earth. Calvin taught that destiny for heaven or hell was predetermined, but that success in life through moral and

[2] Erich Fromm, *Escape from Freedom*, Holt, Reinhart and Winston, Inc., New York, 1941, pp. 73–74.

effortful living indicated predestined salvation. Luther and Calvin both emphasized the powerlessness and baseness of man and the need for faith in the submission to God. The theology of both resulted in stronger self-reliance and responsibility for salvation. Thus, both doctrines succeeded in placing the burden of salvation on the individual—one by enabling man to earn his way to heaven, and the other by enabling him to prove to himself and others that he was predestined for heaven. Man became responsible for his own fate; no longer could the church lift the burden from his shoulders. Hence, the overdeveloped conscience and the latter-day Horatio Alger "rags to riches" theme were born. According to Fromm[3]:

> This new attitude towards effort and work as an aim in itself may be assumed to be the most important psychological change which has happened to man since the end of the Middle Ages. . . . What was new in modern society was that men came to be driven to work not so much by external pressure, but by an internal compulsion which made them work as only a very strict master could have made people do in other societies. The inner compulsion was more effective in harnessing all energies to work than any outer compulsion can ever be. Against external compulsion there is always a certain amount of rebelliousness which hampers the effectiveness of work or makes people unfit for any differentiated task requiring intelligence, initiative and responsibility. The compulsion to work by which man was turned into his own slave driver did not hamper these qualities. Undoubtedly, capitalism could not have been developed had not the greatest part of man's energy been channeled in the direction of work. There is no other period in history in which free men have given their energy so completely for the one purpose: work.

The Industrial Revolution

As a result of religious and political oppression in western Europe, the industrious rebels of the Reformation transferred their efforts to improve their lot to America. Firmly believing that God helps those who help themselves, members of the Protestant faith became associated with the rising commercial class. In a remarkably short time, they and their decendants had brought about the Industrial Revolution. Because of its impact on the economy and the people, perhaps the most far-reaching effect of the Industrial Revolution was the development of large industrial organizations.

Stimulated initially by the iron and steel mills, and nurtured by the

[3] *Ibid.*, pp. 112–114.

railroads and entrepreneurs, big business was built across the country. Accompanying big business was the development of mass markets and mass-production techniques, including standardization of parts and processes, division of labor, and repetitive production of standard items, manufacture of interchangeable parts, and assembly of parts into finished products. And while big businesses mushroomed, many small businesses disappeared, their owner-managers being forced to sell their labor for nothing more than wages. Caught in a trap of specialization, division of labor, wage systems, and pyramidal authoritarian organizations, dissatisfied workers in the 1860s formally joined forces in the National Labor Union and Knights of Labor in an unsuccessful attempt to regain some of their former status as owners of enterprise. The wage system became permanent, however, in spite of their efforts to destroy it. Accepting this fact, then, a new labor organization, the American Federation of Labor (AFL) was formed in 1886 to help workers improve their position within the system. Organized on the basis of trades and inspired by Samuel Gompers, the AFL differed from previous unions in that it *rested upon the assumption of an inherent conflict of interest between labor and management and the permanent ban of most employees from the ranks of management.*

Early Attempts at Scientific Management

Threatened by the aggressive role of labor and the continuing need for new responses to industrialism, managers of business and industrial organizations sought better management techniques—not for altruistic reasons, but for increased efficiency and productivity. They were influenced first by Max Weber's concept of bureaucracy, introduced in 1900. Opposed to loosely structured organizations run by whim, Weber proposed highly structured organizations run by rules. Although bureaucracy was understandable as a reaction to arbitrariness, it proved to be inefficient and cumbersome in an environment of rapidly changing technologies.

More attractive to management at that time was Frederick W. Taylor's concept of scientific management, which placed more emphasis on efficiency and productivity. Believing that the nature of work had gradually evolved from an art to a science, Taylor recommended that each job should be fractionated, analyzed for efficiency techniques, and given to the highest-aptitude employees trained for one specific task. To maximize efficiency, Taylor further recommended that employees be motivated through piecework incentive systems of pay, by which the most productive would earn the highest wages. Taylor's research, coupled with that of his successor, Frank B. Gilbreth, is now often known as time and motion study.

Taylorism and expressions of its philosophy linger on in many of today's organizations in the forms of engineered labor standards, time and motion study, piecework incentive, paid suggestion plans, and a myriad of manipulative programs for "communication," "zero defects," "attitude measurement," "merit rating," "motivation," "recognition," and "morale." Though the application of these concepts may yield sporadic short-term gains, its ultimate impact is alienation and net loss.

The discovery that incentives other than wages, hours, and working conditions motivated employees came as a surprise to many managers when Elton Mayo uncovered the importance of the attitude of the worker toward his job at Western Electric's Hawthorne Plant in 1927. Moreover, he called attention to the effects of groups on productivity, noting that cohesive groups had the power to raise or lower production according to their attitudes toward their jobs and the company.

The shift in emphasis away from improving individual efficiency to human relations and improved group processes was a natural consequence of trends toward mass production and automation. While machines and processes have been made increasingly complex, the workers who monitor the machines are experiencing diminishing demands on their intellect, initiative, and creativity. Recognizing that automation is making man an appendage of machines, Charles Walker[4] calls attention to the need to return the machine to its proper role as an appendage of man. Attempts to remedy the stultifying relationship between man and machines initiated the concepts of human engineering and job enrichment, whereby machines are designed to meet the abilities and limitations of man, and humans are taught to amplify the efficiency of machines.

Emergence of Formalized Job Enrichment

Realizing that the dimensions of a job exceed the conventional formula of wages, hours, and working conditions, Walker cites several other work dimensions useful as analytic tools in determining both

[4] Charles R. Walker (former director, Yale Technology Project), "Changing Character of Human Work under the Impact of Technological Change" (multilith), Wellfleet, Mass., 1965.

productivity and satisfaction on the job:
1. Knowledge and skill requirement
2. Pacing or rate of performance
3. Degree of repetitiveness or variety
4. Relation to the total product or process
5. Relationships with people as individuals or as groups
6. Style of supervision and of managerial controls
7. Degree of worker's autonomy in determining work methods
8. Relation of work to personal development

To the extent that these dimensions are known about a job, and improved in accordance with technological and psychological changes, there is potential for putting meaning back into work. As employers recognize the need to design machines to fit man, they also see the importance of designing jobs to meet man's needs. In answer to the question of how the design of a job affects the meaningfulness of a job, Peter Vaill[5] concluded, on the basis of research on the working lives of fifty factory workers, that jobs are more meaningful when (1) they offer the worker continuous opportunity to learn on his job, (2) they encourage quality workmanship, (3) they allow the worker to set his own standards and goals, (4) they are experienced by the worker as psychologically "whole," and (5) they show the relationship between the goals of a particular jobholder and company goals.

Regarding the relationship between the design of a job and the working environment, Vaill concluded that there is an inverse relationship between the degree of concern with wages, hours, and working conditions and job challenge and complexity. Vaill found the effect of improved job design resulted in greater willingness on the part of the workers to take an active, rather than a passive, role in the organization, thus leading to their increased commitment and self-confidence. Though all job enrichment is based on strategies for facilitating the greater utilization of human talent at work, not all proponents of job enrichment agree that eradication of the management-labor dichotomy is feasible or even desirable.

The Job Ahead

The evolutionary process of the nature of work and the worker, from the days of the caveman and the stone ax to the days of technicians and the computer, has offered man the opportunity to move upward

[5] Peter B. Vaill, "Industrial Engineering and Socio-Technical Systems," Paper presented before the AIIE, San Francisco, May 26, 1966, pp. 13–15.

through his hierarchy of need satisfactions. However, he is stopped short of self-actualization by a factor that has remained curiously constant throughout the ages: his dependency on powers beyond his influence. Mason Haire[6] traces the source of power through several stages. Primeval man, of course, lived in a bewildering and overwhelming world in which his survival depended on his wariness in reacting to unpredictable and sometimes uninterpretable threats. *Fear of the unknown* was the major source of power to the caveman. In medieval times the *state,* often identical with the official religious organization, was the source of power. Conformity and servility were keys to acceptance. The late Middle Ages ushered in entrepreneur activity, with *ownership* or equity as the source of power. Loyalty and industriousness were keys to success. The Industrial Revolution placed a premium on production, and *production technology,* coupled with the Protestant's attitude toward industriousness, was the source of power. Midcentury emphasis on professional management and staff expertise has made the *professional manager and his systems* a velvet-gloved source of power. Success is usually measured in terms of professional competence and advancement in the organization. However, there is not room for all to succeed in these terms, and large numbers at the lower levels resort to emotional disengagement, if only to maintain their sanity. Tomorrow's manager will shun the use of authority and will organize physical resources and manpower to enable human talent at all levels to find expression in solving problems and achieving goals. The source of power, then, will be *human competence,* applied toward the synergistic achievement of the goals of the organization and its members. Only under conditions of responsible self-direction and self-control can self-actualization be realized.

MEANINGFUL WORK

Meaning is given or returned to work through processes known as job enrichment or job enlargement. Applications of job enrichment in many organizations have shown tangible improvements in terms of diverse criteria such as reduced costs, higher yields, less scrap, accelerated learning time, fewer complaints and trips to the health center, reduced anxiety, improved attitudes and team efforts, and increased profits. Though "job enrichment" has become a shibboleth of today's

[6] Lecture by Mason Haire to Fellows of Salzburg Seminar in American Management Dynamics, Salzburg, Austria, March 21, 1969.

managers, few have had firsthand experience with it, or would know how to apply it to their own work groups. Hence, the desirability for job enrichment is no longer in question; rather, the quest now is for definitions and implementation procedures.

Definition of Job Enrichment

Most reports on job enrichment are situational descriptions which offer little guidance for supervisors in dissimilar circumstances, and slavish emulation of inappropriate models usually leads to failure. Job enrichment may result from horizontal or vertical job enlargement, or a combination of both, as illustrated in Figure 3-1. Horizontal job enlargement is characterized by increasing the variety of functions performed at a given level. As an intermediate step, it serves to reduce boredom and broaden the employee's perspective, thereby preparing him for vertical job enlargement. Vertically enlarged jobs enable employees to take part in the planning and control functions previously restricted to persons in supervisory and staff functions.

Management Functions

The functions of management are commonly defined in business school terminology as planning, organizing, leading, and controlling, as illustrated in Figure 3-2. For the average manager, management functions refer to the job of a "manager," but not to the job of the "worker." For example, a manager in a typical automobile assembly plant might describe his own job in terms of planning, organizing, leading, and controlling, and would see his fifty foremen as concerned primarily with leading and controlling. Their main responsibility is supervising the 2,000 workers on the assembly line who are doing the work. This concept is reflected in Figure 3-3.

The Management-Labor Dichotomy

This typical management point of view excludes employees from the realm of management and creates, subconsciously if not deliberately, a dichotomy of people at work: workers are perceived as unintelligent, uninformed, uncreative, irresponsible, and immature persons dependent upon the direction and control of intelligent, informed, creative, responsible, and mature managers. Consequences of this viewpoint are widely evident in industry and are reflected in Figure 3-4, which shows the cleavage between management and labor in terms of social distance and alienation.

Horizontal

1 - Assemblers on a transformer assembly line each performed a single operation as the assembly moved by on the conveyor belt. Jobs were enlarged horizontally by setting up work stations to permit each operator to assemble the entire unit.
Operations now performed by each operator include cabling, upending, winding,
soldering, laminating and symbolizing.

2 - A similar transformer assembly line provides horizontal job enlargement when
assemblers are taught how to perform all operations and are rotated to different
operations periodically, or as permitted by peer and supervisory consensus.

Vertical

3 - Assemblers on a radar assembly line are given information on customer contract commitments in terms of price, quality specifications, delivery schedules,
and company data on materiel and personnel costs, breakeven performance, and
potential profit margins. Assemblers and engineers work together in methods and
design improvements. Assemblers inspect, adjust, and repair their own work, help
test completed units, and receive copies of customer inspection reports.

4 - Female electronic assemblers involved in intricate assembling, bonding,
soldering, and welding operations are given training in methods improvement and
encouraged to make suggestions for improving manufacturing processes. Natural
work groups of five to 20 assemblers each elect a "team captain" for a term of six
months. In addition to performing her regular operations, the team captain collects
work improvement ideas from members of her team, describes them on a standard
form, credits the suggestors, presents the recommendations to their supervisor and
superintendent at the end of the week, and gives the team feedback on idea utilization. Though most job operations remain the same, vertical job enlargement is
achieved by providing increased opportunity for planning, reorganizing and controlling their work.

Horizontal Plus Vertical

5 - Jobs are enlarged horizontally in a clad metal rolling mill by qualifying
operators to work interchangeably on breakdown rolling, finishing rolling, slitter,
pickler, and abrader operations. After giving the operators training in methods
improvement and basic metallurgy, jobs are enlarged vertically by involving them
with engineering and supervisory personnel in problem-solving, goal-setting
sessions for increasing production yields.

6 - Jobs in a large employee insurance section are enlarged horizontally by
qualifying insurance clerks to work interchangeably in filing claims, mailing
checks, enrolling and orienting new employees, checking premium and enrollment reports, adjusting payroll deductions, and interpreting policies to employees.
Vertical enlargement involves clerks in insurance program planning meetings with
personnel directors and carrier representatives, authorizes them to sign disburse-
ment requests, attend a paperwork systems conference, recommend equipment replacements and to rearrange their work layout.

FIG. 3-1   Examples of horizontal and vertical job enlargement.

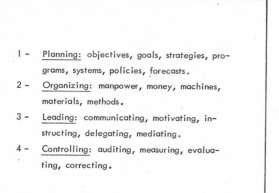

1 –   <u>Planning</u>: objectives, goals, strategies, pro-
        grams, systems, policies, forecasts.

2 –   <u>Organizing</u>: manpower, money, machines,
        materials, methods.

3 –   <u>Leading</u>: communicating, motivating, in-
        structing, delegating, mediating.

4 –   <u>Controlling</u>: auditing, measuring, evalua-
        ting, correcting.

FIG. 3-2   The functions of management.

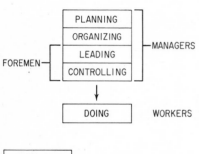

**FIG. 3-3   The manager's traditional perception
of his job.**

FIG. 3-4   The management-labor dichotomy.

Though the gap between the employer and the employed has a long heritage and, in some respects, seems inescapably inherent to the relationship, it has become more formalized and widened through the efforts of labor unions whose charters depend on their success in convincing labor that management is their natural enemy. The union, while pressuring management to share its affluence and relinquish its prerogatives, has at the same time clearly defined the laboring man's charter as being separate from, and indeed in conflict with, that of management. Managers typically and naturally align themselves with the goals of the company, but workers divide their allegiance between the union and the company, often with a feeling of closer identification with the union than with the company.

Though reductive management, tradition, and labor union strategy all tend to perpetuate the two-class concept, two forces in America have the potential for narrowing or obliterating the gap between labor and management. One is the improving socioeconomic status and the consequent rising aspirations of the less privileged, accelerated by legislated equality and increasing enlightenment in a democratic and increasingly affluent society. The second force is a growing awareness by managers of the inevitability of democracy as the pattern for successful competition in an entrepreneurial society, and their acceptance of their role in initiating and supporting it. This chapter is devoted mainly to this second force: defining a concept of meaningful work to guide tomorrow's managers in redefining their roles.

The Changing Needs of Man

Maslow's[7] hierarchy-of-needs theory is useful in understanding the consequences of the increasing affluence of man. Primeval man's efforts were directed primarily toward survival needs—safety, food and shelter—leaving little time or energy for preoccupation with his latent higher-order needs. As his survival needs were satisfied, he became sensitized to social and status needs. Finally, in the affluence of recent decades, these lower-order or maintenance needs are being satisfied to the point that he is ready to realize his potential, to experience self-actualization in terms of intellectual, emotional, and aesthetic growth, or to satisfy his motivation needs.

Management and the union both have contributed to the worker's readiness for self-actualization. Efficiency engineers of the Industrial Revolution, under the label of "scientific management," simplified tasks and created the mass-production technology. Jobs were fractionated for efficiency in training (and to escape management's dependency on prima donna journeymen) and to satisfy the implicit assumption that workers would be happy and efficient doing easy

[7] Abraham H. Maslow, *Toward a Psychology of Being*, 2d ed., D. Van Nostrand Company, Inc., 1968.

work for high pay. And though mass-production technology made man an appendage of tools and destroyed his journeyman's pride and autonomy, it helped to price automobiles, washing machines, refrigerators, and other consumer products within his reach. These and other effects of the mass-production economy accelerated the satisfaction of man's lower-order needs and readied him to become aware of his dormant and unfulfilled self-actualization needs.

The union's role was just as vital in readying the worker for self-actualization, for it forced industrial managers to share company success with the worker, thereby narrowing the economic gap between the manager and the worker and further enabling him to buy the products of mass production. However, as noted on pages 65–66, the union, for reasons of self-preservation, sharpened the worker's identity as a member of labor rather than a member of management—preserving the social gap that might otherwise have been reduced through economic trends.

When Work Is Meaningless

Though jobs may satisfy certain personal needs of people at work, in the eyes of many workers, work itself is a form of punishment. It is uninteresting, demeaning, oppressive, and generally unrelated to, or in conflict with, their personal goals. But it is an activity which they take in stride, or an unpleasantness they are willing to endure, to get the money needed to buy goods and services which are related to personal goals. The income itself, however, is not the sole motive for working.

Apart from the needs satisfied through income earned on the job, work itself, however dull and menial, satisfies a wide variety of motives:

- Work reduces role ambiguity. It establishes the worker's identity and, though the self-image may not be an attractive one, for most it is better than an undefined role. For some it is an "escape from freedom" which Eric Fromm[8] shows to be necessary for people who are culturally conditioned to associate security with roles prescribed by authority.
- Work offers socializing opportunity. Close and sustained association with others having similar job goals, socioeconomic backgrounds, and interests are natural conditions for social

[8] Fromm, *op. cit.*, pp. 73–74.

compatibility. However, social relationships, in the absence of a unifying achievement mission, can result in group pressures disruptive to productivity. Broad-scale group cohesiveness and social interaction sometimes occur among the members of a work force who can find no better basis for uniting than to defy the management Goliath.

- Work increases solidarity. The performance of similar tasks, however routine, is a shared ritual which provides a basis for equality and role acceptance. "Misery loves company" only because of the solidarity created by shared misery. The individual who is promoted or transferred from the unifying circumscribed role becomes an outsider whose solidarity needs must be satisfied elsewhere. The saying, "God must have loved common man because he made so many of them" finds grateful acceptance by people who need solace for their inescapable commonness.

- Work bolsters security feelings. Apart from the security related to economics, for many persons, feelings of security require continuous affirmation from authority figures. Authority-oriented people, particularly when deprived of meaningful work roles, have unusually high requirements for feedback from the supervisor to satisfy their security and achievement needs. Dependency relationships to authority figures are also manifested, of course, by achievement-oriented people with thwarted achievement needs.

- Work is a substitute for unrealized potential. "Keeping busy" channels energy or thwarted intellectual capability and helps obscure the reality of unfulfilled potential. Though it is an escape mechanism, at least it is less punishing than alcoholism or other means of escape, and it helps to buy freedom and the opportunity off the job which gives better expression to talent. Furthermore, fatigue from an "honest day's work" evokes social approval.

- Work is an escape from the home environment. Particularly for women whose homemaking roles are unfulfilling or completed, a job provides an opportunity for getting away from the home. Other reasons for wanting to get away from home include domestic conflict, neighborhood friction, unattractive home facilities, and loneliness.

- Work reduces feelings of guilt and anxiety. In an achieving society where dignity and pride are earned through the traits of ambition, initiative, industriousness, and perseverance, idleness violates deep-seated values, and work for work's sake is virtuous. By Horatio Alger or Protestant ethic standards, idleness is the equivalent of stealing, and a strong conscience is a key motive for staying on the job.

Though the roles of meaningless work defined above relate to the personal needs of individuals, they are not constructively aligned with company goals. Moreover, these roles thwart long-range personal goals, as they increase dependency relationships and discourage the development of talent. However, work itself, properly designed, can satisfy other needs which are related to the achievement of long-range personal and organization goals.

For example, the manager's job is usually found to be challenging, related to company goals, and generally aligned with his long-range personal goals. The difference in job attitude between manager and worker is usually ascribed to immaturity of the worker, overlooking the fact that maturity is developed or impaired as a function of opportunity to manage one's job.

Managers manage their jobs, while workers are managed by their jobs. Workers are frequently only appendages of tools or links between them—doing what is necessary to satisfy the requirements of inflexible, inanimate monsters.

The Dimensions of Meaningful Work

Work itself, to be meaningful, must make tools the appendage of man and place man in a role not restricted to obedient *doing*. It must include *planning* and *controlling*, as well as *doing*, as illustrated in Figure 3-5.

The *plan* phase includes the planning and organizing functions of work and consists of problem solving–goal setting and of planning the use of manpower, materiel, and systems. Planning is the ingredient of work which gives it meaning by aligning it with goals. The *do* phase is the implementation of the plan, ideally involving the coordinated expenditure of physical and mental effort, utilizing aptitudes and special skills. *Control* includes measurement, evaluation, and correction—the feedback process for assessing achievements against goals. Feedback, even to a greater extent than planning, gives work its

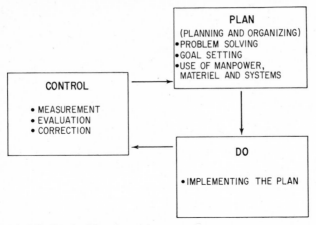

FIG. 3-5 Meaningful work model.

meaning, and its absence is a common cause of job dissatisfaction. The control phase is the basis for recycling planning, doing, and controlling. People who work for themselves generally have meaningful work in terms of a complete cycle of plan, do, and control.

The self-employed farmer, for example, plans and organizes in terms of market evaluation, crop rotation, seed selection, utilization of land, purchase of equipment, and the employment of manpower. He typically has a major role in implementing his plan—planting, cultivating, irrigating, harvesting, and marketing. Finally, he measures, evaluates, and corrects his program as necessary to provide for a better future cycle. A similar analogy may be drawn for others in the entrepreneurial situation of working for themselves.

The Meaningful Work of Managers

Managers in industry, though seldom having as much autonomy as self-employed entrepreneurs, typically have jobs rich in plan, do, and control phases, particularly at the higher levels. Three typical management jobs out of a seven-level hierarchy in a manufacturing organization are identified below for analysis in terms of their usual plan, do, and control phases.

> President
> → Operating vice-president
> Department manager
> → Manufacturing manager

Superintendent

→ Foreman

Operator

Figure 3-6 shows that the operating vice-president, as division manager, plans in the realm of economic and technological trends, facilities expansion, manpower and management systems, and policy formulation. The doing aspect of his job involves him routinely with key customers, in public relations roles, with visits to various operating sites, and in the exchange of business information. His control functions include the measurement, evaluation, and correction of factors associated with customer satisfaction, net sales, profits, cash flow, facilities utilization, return on investment, morale, and manpower development. Hence, the division director's job is rich in plan, do, and control, much as the self-employed individual's work is.

Similarly, Figure 3-7 shows the manufacturing manager's job to be relatively rich in the meaningful aspects of work. Though his job is narrower in scope and two levels below the division manager's position, it is nonetheless rich in plan, do, and control. A company is rarely plagued with the lack of commitment of a manufacturing manager or the people above him.

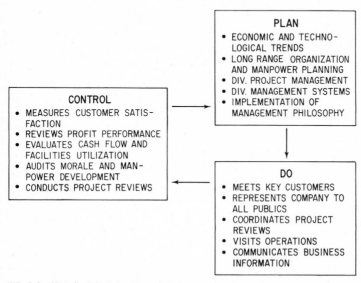

FIG. 3-6   Meaningful work—operating vice-president.

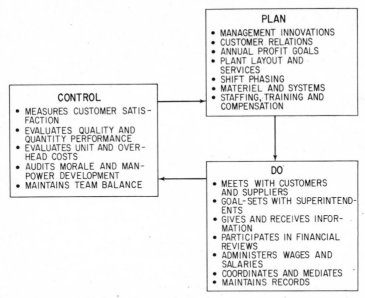

PLAN
- MANAGEMENT INNOVATIONS
- CUSTOMER RELATIONS
- ANNUAL PROFIT GOALS
- PLANT LAYOUT AND SERVICES
- SHIFT PHASING
- MATERIEL AND SYSTEMS
- STAFFING, TRAINING AND COMPENSATION

CONTROL
- MEASURES CUSTOMER SATISFACTION
- EVALUATES QUALITY AND QUANTITY PERFORMANCE
- EVALUATES UNIT AND OVERHEAD COSTS
- AUDITS MORALE AND MANPOWER DEVELOPMENT
- MAINTAINS TEAM BALANCE

DO
- MEETS WITH CUSTOMERS AND SUPPLIERS
- GOAL-SETS WITH SUPERINTENDENTS
- GIVES AND RECEIVES INFORMATION
- PARTICIPATES IN FINANCIAL REVIEWS
- ADMINISTERS WAGES AND SALARIES
- COORDINATES AND MEDIATES
- MAINTAINS RECORDS

FIG. 3-7 Meaningful work—manufacturing manager.

Where Meaningful Work Usually Stops

Even the foreman's job, two levels below the manufacturing manager, may be rich in terms of the ingredients of meaningful work. Figure 3-8 indicates that the foreman's job, though narrower in scope than the manufacturing manager's, offers him considerable latitude in managing his work. This example depicts a traditional authority-oriented supervisor, who will be contrasted with a goal-oriented supervisor in Figure 4-2.

Though this foreman's job portrays a complete plan-do-control cycle, it is nonetheless unsatisfying to the incumbent because its authority orientation prevents the delegation of a complete plan-do-control cycle of responsibility to the operator. Under this foreman, the operator lives in a world circumscribed by conformity pressures to follow instructions, work harder, obey rules, get along with people, and be loyal to the supervisor and the company, quashing any pleasure that work itself might otherwise offer. His role puts him in a category with materiel, to be manipulated by managers exercising their "management prerogatives" (as kings once exercised their "divine rights") in pursuit of "their" organizational goals. Conformity-oriented workers tend to behave like adolescent children responding to punishments and rewards of authoritarian parents, and their prerogatives, which are generally expressed in terms of rights wrested from management, are only incidentally aligned with company goals.

The Impact of Supervisory Style

Job enrichment sometimes results naturally from the intuitive practices of goal-oriented, emotionally mature managers who evoke commitment through a "language of action" which grants freedom and reflects respect, confidence, and high expectations. Unfortunately, many managers still see job enlargement as a form of benevolent autocracy, and their unguided attempts to enlarge jobs fall more within the realm of manipulation than within that of job enrichment. When job enrichment is attempted by reductive, authority-oriented managers, they usually fail to inspire the level of involvement and commitment achieved by goal-oriented managers. Their motives are suspect and their "language of action" comes through as manipulation and exploitation rather than as acts of trust, confidence, and respect.

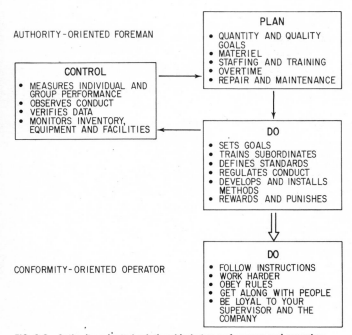

FIG. 3-8 Authority-oriented relationship between foreman and operator.

Hence, job enrichment depends on style of supervision as well as job requirements and is not simply a matter of duplicating patterns of work and relationships found to be successful elsewhere.

HOW TO ENRICH JOBS

The foregoing examples show that meaningful work includes planning and controlling, as well as doing, and that conformity pressures by the authority-oriented supervisor defined in Figure 3-8 tend to prevent the break with tradition necessary for people under his supervision to experience the full plan-do-control cycle of work. Hence, the role of the supervisor is the key to job enrichment. The involvement of the supervisor in the enrichment process is necessary, if only because he is usually the person most familiar with all jobs in his work group. But, more importantly, his participation involves him in the redefinition of his role and leads to self-initiated changes in his managerial style.

Job enrichment is a never-ending process, and particularly in a large organization, the logistics of correcting all jobs simultaneously would be overwhelming. A realistic initial mission is to involve each supervisor at least once in a formal way, so that he can take the initiative in testing and implementing enrichment techniques with other jobs under his supervision.

Use of the Checklist

As part of the intellectual conditioning process described on pages 10 to 16, supervisors can analyze the meaningfulness of jobs under their supervision by answering questions related to each of the three phases of work, as illustrated in Figure 3-9. A supervisor's involvement in answering questions in this checklist may for the first time make him aware of the gross disparity between the reality of his own work group and the theoretical model. The plan and control items in particular may at first appear unrealistic to him in terms of his perception of his people's competence, but he can be helped to a more realistic view by having him make a comparative analysis of a similar job managed by a person of similar talents in business for himself.

For example, analysis of a company oil driller's job in the field may show it to be largely devoid of planning and control phases when compared to the job of his free-lance counterpart who manages his own drilling rig. The self-employed driller, who must manage the

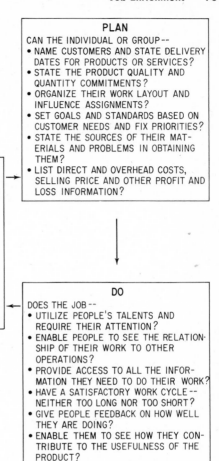

PLAN

CAN THE INDIVIDUAL OR GROUP--
• NAME CUSTOMERS AND STATE DELIVERY DATES FOR PRODUCTS OR SERVICES?
• STATE THE PRODUCT QUALITY AND QUANTITY COMMITMENTS?
• ORGANIZE THEIR WORK LAYOUT AND INFLUENCE ASSIGNMENTS?
• SET GOALS AND STANDARDS BASED ON CUSTOMER NEEDS AND FIX PRIORITIES?
• STATE THE SOURCES OF THEIR MATERIALS AND PROBLEMS IN OBTAINING THEM?
• LIST DIRECT AND OVERHEAD COSTS, SELLING PRICE AND OTHER PROFIT AND LOSS INFORMATION?

CONTROL

CAN THE INDIVIDUAL OR GROUP --
• STATE CUSTOMER QUALITY REQUIREMENTS AND REASONS FOR THESE STANDARDS?
• KEEP THEIR OWN RECORDS OF QUALITY AND QUANTITY?
• CHECK QUALITY AND QUANTITY OF WORK AND REVISE PROCEDURES?
• EVALUATE AND MODIFY WORK LAYOUT ON THEIR OWN INITIATIVE?
• IDENTIFY AND CORRECT UNSAFE WORKING CONDITIONS?
• OBTAIN INFORMATION FROM PEOPLE OUTSIDE THE GROUP AS A MEANS OF EVALUATING PERFORMANCE?

DO

DOES THE JOB --
• UTILIZE PEOPLE'S TALENTS AND REQUIRE THEIR ATTENTION?
• ENABLE PEOPLE TO SEE THE RELATIONSHIP OF THEIR WORK TO OTHER OPERATIONS?
• PROVIDE ACCESS TO ALL THE INFORMATION THEY NEED TO DO THEIR WORK?
• HAVE A SATISFACTORY WORK CYCLE -- NEITHER TOO LONG NOR TOO SHORT?
• GIVE PEOPLE FEEDBACK ON HOW WELL THEY ARE DOING?
• ENABLE THEM TO SEE HOW THEY CONTRIBUTE TO THE USEFULNESS OF THE PRODUCT?

FIG. 3-9. Sample questions for analyzing meaningful work.

total plan-do-control cycle of his work to succeed in business, thus serves as a model for planning the enrichment of the company driller's job.

Task-force Approach[9]

Job enrichment may be approached through a task force composed of a vertical cross section of supervisors extending from the job incum-

[9] The task-force approach is a combination of Texas Instruments' motivation seminar and plan-do-control concepts with Robert Ford's process, defined in "The Art of Reshaping Jobs," AT&T, *Bell Telephone Magazine,* pp. 29–32, September-October, 1968.

bent's supervisor to the highest level possible. This slice is made up of people in line management of a given product or service, and may include horizontal cross sections at the lower levels. Ideally, the first job-enrichment workshop should be limited to fewer than ten people. Later on, larger task forces may be practical, with perhaps twenty members as an upper limit. The task-force approach of job enrichment is outlined in Figure 3-10.

These work groups should be isolated from their daily jobs, off the premises if feasible, away from interruptions. Resistance to removing supervisors for two days is to be expected, particularly when they are deeply involved in day-to-day efforts for which they believe themselves indispensable. Of course, their "inescapable" problems are the ones most likely to be solved through job enrichment.

Supervisory training is a prerequisite to this process, and all participants in the task force should have completed at least 16 hours of orientation consisting of:

1. Motivation theory
2. Meaningful work
3. Work simplification
4. Conference leadership

Motivation theory provides a foundation for understanding constructive and reactive behavior as a symptom of satisfied or thwarted needs. "Meaningful work" defines the proper or ideal balance of plan-do-control functions that give work its meaning. Work simplification familiarizes the supervisor with techniques and principles which enable people to become their own industrial engineers in analyzing and improving their jobs. Conference leadership skills enable supervisors to avoid quashing individual initiative and creativity, and to obtain goal-directed involvement of the group in problem solving and goal setting.

The mission of the supervisory group is to translate the abstractions of responsibility, achievement, recognition, and growth into tangible factors. Initial effort is focused on the first two. How can *responsibility* be added to this particular job? Who is responsible now for planning and assigning work and measuring results? Can any of this responsibility be moved down to the job incumbent? How can the job be enriched to provide a greater sense of *achievement*? Are accomplishments clearly definable or measurable and, if not, what is obscuring goals or feedback? Bob Ford cited a case in AT&T where a super-

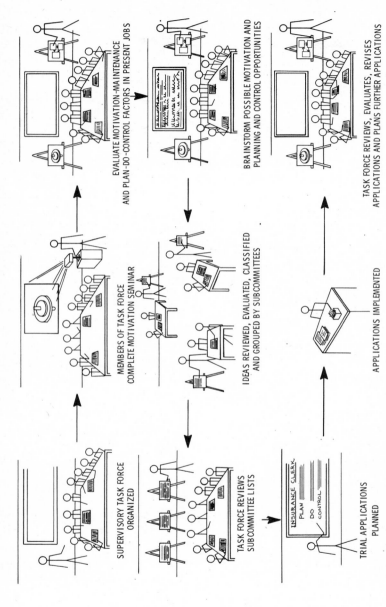

EVALUATE MOTIVATION-MAINTENANCE AND PLAN-DO-CONTROL FACTORS IN PRESENT JOBS

BRAINSTORM POSSIBLE MOTIVATION AND PLANNING AND CONTROL OPPORTUNITIES

TASK FORCE REVIEWS, EVALUATES, REVISES APPLICATIONS AND PLANS FURTHER APPLICATIONS

MEMBERS OF TASK FORCE COMPLETE MOTIVATION SEMINAR

IDEAS REVIEWED, EVALUATED, CLASSIFIED AND GROUPED BY SUBCOMMITTEES

APPLICATIONS IMPLEMENTED

SUPERVISORY TASK FORCE ORGANIZED

TASK FORCE REVIEWS SUBCOMMITTEE LISTS

INSURANCE CLERK
PLAN
DO
CONTROL

TRIAL APPLICATIONS PLANNED

FIG. 3-10 Job enrichment—task-force approach.

77

visory task force found sixteen new ways of giving each service representative her own performance results. In another example, an operator was given copies of only her own defective toll tickets with the
request to analyze and classify the defects.

Recognition and growth result from responsibility and achievement. Traditionally, the job incumbent is dependent on authority
figures for *recognition*. But jobs can be designed so that participation in
plan and control responsibilities give the job incumbent natural opportunity for recognition, without reinforcing a dependency relationship to his supervisor. How can the worker get natural recognition from upper management, supervisors, peers, and others without
relying unduly on the value judgments of supervisors?

Personal and professional *growth* is a natural consequence of
progressive or varied challenges. People with greater ability thrive on
a progression of increasingly difficult tasks or skills to master, and
need opportunity for advancement to more challenging jobs. Some
jobs, such as those in medicine, research, and top management, have
a lifetime of challenge in them. The challenge of the supervisor is to
vary job content flexibly to enable people of varying abilities to experience job satisfaction as much as the professional man does.

A brainstorming session (with ground rules against criticism,
ridicule, and inflexibility) for loading jobs with responsibility,
achievement, recognition, and growth usually lasts a whole day, and
may extend into the second day. Proceedings are summarized on
large easel pad sheets and displayed around the conference room.

First-day guidelines include the instructions, "Think radically about
the work flow and the purpose of the jobs involved in satisfying customer needs. What can be done to create more complete jobs for
these employees?" Diagnose jobs in terms of the plan, do, and control
phases—for both the job incumbent and his supervisor. Which *do*
functions are perpetuated by tradition, and what would happen if
they were eliminated? Which *plan* and *control* functions could be
moved across or down to a job incumbent? Brainstorming sessions
purposely preclude concern with the feasibility of implementing
changes or the consequences of manpower surplus that might result
from these changes.

Following the brainstorming session, which takes up most of a day,
an evaluation of the brainstorming list is begun. If the list is short
(fewer than fifty items), the group usually works together to classify

each suggestion into either motivation or maintenance categories, as defined in Figure 1-2 on page 10. If the list is long (more than fifty items), and if conference time is limited, the task can be subdivided for subgroup assignment, each group reviewing all items for possible inclusion in one category. Motivational items are designated as horizontal or vertical job enlargement, as illustrated in Figure 3-1 on page 64, and their impact is specified in terms of growth, achievement, responsibility, and recognition.

Maintenance items may be diagnosed in terms of economic, security, orientation, status, social, physical factors, or, more simply, in terms of administrative roadblocks and other maintenance factors.

When all items have been classified by category, they are rated by consensus as excellent, good, fair, or poor. The fair and poor ideas are reviewed and some are eliminated. Remaining items are listed by category on a clean easel sheet; excellent ideas first, followed by the good, fair, and poor items.

The workshop then reconvenes as a total group, and each team reports on the strengths and deficiencies of each item on its list and evokes and incorporates new ideas from the group. Also, at this point, for the first time, conferees are asked to designate the items in their list which they believe could and should be implemented. Job restructuring begins at this stage, especially if motivation factors are strongly represented in the items.

If the list is strong on roadblock items but weak in motivation categories, it may imply a basically or potentially rich job that has become hemmed in by rules and regulations. If so, motivation factors might be liberated by eliminating roadblocks.

Some maintenance items, because of their uniform application across the organization, cannot be altered for a job or a group. However, some changes can be spearheaded in small groups, and group efforts can sometimes lead to more broadly applied changes throughout the organization.

Near the end of the second day, the group decides whether a job-improvement trial is to be undertaken and which items are to be implemented. Supervisors, individually or in groups, are asked to pick a few items for trial application. They list obstacles and problems anticipated in implementing each item, with specific steps for overcoming them.

During trial applications—usually extending through a four- to six-week period—supervisors meet periodically to review progress, discuss problems, and continue brainstorming of additional jobs. Also during this period, implementation procedures and schedules are planned. Participation and support of top management are helpful ingredients in planning the strategy.

In beginning job enrichment, much can be done just by improving existing jobs. This is least threatening or disrupting to job incumbents and their supervisors. The next step might involve the collapsing or merging of several allied jobs. In both instances, it is helpful to itemize the planning and control functions of higher jobs which can be pulled down to make lower jobs more complete. When possible, routine functions are eliminated, perhaps through automation, or placed in less oppressive combination with more interesting functions.

One key, but elusive, concept in making work more meaningful is the natural module of work; that is, all the work in connection with a particular assignment. For example, in one of the AT&T studies, a group of ten girls was responsible for mailing out toll billings on staggered dates throughout the month. All bills for telephone numbers starting with 392 were due out on the first of the month, 395 on the fifth, 397 on the 13th, and so on. Working as a team, they would finish 392 and then start 395 under the scheduling and direction of the supervisor. But productivity was low, due dates were missed, and overtime costs were high. Recognizing each block of billings per due date as a natural module of work, responsibility for each module was assigned to an individual. One girl was responsible for getting out 392, another for 395, and so on. The individual was responsible for the plan, do, and control functions necessary to meet deadlines. The girls were making their own decisions and working out mutually supportive relationships with each other. Each could succeed or fail, but her performance and fate were under her control. Results were dramatically good: schedules were met, overtime was eliminated, and job satisfaction increased.

Other applications of the modular idea in Ford's studies included:

- A frameman was given responsibility for handling all cross-connection work for specific groups of customers, rather than miscellaneous and unrelated wiring assignments.
- A keypunch operator was made responsible for preparing all cards from a certain geographic area or for certain kinds of

reports, rather than whatever cards needed to be punched next.

■ An equipment engineer was made responsible for handling all contacts from initial request to final installation in a certain area and/or for certain kinds of equipment, rather than whatever job came along next.

In each case, the key was to give each person the knowledge that he had a job to manage to satisfy "his" customer or set of customers.

Problem Solving–Goal Setting[10]

Perhaps the most effective approach to job enrichment is through the participation of job incumbents themselves. However, rather than involve them in the unnatural task of analyzing the dimensions of work and other factors related to motivation, their supervisor involves them in the un-self-conscious process of solving everyday customer problems and setting new goals, as illustrated in Figure 3-11.

The supervisory training described on page 76 is a prerequisite to the problem-solving–goal-setting process. Without this background of information, supervisors can inadvertently and innocently confuse motivation and manipulation techniques.

A problem-solving–goal-setting session is initiated by the supervisor when he has a customer problem which he and the usual support personnel cannot solve adequately. He convenes the group concerned with the problem—usually a natural work group under his supervision—and presents them with the customer problem. On initial applications, he may have to spend up to an hour just in briefing the group on background information. For example, he provides historical information on the product or service, naming competitors and customers and defining the problem in terms of costs, quality, and schedules. He should be as specific and open as possible in defining the problem and answering questions. He should define costs, for example, in terms of overhead, materials or services, and labor. He should enumerate the factors contributing to each of these costs and should show the relative influence of each in determining the unit cost of the product or service. Quality and quantity factors can also be

---

[10] The problem-solving–goal-setting approach was developed in Texas Instruments. Further examples of job enrichment in Texas Instruments are detailed in Fred K. Foulkes' *Creating More Meaningful Work*, American Management Association, New York, 1969.

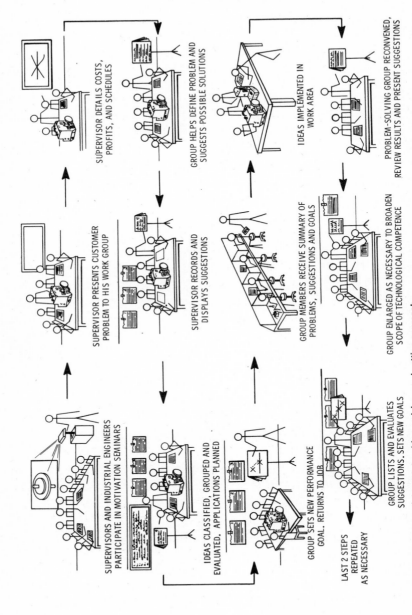

SUPERVISORS AND INDUSTRIAL ENGINEERS PARTICIPATE IN MOTIVATION SEMINARS

SUPERVISOR PRESENTS CUSTOMER PROBLEM TO HIS WORK GROUP

SUPERVISOR DETAILS COSTS, PROFITS, AND SCHEDULES

GROUP HELPS DEFINE PROBLEM AND SUGGESTS POSSIBLE SOLUTIONS

SUPERVISOR RECORDS AND DISPLAYS SUGGESTIONS

IDEAS CLASSIFIED, GROUPED AND EVALUATED. APPLICATIONS PLANNED

GROUP SETS NEW PERFORMANCE GOAL. RETURNS TO JOB

GROUP LISTS AND EVALUATES SUGGESTIONS. SETS NEW GOALS

GROUP MEMBERS RECEIVE SUMMARY OF PROBLEMS, SUGGESTIONS AND GOALS

GROUP ENLARGED AS NECESSARY TO BROADEN SCOPE OF TECHNOLOGICAL COMPETENCE

IDEAS IMPLEMENTED IN WORK AREA

PROBLEM-SOLVING GROUP RECONVENED, REVIEW RESULTS AND PRESENT SUGGESTIONS

LAST 2 STEPS REPEATED AS NECESSARY

FIG. 3-11 Job enrichment—problem-solving—goal-setting approach.

82

translated into costs of rework, scrappage, overtime, and customer alienation. With this information, members of the group are able to view the problem as the supervisor sees it, and armed with their new insights, they can begin making suggestions.

When the supervisor begins with the customer problem, sharing with the group all the information available to him, they are able to see the problem as he sees it, but they have the additional advantage of detailed familiarity with job operations. Hence, they are generally more effective in coming up with new solutions to the problem. In a typical session of 1 to 2 hours, it is not unusual to compile forty to fifty suggestions. The supervisor's role during this problem-definition phase is that of a conference leader. He makes no value judgments regarding the merit of the suggestions, but rather serves primarily as a recorder of the ideas, using a blackboard or flip chart. He may ask questions of clarification or for expressions of opinion from other members of the conference, but not in a manner that would reflect his own values.

A pitfall in the problem-solving–goal-setting process is to begin a meeting without a defined problem. Supervisors who begin meetings with the announcement, "This is a problem-solving conference, what are your problems?" have little trouble getting a list of problems. However, these problems tend to be related to factors such as eating facilities, parking facilities, air conditioning, coatracks, and other maintenance items. The participants usually enjoy the meeting, sometimes only as an opportunity to escape their jobs, and also because it has some cathartic effect. But beginning a session with a list of maintenance problems is an inefficient approach to focusing on customer problems.

However, maintenance problems may arise even when the focus in this conference is on customer problems. If, for example, a shortage of parking spaces or congested cafeteria lines are causing tardiness and delayed start-ups on the assembly line, these maintenance problems must be dealt with. However, having dealt with them, it is natural to return to the main mission of the conference; namely, solving customer problems and setting goals.

The problem-definition and suggestion-listing process in the first meeting usually continues for an hour or more, or until the flow of new ideas drops off. The next step is to review all suggestions and group them into natural families, such as inspection, inventory shortages, defective materials, machine maintenance, training, and engineering changes. Rather than try to implement all the ideas, the supervisor will ask the group to review the lists and select the suggestions that offer the richest opportunity for immediate return. The group are then asked to set a goal, based on the assumption that their selected changes will be implemented. They are assured that this goal is contingent on the support of supervision and technical support personnel. Typically, the group will work through the revised procedure, making estimates of the savings in time and material, and will set a goal. A goal must, of course, have quantitative and time dimensions. For example, it might be to reduce the average time per unit from 36 to 25 hours in 3 weeks, or to reduce the feedback time in technical data reports to the customer from 7 days to 3 days within a 6-month time period, or to increase the yield from 85 to 95 percent in 3 months.

Once these goals are set, the meeting adjourns and the people return to their work areas to meet the demands of daily production requirements and at the same time begin implementing their new plan. Their commitment to achieve their new goal is, of course, dependent on the supervisor's commitment to provide the necessary freedom and technical support to make changes. Problem solving–goal setting is a never-ending process. It continues on an *ad hoc* basis, often quite informally in the work area whenever needed. However, it is usually desirable to return to the conference room from time to time in order to give more deliberate consideration to ideas from a variety of sources.

A natural work group consisting of operators and their supervisor involved in a problem-solving–goal-setting session will usually discover their limitations before long and will see a need to invite other people into the meeting. In manufacturing operations, for example, it may become necessary to expand group membership to include industrial engineers, manufacturing engineers, inspectors, members of other assembly lines, and personnel specialists. The "invited guests" are included, of course, only if their particular competence is needed, and care should be taken to avoid expanding the membership needlessly. Justifiable expansion of membership, however, broadens the perspective of the group, enabling them to deal with problems that they would normally consider to be outside their realm of influence. More importantly, broadened membership enables the participants to appreciate their interdependence in achieving customer goals.

In common practice, the mixing of professional staff with people in manual occupations would create an unnatural situation. Their unequal educational levels and memberships in unequal job grade levels are normally deterrents of fluid communications between them. But their joint membership in the problem-solving–goal-setting conference changes their attitudes toward each other and toward their own roles. The engineer, for example, learns to perceive the female assembler, not as a "drone working to buy a television set," but in fact a creative person who generates ideas undiscovered by the engineers. In turn, the assemblers come to see the engineer less as an arbitrary authority figure and more as a person who has useful technical information that enables them to solve their problems more effectively.

Similarly, the inspector comes to appreciate the importance of immediate feedback to the operators, if they are to behave in a responsible fashion. Typically, the inspectors give quality reports to the supervisor, who transmits this information to the operator. There are two disadvantages to this two-step process. First, the relaying of information through a second person (the supervisor) to the operator delays and sometimes distorts it. Second, feedback from a supervisor is commonly perceived as criticism which tends to evoke defensiveness. The ideal feedback is the immediate transmittal of objective data directly to the individual whose skills produce the service or product. Hence, direct feedback from the inspector to the operator is better than relaying it through the supervisor, though the supervisor's responsibility may require simultaneous receipt of the same feedback. Even better, the system should be designed to enable operators to measure their own performance as a basis for self-control.

The definition of a natural work group changes as problem solving–goal setting progresses. In the beginning, a supervisor and those under his supervision may seem like the natural entity. But as the group expands to include members of interdependent functions, their common concern fuses them into a natural work group. United by their joint mission of providing a superior product or service to a common customer, they develop relationships in the conference room which are carried back to the work place, and a natural, fluid communication process continues among the operators, engineers, inspectors, and representatives of other functions on whom their effectiveness depends. No longer is the natural work group defined by the jurisdiction of supervisory authority. Rather, the expression of competence and commitment by individuals with a joint stake in the success of the mission becomes the influence for defining and uniting the natural work group.

The focus of these problem-solving–goal-setting sessions is on the achievement of customer goals. Every work group has a customer, but not all customers are the ultimate or outside customer. Sometimes the customer is an intermediate or inside customer—another division or department, or simply an adjacent production line. A staff group's customer is often a line operation. But every group is involved in providing either a product or a service for a customer. One of the important keys to problem solving–goal setting is providing group members with cost data, reliability standards, delivery schedules, and other necessary information usually retained by supervision and upper levels of management.

The sequence for expanding a natural work group is sometimes a key factor. If the initial problem-solving–goal-setting session includes participants from a variety of functions and levels of management, it will often get off to a poor or even unsuccessful start. In such sessions, the technically trained, or higher-level, people tend to dominate the meeting, and the operators are reticent about speaking up. Though they may have ideas, their unaccustomed inclusion in this "management meeting" evokes an understandable hesitancy about expressing themselves before their "superiors." But if the meeting is begun with the operators and carried on until they exhaust their ideas or discover their limitations, it is meaningful for them to suggest other people as resources, to be invited as guests or advisers into the conference. Having begun the sessions, the operators have proprietary feelings about the mission and have developed a confidence that enables them to continue contributing and to develop natural working relationships with the professionally trained people whom they were instrumental in bringing to the conference.

Needless to say, the problem-solving–goal-setting process depends on the competence of supervision. A supervisor who naturally shows respect and consideration to others (a theory Y manager) and who has done his homework in learning motivation theory, the characteristics of meaningful work, the techniques of work simplification, and the process of conference leadership will experience success. But the supervisor who lacks these skills and knowledge and who has low regard for his fellow man (a theory X manager) is bound to fail. This kind of person's attempts at problem solving–goal setting usually emerge as manipulation. Assuming that his people are incapable of coming up with ideas, he will "protect himself against failure" by coming to the conference room with a hidden agenda. He will present the problem to the employees and attempt to lead them into discovering his secretly predetermined solution to the problem. He is further reflecting his theory X orientation by assuming that they will fail to see through his shallow play. This kind of supervisor fails to realize that motivation springs not simply from *feelings* of involvement or responsibility, but rather from *actual* involvement and responsibility.

HOW WORKERS BECOME MANAGERS

A creative amalgamation of behavioral theory and technique was developed by Irving Borwick[11] and his associates in Steinberg's Limited, a major food chain headquartered in Montreal. It uniquely offers "management development" to rank-and-file employees to give substance to the concept "every employee a manager." It is probably one of the first programs to attempt systematically to develop wage earners so that they can assume managerial responsibility for the jobs they are now doing.

Borwick's "team improvement laboratory" (TIL), described in the following pages, is based upon the "grid" program of Blake and Mouton and the principles of Work Simplification of Allan Mogensen. Approximately one-third of the program is devoted to learning concepts of management and managerial styles, while two-thirds of the course is devoted to problem solving and managerial training. Though subsequent applications in more than 100 stores have differed experimentally from the model described here, and are implemented under different program names, the same basic principles and techniques are applied.

A typical TIL would involve about twenty persons, including the store manager, department managers, cashiers, and clerks.

Group activity is carefully scheduled for lectures and workshop

---

[11] Irving Borwick, "Team Improvement Laboratory," *Personnel Journal,* pp. 18–24, January, 1969.

activity, allowing participants freedom to learn on their own within this schedule. The program is run mainly on company time with straight-time pay for the regular work week. Because the majority of employees were in the bargaining unit, union officials were consulted about the program. They indicated they would have no objections as long as employee enrollment was voluntary.[12] There is, in fact, a strong demand by employees to participate; numerous comments indicate that participating in the program is viewed as an honor.

Supervisors assemble the employees at least a month before the start of the program and give a general outline of what will take place. They give each participant a collection of readings and questionnaires to complete as prework:

1. Synopsis of Blake and Mouton's theory of managerial grid, and questionnaire
2. *Every Employee a Manager* by Scott Myers
3. *Work Simplification and People* by Allan Mogensen, and questionnaire
4. *The Management of Change* by Leo Moore[13]

At the conclusion of the briefing session, each supervisor asks his team to select a project they would like to work on and improve. It is carefully explained that projects need not be problem areas, but can be any work situation that is functioning well which they might like to try to improve.

Employees read the material and complete the questions during the intervening month.

The educational level of employees in the program usually ranges from grades 7 to 12, and averages at grade 10. While some participants express some difficulty in reading the material, typically everyone completes it, and their performance puts them on a par with managers who have participated in similar exercises in other programs.

The TIL is usually held at a hotel located in the vicinity of the stores. Facilities include a general conference room and four rooms for the discussion teams. The session leader welcomes the group, advises them of the informality of the program (no suits or ties), and introduces the most senior man present, who outlines the objectives of the program:

---

[12] The union's consent is a testimonial to the success of earlier union-company development activity described on page 219.

[13] Leo B. Moore, "How to Manage Improvements," *Harvard Business Review*, pp. 75–84, July–August, 1958.

1. To provide an opportunity for people to make use of their capabilities and their creative and imaginative skills, in improving the work they are doing.
2. To enrich the jobs of these employees and to give them managerial control over their areas of responsibility.
3. To unleash the ideas and know-how of employees to bring about useful improvements in the work situation.
4. To bring about cost savings through improvements made on the job by individual employees.
5. To create an atmosphere conducive to open communication and mutual trust among people at various levels of the organization.
6. To create an atmosphere and frame of mind which challenges present methods of operation and is conducive to constant change for improvement.
7. To create project teams which provide the optimum opportunity for employees to participate in and work together on planning, controlling, doing, critiquing, and improving their work.

Following the objectives, they are assigned the task of reaching agreement on the forty-nine questions, which they completed individually as prework, concerning the concepts of the managerial grid. An hour is allocated.

Teams adjourn to the team room to complete this task. They return to the conference room following this session and score their results.

This session is followed by a 45-minute lecture which introduces the assumptions on which the TIL is based:

ASSUMPTIONS

1. People do not resist change; they resist being changed.
2. Every job is capable of being improved.
3. Every employee has the basic ability to improve his job.
4. People like to improve their work, and get satisfaction from their work.
5. People like to participate in groups.
6. Improvements are best made by those who perform the job.
7. Employees should be provided with the basic skills for job improvement through an educational program.

8. The role of the supervisor is one of adviser, consultant and coordinator.
9. The role of the employee is manager of his own area of responsibility.

Acceptance of these assumptions is the foundation for assuming managerial responsibility in their job. The first assumption, "People don't resist change; they resist being changed," emphasizes the objective of constantly changing the system rather than the man. Too often criticism of an operation is directed at, or is perceived as being directed at, the man who does the job rather than at the job itself. It is important to disassociate the two and objectify the analysis of the job. This prevents defensive behavior on the part of the operator, who is no longer the butt of adverse criticism and can willingly participate in altering the job and introducing change.

This last point is fundamental. Changes introduced by an individual not responsible for performance of the job are not likely to gain the same commitment as changes generated through employee involvement. Involvement is not a façade to suggest the illusion of reality but participation in the real sense of the word.

In the light of an understanding of assumption 1, assumption 6 becomes a corollary, "Improvements are best made by those who perform the job." Besides increasing the prospects of a committed and motivated person, such an assumption rests on the principle that he who does the job knows it best. This is not true in all cases, but it appears to be true more times than not. The person who performs a task usually has knowledge in depth not readily available to a supervisor or an outsider. With his technical proficiency and knowledge, he is the man most suited to change the job.

This assumption is tied into two other concepts, "Every job is capable of being improved" and "Every employee has the basic ability to improve his job." The latter is another case where the exceptions to the rule are minimal to such a degree as to be practically nonexistent. Any employee capable of performing a task has the capability to improve that job. The exceptions are likely to be jobs in which retarded individuals perform menial tasks under supervision. These exceptions are rare and do not invalidate the principle. On the other hand, the assumption leads one to the conclusion that there is a reservoir of untapped intellectual power. This tremendous reserve of people who perform rote tasks and whose energies and abilities are hardly utilized can effect a total revolution in the manner in which business is conducted.

It is important to stress this capability. Many employees, blinded to their own abilities by years of conformity to outmoded managerial practices, and blinded because of the authoritarian nature of their primary education, have lost faith in their capacity to alter the world in which they live. Allusions in the lectures and sessions to the work of Argyris, Blake, Herzberg, Likert, McGregor, Mogensen, Moore, and Myers reinforce the scientific underpinning on which such assumptions are made and give additional confidence to those small sparks of individuality that are thought to be alive in everyone, no matter how limited his experience.

To illustrate that every job is capable of being improved, allusion is made to work experience with which the group is familiar. A classic example frequently quoted is the experience of Procter & Gamble with pallets.

Procter & Gamble used regular wooden pallets to handle its products. While there was no problem in the efficiency or capability of such pallets, there was a cost factor involved. Procter & Gamble developed the paper pallet to replace the wooden pallet and reduced operational costs while maintaining efficiency. Efficiency was improved further when the palletless pallet was developed, a redesigned fork truck which now had two broad parallel plates which lifted a load by applying pressure from the sides. This eliminated the use of pallets for approximately 90 percent of Procter & Gamble products.

This type of case history illustrates three principles in work improvement:

1. That every job is capable of being improved.
2. That you do not select problem areas for improvement. It is even preferable to select jobs which are functioning well. There is no such thing as perfection.
3. That the ultimate goal in improving a job is to eliminate the task altogether.

Illustrations of this type, usually selected for their relevance to the areas in which employees work, demonstrate the validity of the concept that every job is capable of being improved.

The assumption that people like to improve their work and get satisfaction from it is supported by reference to McGregor's theory X and theory Y, Herzberg's hygiene and motivation studies, and Myers' "Who Are Your Motivated Workers?" [14]

In the same lecture, participants are introduced to Mogensen's "five-step pattern" for problem solving:

THE FIVE-STEP PATTERN

1. Select a job to improve.
2. Get all the facts.
3. Challenge every detail.
4. Develop the preferred method.
5. Install it—check results.

In conjunction with the five-step pattern, participants are also taught the rudiments of flow-process charting. This technique is an aid for analyzing their present jobs in the effort to improve what they are now doing. The teams are given a task to perform in which they apply the five-step pattern. In the case of the flow-process chart, once they have learned the rudiments of analysis, they immediately set to work using the five-step pattern and the charting technique to tackle their projects.

Teaching techniques place emphasis on team participation and direct involvement by participants. Every effort is made to avoid "telling" the student, and emphasis is placed upon students' discovering ideas for themselves. The four lectures occupy only 2 of the 38 hours normally spent in the TIL.

The teaching sequence is:

1. Assign prereading and exercises for completion before the sessions begin.
2. Task assignment is based on prework, completed first by individual and then by team.
3. Scoring of results, where appropriate, or a verbal exchange of results by a representative of each team.
4. Critique by the team of the results and their methodology in achieving these results.

The function of the laboratory leader is to coordinate these activities, act as a resource for problem situations and deliver the four lectures. Most of the learning is done without the leader's intervention.

[14] Myers, *op cit.*, p. 10.

Films are also used during the laboratory to introduce new information not covered in the prereading and are the object of further task assignments. In this laboratory, three films are used to teach management styles, the flow-process chart, and one approach to team job improvement.

The four lectures are interspersed with laboratory experience in the following sequence:

1. Assumptions and the five-step pattern (Borwick, Mogensen)
2. Managerial styles (Blake and Mouton)
3. Every employee a manager (Myers)
4. How to manage improvement (Moore)

At the end of the program, the employees, working in teams, establish an improvement program to be implemented upon their return to the work situation. The teams determine objectives, design a strategy for achieving the objectives, and then implement the tactics that will accomplish the goal.

It is made clear to employees during the lecture on change that the task of developing a program for change is a team effort and is clearly related to their new role as managers. Through examination of the managerial functions already outlined in the lecture "Every employee a manager," correlation is made between the management functions (planning, doing, and controlling) and the development of a regular program of planned improvement on a systematic basis. Figure 3-12 illustrates the scope of the management functions for an enriched clerk-packer job in the supermarket.

Change should not occur as the effect of random events upon current practice, but rather as the effect of planned efforts by managers in control of their own areas of responsibility. To implement this concept, teams are asked to define operations they would like to improve in their respective work areas. This task follows immediately after they have undergone training in flow-process charting as a technique for analysis. Armed with their new knowledge of managerial responsibility, team activity, problem solving, and analysis, project teams begin a determined assault on their projects. Teams spend approximately 8 hours working on projects.

There are a number of reasons for devoting so much time to these projects. In the first place, sufficient time must be allocated for analysis and improvement. Second, the aim of the TIL is to develop every employee as a manager. It is not sufficient to "tell" employees how to

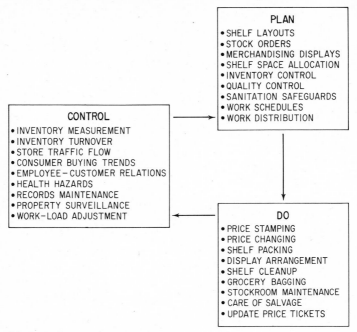

FIG. 3-12   Supermarket clerk-packer.

manage. If they are ever to be managers, they must begin to assume managerial responsibility.

TIL graduates assume managerial responsibility for assigned areas immediately upon completion of the program. Eventually, individuals and/or teams will be responsible for scheduling, budgeting, controlling, ordering, critiquing, and improving their own areas. They will also be provided with sales objectives, margins, product turns, and costs. The initial program has envisaged a slow development of these responsibilities based upon a growing demand by trained employees for greater managerial responsibility. Moreover, employees get additional skill training on the job and off, in order to increase their efficiency and productivity and also in order that they may assume greater responsibility.

The final session is designed to allow the employees and their senior supervisor, the store manager, to meet together and work out the details of implementing the TIL in their stores. The store manager, who has been a participant until now, becomes the discussion leader. Employees know that this program is not a one-shot affair, that following conclusion of the laboratory, they will continue to meet once a week in the same teams in their respective work areas.

Store personnel have been provided with a model of how the program should work, but every model must be altered to suit the individual circumstances of the store. The details of future meeting logistics are agreed upon before personnel return to the work situation. Together, the entire staff including department heads, manager, and all employees, work out how the program will operate when they will meet, and how projects will be implemented on an ongoing basis.

People who have gone through the TIL program are excited and actively participating. Employees not yet involved in the program are actively interested and excited at the possibilities of the program. When a TIL meeting was cancelled because it conflicted with a union membership meeting, employees got the union to call and confirm that the meeting would be rescheduled.

Jobs have been enriched, new ideas have been unleashed, and a greater openness of communication has come about. More and more the employees are influencing the management of the operation. Improvements generated through the program include a productivity increase of approximately $2 in sales per man-hour. Though other improvements are realized, it is difficult to measure improvements directly attributable to TIL efforts. For example, though observations have indicated that courtesy and concern for the customer and rise in sales were both above normal, it may be premature to interpret these effects as cause-and-effect results arising from the TIL; or if a cause-and-effect relationship does exist, it may be premature to assume that the results will be lasting. However, in terms of the intervening variables of changing attitudes, educating employees, developing managerial skills, and introducing control of change, the program is already successful.

chapter four

The Changing Roles of Management

Management of change is the key function of the manager, in regard to both human effort and technology. The responsibility is not new, of course, but it is becoming increasingly complicated by the accelerating rate of change in all media. Because change requires adaptation at all levels of the organization, the manager is confronted with the circular problem of encouraging innovation, while introducing changes in a manner that will not threaten the innovators. Being human, the manager, too, is vulnerable to change, and he must be able to monitor and evaluate his own effectiveness and take measures to prevent his own obsolescence. Through the media of supervisory style, management systems, and other factors affecting the organization's climate, he must gradually shift the source of influence from authority to competence so that initiative and freedom at all levels of the organization will find responsible expression.

He is challenged further by the requirement for applying principles of human effectiveness in operations in other cultures. The role of the American abroad is defined, with particular reference to his relationships with indigenous personnel. In part, the role of the

American abroad is a response to Servan-Schreiber,[1] who sees America's industrial invasion as a threat to other countries' economic and cultural sovereignty, and articulates a plea for Europeans and other international associates to unite against the omnipresent expatriate American entrepreneur.

THE ROLE OF THE SUPERVISOR

The preceding chapter presents a framework to erase the management-labor dichotomy and give substance to the slogan "Every employee a manager"—a manager being defined as one who manages a job. A self-managed job is one which provides a realistic opportunity for the incumbent to be responsible for the total plan-do-control phases of his job. Though many jobs in their present forms cannot be fully enriched, most can be improved and some can be eliminated. Whether the supervisor's mission is to enrich, to improve, or to eliminate the job, he achieves it best by utilizing the talents of the incumbents themselves.

The supervisor must be able to understand the conditions which promote and inhibit expression of talent in terms of interpersonal competence, meaningful goals, and helpful systems, as defined on pages 24 to 54. In satisfying these conditions, he must be able to hold the mirror up to himself and see himself objectively—to find out what new responsibilities and activities he should be involved with, and which of his traditional roles should be modified or discontinued. As he is human, changes in his role are unsettling or threatening, particularly if they are imposed by authority. His dilemma is ameliorated if he himself is the initiator and agent of his changing role.

Self-imposed Role Ambiguity

When production supervisors in Texas Instruments introduced the problem-solving–goal-setting process, they did so in an attempt to invoke the talent of their groups in achieving difficult production goals. Their efforts were rewarded when the job-enrichment process led to the successful attainment of goals. Moreover, they noted that, in addition to the increase in production, the quality of workmanship improved; complaints about maintenance factors decreased; and

[1] J.-J. Servan-Schreiber, *The American Challenge*, Atheneum Publishers, New York, 1969.

absenteeism, tardiness, and trips to the health center, restrooms, and personnel department diminished. In some cases, they found commitment so high it became essential to remind employees to take the legally required rest periods in midmorning and midafternoon.

With their increased freedom and involvement in managing their own work, operators began working directly with the engineers in methods improvement, value analysis, and rearranging their work place. Supervisors permitted these new work roles of the operators primarily because they resulted in improved performance. But the operators' activities did not always of necessity involve the supervisors, who became understandably uncomfortable with the resultant ambiguity of their own roles. One supervisor's anxiety reached a new high when a problem-solving group told him that he was free to attend to other matters and that they would keep him posted on their progress. Consequently, a group of these disfranchised supervisors, with the assistance of the division training director, undertook the task of defining their new role.

Role Redefinition

The results of this group's efforts are reflected in Figure 4-1. Initial efforts of the group produced the traditional authority-oriented role detailed in the left column—not because they were committed to this role, but, rather, because their anxiety and haste regressed them temporarily to the typical textbook definition of the role of supervision. After evaluating and then rejecting this traditional role as an inaccurate description of their emerging role, they restated their supervisory responsibilities, thereby defining the goal-oriented role column.

Though most of the items in the left column are acceptable in the light of tradition, their collective effect tends to reinforce the authority-oriented relationship, depicted in the diagram at the foot of the column, in which people conform to the plan-lead-control directions received from their supervisors. Items in the goal-oriented column do not differ completely from those in the authority-oriented column, but their net effect provides opportunity for people to manage the full plan-do-control phases of their work, involving supervisors as resources.

During the discussion of the emerging role of the supervisor, the group concluded that an effective supervisor is one who provides a climate in which people have a sense of working for themselves. In

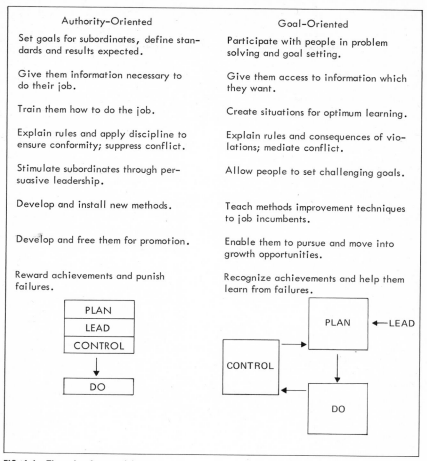

Authority-Oriented

Set goals for subordinates, define standards and results expected.

Give them information necessary to do their job.

Train them how to do the job.

Explain rules and apply discipline to ensure conformity; suppress conflict.

Stimulate subordinates through persuasive leadership.

Develop and install new methods.

Develop and free them for promotion.

Reward achievements and punish failures.

Goal-Oriented

Participate with people in problem solving and goal setting.

Give them access to information which they want.

Create situations for optimum learning.

Explain rules and consequences of violations; mediate conflict.

Allow people to set challenging goals.

Teach methods improvement techniques to job incumbents.

Enable them to pursue and move into growth opportunities.

Recognize achievements and help them learn from failures.

FIG. 4-1   The role of supervision.

terms of their day-to-day relationships, they defined the supervisor's role as:

- Giving visibility to company goals.
- Providing budgets and facilities.
- Mediating conflict.
- Staying out of the way to let people manage their work.

Giving visibility to company goals means sharing information with the members of the group who are to be involved in achieving a specific customer goal. In a production line, for example, it means defining the group's mission to provide a product for a customer, including cost, quality, and schedule requirements. It means detailing the overhead, materiel, and labor costs associated with providing the product or service, showing the percentage each contributes to the total cost, and distinguishing between the fixed and variable costs. All members of the group should be able to see the problem essentially as the supervisor sees it and should have access to any information needed to achieve their goal. The key to this function is emphasizing the facts that everyone has a customer, whether this customer is the ultimate customer or another department or assembly line within the company, and that the group goal is to satisfy the customer's need.

Providing budgets and facilities does not mean financing every improvement or capital investment suggested by the members of the group. It does mean sharing with them the rationale for managing a budget and, if a capital investment is suggested, explaining the amortization process and exploring with them its application to a suggested expenditure. When the group is involved in assessing a proposed investment in terms of increased efficiency, the duration of the project, change in quality, etc., they can see whether or not it is a sound economic investment, and a decision to buy or not to buy is a matter of logic rather than an arbitrary decision based on authority.

The mediation of conflict is an ongoing and often misunderstood role of supervision. Conflict always exists; however, the nature of conflict varies. In the environment of meaningless or oppressive work, conflict naturally arises as a form of displaced aggression or as a means of breaking the monotony. In an environment of challenging and interesting work, conflict may arise as a result of competition and efforts to overcome barriers to individual and group goals. This type of conflict is not harmful, as long as it is surfaced and group members are able to cope with it. Supervisors too often believe that conflict is undesirable and must be suppressed—not realizing that such a strategy deals only with symptoms.

Staying out of the way to let people manage their work does not mean abandoning the group, but it does mean being sensitive to the needs of individuals in regard to their desire and ability to be responsible for many planning and control functions of their job. When delegation is done successfully, people are not subjected to imposed direction and control, but have the freedom to pursue goals which they have helped define. They will seek help from any source to achieve this goal, including the supervisor if he has earned their acceptance and has something to contribute in the nature of needed business information or technical competence. The intervention of authority in a team effort is usually felt more as an inhibiting than as a facilitating influence.

Goals Replace Conformity

This redefinition of the supervisor's role to provide opportunity for people to manage their own work is portrayed in Figure 4-2. In contrast to the authority-conformity-oriented roles of the supervisor and operator shown in Figure 3-8, each now has a goal-oriented role in which the revised *do* phase of the supervisor and *plan* phase of the operator compose the realm of interface between them. Figures 4-1 and 4-2 both show the goal-oriented supervisor to be a resource person whose involvement is invoked primarily at the initiative of the operator.

This role of the leader, evolved initially to illustrate the relationship between the foreman and operators, is a model representing ideal supervisory relationships at any level. Furthermore, enriching the operator's job has changed higher-level jobs, in some cases making it possible to reduce the number of levels in the management hierarchy. The foreman, now freed of many detailed maintenance and control functions, has more time to be involved with his supervisor in higher-level planning functions and is also more available to meet his responsibility as a mediator and resource person when needed by the natural work group under his supervision.

The application of meaningful work offers substantial short-range incentive for managers to support it. Judged as they are, periodically, in terms of profit, cost reduction, cash flow, share of the market, and return-on-investment criteria, job enrichment is valued as a process for achieving success. But it offers even greater rewards on a long-term basis, particularly if criteria of success are broadened to include aspects of human effectiveness such as better utilization of employee talent, responsible civic and home relationships, and the profitable and self-renewing growth of the organization.

Responsibility Replaces Prerogatives

Gone are management prerogatives. Management prerogatives, by definition, are exclusive rights based on authority. The specifying of

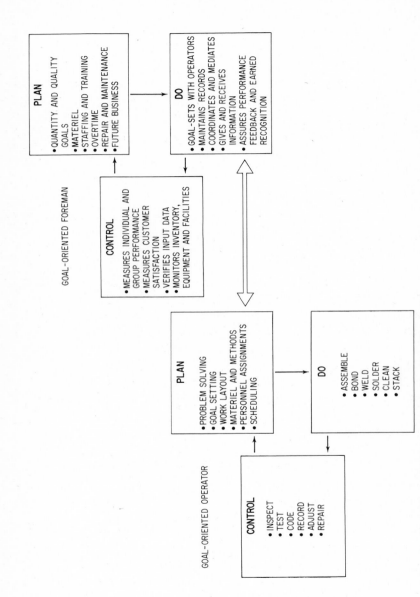

FIG. 4-2 Goal-oriented relationship between foreman and operator.

GOAL-ORIENTED FOREMAN

PLAN
• QUANTITY AND QUALITY GOALS
• MATERIEL
• STAFFING AND TRAINING
• OVERTIME
• REPAIR AND MAINTENANCE
• FUTURE BUSINESS

CONTROL
• MEASURES INDIVIDUAL AND GROUP PERFORMANCE
• MEASURES CUSTOMER SATISFACTION
• VERIFIES INPUT DATA
• MONITORS INVENTORY, EQUIPMENT AND FACILITIES

DO
• GOAL-SETS WITH OPERATORS
• MAINTAINS RECORDS
• COORDINATES AND MEDIATES
• GIVES AND RECEIVES INFORMATION
• ASSURES PERFORMANCE FEEDBACK AND EARNED RECOGNITION

GOAL-ORIENTED OPERATOR

PLAN
• PROBLEM SOLVING
• GOAL SETTING
• WORK LAYOUT
• MATERIEL AND METHODS
• PERSONNEL ASSIGNMENTS
• SCHEDULING

CONTROL
• INSPECT
• TEST
• CODE
• RECORD
• ADJUST
• REPAIR

DO
• ASSEMBLE
• BOND
• WELD
• SOLDER
• CLEAN
• STACK

"management" prerogatives evokes a requirement for "labor" prerogatives. Evaluation of labor prerogatives shows them to be un-aligned with, or contradictory to, company goals, as shown in Figure 5-16. Hence, it is self-defeating to articulate and act through the authority of management prerogatives. The divine rights of "King Supervisor" are being relinquished under the self-imposed pressures of enlightenment. The price of management prerogatives in terms of quashed initiative, alienation, and unachieved goals is much too high for all but those seeking satisfaction of pathological needs for power and manipulation.

Prerogatives have given way to responsibility—to customers, share-holders, employees, and the community. To the *customer* the manager is responsible for delivering a superior product or service at minimum cost. To the *shareholder* or owner he is responsible for max-imizing return on investment. To the *employee* he is responsible for providing a meaningful life at work. And the manager's impact is made on the *community* by the emulation in homes of his leadership patterns on the job. Democratic or autocratic managers began the development of their management styles in democratic and autocratic homes under parents whose styles of supervision were often copied from the job situation. Hence, industry represents a potent medium for influencing the philosophy of a culture.

Competence Replaces Authority

Influence is still needed to satisfy this new role; however, it is not the influence of official supervisory authority but, rather, the unofficial influence of all members of the group based on their competence and commitment to goals. Both kinds of influence exist in all organiza-tions, and the manager's supervisory style determines and indicates which is predominant.

For practical purposes, what really matters in industry is not whether the supervisor has official authority or not, but whether he is accepted by the people in his group. The supervisor whose behavior has earned the acceptance and respect of his work group has, in effect, transformed his official authority to unofficial acceptance. He is both the formal and the informal leader of the group, and he succeeds as a leader not by virtue of authority from above, but through the willing acceptance of those below.

Leadership is not a psychological trait but a function of the situation and the nature of the group. In a given situation, the effective leader is the person most fitted to take charge. The supervisor who is the official group leader will try to see to it that he is accepted willingly as the appropriate leader in that situation, rather than grudgingly as the leader forced on the group by virtue of his formal authority.

The manager who insists on using the influence of official authority in today's enlightened society will increasingly be frustrated by negative reactions to his attempted use of arbitrary direction and control. No matter how technically correct and logically insightful the direction given by the manager, his style of dispensing information and influencing the group will be a key determinant of his success. The successful manager has learned to avoid the use of official authority and succeeds through the constructive harnessing of his group's competence. He knows how to organize his materiel and manpower in ways that allow free expression of talent in defining problems, in setting goals, and in managing resources for achieving these goals.

The new role of the supervisor is not always accepted easily. Testimonials from others who solve production problems with the help of operators are often received with mixed reactions. For some managers, the involvement of subordinates in solving management problems is seen as an expression of weakness that is bound to cause loss of respect from subordinates. Such managers oppose worker involvement, as capitulation or as relinquishment of management prerogatives. Reactions of this type are not uncommon, as authority-oriented relationships fostered in many homes, schools, military organizations, and other institutions find natural expression in most job situations. A supervisor does not switch styles by edict or as an immediate consequence of reading a book or hearing an inspiring speech. An intellectual message may sensitize him to his problem, but he must work through the process of self-evaluation, self-acceptance, adjustment of values, and change of behavior at his own pace, in his own way, and only in a climate conducive to change. The pressure of an edict to "be democratic" will only regress him to familiar old authority-oriented patterns, from which stance he will obediently recite the official intellectual message.

Supervisory effectiveness results from job enrichment as a circular phenomenon. In the first instance, job enrichment requires action (or discontinuation of previous action) on the part of the supervisor to supply conditions of human effectiveness. The results of this action in turn reinforce it and encourage its application by others. Its application brings about subtle changes in the perceptions, the values, and finally, the habits of the supervisors, so that in a gradual branching and multiplying process a new way of life at work is put into motion which simultaneously changes and effects changes through the supervisor. Hence, the supervisor is the originator of and the medium for change—providing conditions for the development of others and thereby bringing about his own self-development or obsolescence.

Avoidance of Obsolescence

The manager is both an agent and the potential victim of the accelerated rate of change in evidence throughout society. In industry this accelerated change is shortening the life span of technologies and jobs and placing an unprecedented demand on employees in all functions and levels to adapt to new roles and new job demands. Ernst Weber, president of the Polytechnic Institute of Brooklyn, has illustrated this shortening job life by showing in Figure 4-3 that the engineering graduate of 1900 was able to coast for approximately 35 years before becoming obsolete. The 1930 graduate could go for approximately 20 years before obsolescence. The engineer of today, without ongoing technological training, finds himself obsolete in 10 years or less. This trend suggests that the ever-steepening curve of obsolescence will

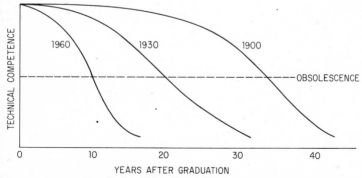

FIG. 4-3 Life span of an engineering degree. (Ernst Weber, president, Polytechnic Institute of Brooklyn, *Electronic News*, Nov. 29, 1965).

make it necessary for the engineer to continue his technological education immediately after graduation and after he has accepted employment as an engineer.

Though criteria for measuring obsolescence are not always as tangible for the manager as they are for the engineer, there is evidence that managerial obsolescence may closely parallel engineering obsolescence. Figure 4-4 presents two management career curves: one for the manager who continues to adapt to, cope with, and effect change, and the other, the "rainbow curve" of an obsolescing manager who experiences progressive disengagement from managerial responsibility. Though actual career curves do not follow such smooth patterns, and seem to have an infinite variety of patterns, these two smoothed curves reflect a common dilemma in industry.

The growth curve reflects an assumption that a manager's effectiveness can continue to improve throughout his career, and that the worst thing that need happen to him is a leveling off during the last 10 years before retirement. Some managers seem to follow such a pattern. A few continue to grow at a steep pace up to sixty-five, and when they are separated from the organization through mandatory retirement policy, they go into new careers.

The obsolescence curve reflects the common plight of the manager who attains his peak effectiveness during his middle years and gradually loses effectiveness, to be retired at age sixty-five or earlier.

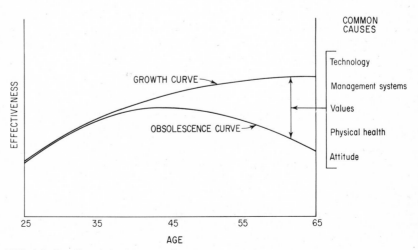

FIG. 4-4   Growth and obsolescence of managers.

The widening gap between the effective manager and the obsolescing manager usually cannot be attributed to a single cause, but usually can be explained in terms of one or more of five common factors:

1. Keeping up with technology
2. Management systems competence
3. Adapting to changing values
4. Physical fitness
5. Overcoming the folklore of aging

Intimate knowledge of *technology* is not seen by many managers as a primary requirement for their success. However, many consider it of at least secondary importance, particularly in research and engineering, if for no other reason than to maintain rapport and team effectiveness within their group. In a world of disappearing management prerogatives, competence is supplanting authority as the source of influence, and the R&D supervisor often feels that his ability to relate to his group as a professional peer enhances the likelihood of team effectiveness in his group. However, the maintenance of technological competence may represent a trap leading to dereliction of managerial responsibilities necessary for effective coordinating and delegating. It may be argued that ignorance of technology, coupled with leadership competence, results in better utilization and development of a group's talents.

In a sense, *management systems* represent the technology of managing, and, like engineers, managers are finding it increasingly difficult to keep abreast of their technology. Management systems, as defined here, are not restricted to EDP-based systems, but more broadly are a "process of people interacting to apply resources to achieve goals" as elaborated on pages 117 to 129. The support of constructive group dynamics in a world depersonalized by automation and bureaucratic controls demands competence in both behavioral theory and EDP technology. The successful manager has learned the futility of imposing masterminded systems and has learned to plan the development and administration of systems in accordance with principles defined on pages 46 to 54 and 117 to 129.

Changing values and expectations are natural consequences of the knowledge explosion. The manager who attempts to manage from the foundation of authoritarian values that were tolerated a generation earlier is obsolete. He is obsolete because a manager's values are the foundation for his style of supervision. The manager who manages through the arbitrary use of authority, as defined on pages 32 to 35, will increasingly encounter resistance and rebellion. The manager who sees technical competence and the broadly shared opportunity for problem solving and responsible behavior as the source of influence is attuned to the trends of the times. Adapting to changing values does not, of course, mean capitulation and relinquishment of moral and ethical standards, but does require sensitivity to, and respect for, the increasing need for freedom and independence.

Though managerial effectiveness and obsolescence are largely mental phenomena, they can be influenced by factors associated with *physical fitness.* Busy executives, in their pursuit of organizational success, commonly overburden themselves, working long hours, eating irregular and unbalanced meals, getting insufficient exercise, and developing the middle-age spread when only halfway through their forty-year careers as managers. As this physical neglect takes its toll through fatigue and health factors, the manager is forcefully hindered and frustrated. He finds himself the unwilling and premature victim of physical obsolescence which forces him to adjust his aspirations and work habits. His usual self-confidence gives way to anxiety and feelings of insecurity. Though preventive maintenance in the form of exercise, adequate rest, and balanced diet can avoid this pitfall, most people prior to physical breakdown have little incentive to change well-established living habits. Dr. Cureton[2] and others have shown that physical health can be retrieved by radically changed and rigorously followed living patterns, but few seem willing to make such adaptations.

The manager's *attitudes,* as shaped by tradition, are often the key to his obsolescence or continuing effectiveness. Many managers seem to accept the cliché "You can't teach an old dog new tricks" and abandon hope in the middle years on the assumption that they are too old to learn. Actually, old dogs can be taught new tricks, but not if they think they cannot! The same is true for managers, and if a manager is only twenty-five and believes himself incapable of learning, for practical purposes he is on his way to obsolescence.

The attitudinal factor is key for two reasons. First, it is essential that a person see the feasibility of avoiding obsolescence and understand its causes and preventive measures. But perhaps more importantly, a

---

[2] Thomas K. Cureton, Jr., *Physical Fitness and Dynamic Health,* The Dial Press, Inc., New York, 1965.

manager must understand that his attitude can influence the obsolescence or growth of his subordinates. The bypassing of older employees in handing out challenging assignments is a language of action that tells the bypassed individual that his supervisor thinks he is "over the hill," raising his own doubts about his continuing effectiveness. In his anxiety to prove himself in his narrowed responsibility, he strives harder to give visibility to his own achievements. His random and ineffective efforts, in a circular fashion, cause his responsibilities to be narrowed further. In a continuing spiral, his anxieties are increased, evoking more random, nonproductive behavior, amplifying and reinforcing his image of ineffectiveness.

But when the aging employee receives a challenging responsibility, it represents a vote of confidence from his supervisor, to bolster his confidence and allay subconscious doubts, providing the opportunity for achievement and continuing growth. Sustained opportunity for success experiences through challenging assignments thus represents a potent antidote to obsolescence.

The causes and correlates of obsolescence enumerated above are not exhaustive, nor can they be assigned relative importance. They tend to be situational to the individual, his job, his organization, or any combination of these and other factors. For one manager, the key may be technology; for another, it may be physical factors; one may need updating in managing systems; for some, all factors may be important. As a generalization, the challenge of continuing human effectiveness in any function or level of the organization is most often satisfied through the opportunities for growth, achievement, responsibility, and recognition afforded by meaningful work.

ORGANIZATIONAL CLIMATE

Every organization can be said to have a climate which colors the perceptions and feelings of people within their work environment. A company's climate is influenced by innumerable factors such as its size, the nature of its business, its age, its location, the composition of its work force, its management policies, rules and regulations, and the values and leadership styles of its supervisors. Many of the factors influencing an organization's climate are dynamic and interactive, resulting in ever-changing "weather" within the organization. However, some factors remain relatively constant, tending to stabilize other factors around a modal or characteristic climate for the organization. Some of these pivotal factors are defined below.

Growth Rate

Rate of growth is a climate factor. In a rapidly expanding organization, the sense of urgency and speed of change create rich opportunities for individual growth, achievement, responsibility, and recognition. Domineering supervisors who would seem oppressive in a stable organization are tolerated in the growth climate, perhaps because their roles are seen as transitory. Also, the sheer pressure of expanding responsibility reduces the authoritarian manager's ability to maintain tight controls, and delegation occurs, if only by default.

In the stabilized or retrenching organization, a condition which often coincides with economic pressures, managers frequently resort to reductive supervisory practices. Delegation is curtailed and growth opportunities are interrupted or deferred, and the more talented members of the work force become impatient and discouraged. Eager to forge ahead, they seek greener pastures, and gradually abandon the organization to those who have less ability either to relocate themselves or to revive the organization. The loss of top talent to competitor organizations, of course, further handicaps the plateaued organization. Hence, growth itself is needed if for no other reason than to retain the talented personnel upon whom the continuing success of the organization depends.

Delegation

Delegation, as a climate factor, is expressed both through style of supervision and through organization structure. Managers operating on the basis of goal-oriented assumptions, as defined on page 31, delegate naturally and willingly—particularly managers who are themselves the recipients of delegated authority. Authority-oriented managers, in contrast, fail to delegate and do little to encourage delegation below them.

The business organized around decentralized semi-autonomous product-customer centers tends to foster delegation better than the functionally layered organization. In a functionally layered organization, for example, the manager of manufacturing with five plants under his jurisdiction has limited freedom to exercise his judgment in setting goals and managing plant resources if another manager is responsible for the sale of his products and another is responsible for research in the five plants. In contrast, a plant manager who has the threefold responsibility of creating, making, and marketing products or income-producing services has more flexibility in managing his resources and in making decisions necessary for organizational success. He is less hampered by the bureaucratic constrictions of poorly coordinated jurisdictions, and can more naturally delegate to others the freedom necessary for building an empire on a foundation of entrepreneurial principles.

Innovation

The spontaneous and constructive expression of creativity is a desirable characteristic of an organization's climate—in the management process as well as in the laboratory. Though managers readily enough accept the principle that they are managers of innovation, few plan for it or demonstrate constructive creativity in their normal day-to-day behavior. Worse yet, official commitment to the support of innovation may foster formidable official systems for "managing innovation" which tend to quash it. Rewards in the form of raises, bonuses, and promotions more often go to those who support the "system," while those who might be involved in the constructive departure from the *status quo* tend to be punished or expelled from the system.

Innovation exists in great abundance in every organization, but not always to the benefit of the organization. In the democratic organization in which people at all levels have opportunity to receive information, solve problems, and set goals, innovation finds positive expression. In organizations characterized by tight supervision, inflexible rules, engineered labor standards, and other authority-oriented controls, creativity finds reactive expression, usually to the detriment of the organization. The tighter the controls, the more innovativeness is directed toward circumventing them. Hence, the problem is not one of evoking innovativeness as much as it is one of providing outlets which give positive expression to innovativeness.

Constructive innovation is encouraged not only by style of management, but also by appropriate systems for managing innovation. The hierarchy of objectives, strategies, and tactical action programs described on pages 50 and 52 provides a framework in which the efforts of task forces can find creative expression in achieving organizational goals. The work-simplification process described on pages 190–191 teaches problem-solving–goal-setting techniques and philosophy to give expression to creativity at all levels of the organization. The task-force analysis of attitude survey results, as described on pages 203 to 212, is a system for better utilization of talent at all levels. A climate of innovation is also enhanced by the avoidance of authority-based systems such as engineered labor standards, chain-of-command communication, defensive expense reporting, and elaborate status symbols.

Authority Orientation .

An organization's climate may be described in terms of goal orientation or authority orientation. An employee may be described as goal-oriented if he understands his job in terms of what it does for the customer, but he is authority-oriented if he performs his job in blind obedience to an order from his boss.

The reductive use of authority, as described on pages 32 to 35, is not an indictment of authority per se. Authority is freedom to act, and it is needed by every member of the organization. However, it is damaging when people at higher levels, deliberately or in ignorance, create systems or behave in ways that deprive people lower in the organization of the information and freedom necessary for goal orientation.

Without deliberate efforts to prevent it, growing organizations drift inexorably toward an authority-dominated climate. The worker parks on the company parking lot according to rules established by a nebulous "management," and the lower his rank, the farther out his parking space. He records his entry and departure from the plant by official timekeeping procedures, he is told by his supervisor what his job is and perhaps by his union steward what his job is not. Industrial engineering defines "correct" procedures and specifies his quantity and quality goals. A signal bell authorizes the beginning and ending of his coffee break and lunch period, and posted notices tell him he cannot eat or smoke in the hallways. Information is dispensed by management through the public-address system, official bulletins, the company newspaper, and bulletin boards. His pay is determined through the value judgment of supervision, and his paycheck is prepared by computer, minus deductions authorized by Federal and state laws, the union, and management. His supervisor may review his performance with him, detailing his strong and weak points, and prescribe remedial actions. The United Fund and Savings Bond Drives for "voluntary" participation are administered through a process which would make his nonparticipation threatening to those above him, and hence to him. His recourse in case of injustice is a grievance procedure which he hesitates to use because of the possibility of alienating his superior and incurring subtle reprisals. His request for time off must be justified to his supervisor by what is sometimes a humiliating detailing of personal information. When he seeks transfers and promotions, or decides to terminate, his dependency on his supervisor's goodwill is inescapable. Though deliberate strategies can prevent or counter the oppressiveness of authority in an organization's climate, few large organizations have succeeded in doing so.

Goal Orientation

Goal orientation is the motivational force which gives direction to the systems and relationships defined throughout this book. It is the climate factor created by processes which give visibility to broad organizational goals, and it allows access to information and freedom to act so that individual initiative finds expression in setting goals and measuring achievements. A goal-oriented person manages his job, in contrast to the authority-oriented person who feels he is managed by his job. Goal orientation depends on an integrated balance of meaningful goals, helpful systems, and interpersonal competence, as detailed in Chapter 2. Deliberate and systematic attempts are made in goal-oriented organizations to minimize the status symbols which tend to sensitize people to authority. Dining facilities are shared by all employees; employee identification badges do not reflect rank; parking privileges, office space, and furnishings are assigned on the basis of factors other than organizational level. Mode of attire is not standardized and is often informal. People address each other on a first-name basis and tend to communicate through the informal and fluid grapevine which exists in every organization. The unwritten, but apparent, ground rule followed by members of the organization is that individuals treat each other with the mutual respect and informality of social peers. The supervisor's influence is not a manifestation of arbitrary direction and control but, rather, results from his role as an adviser, consultant, and coordinator. The net effect of such a system is to enable people to relate to each other on a competence basis in the pursuit of common goals, rather than to sensitize them to, and sandwich them into, an authority hierarchy.

Status

Climates differ with regard to the amount and kind of status afforded through organizational membership. Status may be considered as official and unofficial.

Official status is derived from the prestige of having a high job grade and salary or occupying a responsible position in the organizational hierarchy. Increased official status is an incentive for personal and professional growth for those who have the talent and desire to achieve it. But not every person wants a promotion in the sense of a higher job grade or becoming a supervisor or plant manager. However, every person does want the prestige of being a better craftsman and a valued member of his work group.

Unofficial status is a function of a person's contribution to the purposes of his work group, not only in achieving production goals, but also arising from such diverse factors as his skill with certain tools and equipment, his knowledge of a particular process or technology, his generosity, his ability to make others laugh, his contagious enthusiasm, his role as a sympathetic listener, or his willingness to accept an unpleasant task. The advantage of unofficial status is that it contains room for all; respect for a machinist does not detract from respect for a secretary, or engineer, or assembler. Nor does respect for one assembler preclude respect for another; each earns respect on the basis of unique competence factors.

Unofficial status leads to less rivalry and more satisfaction than official status based on power or wealth. Official status is more vulnerable to the whims of politics and happenstance, disappearing with demotions and organizational changes. Unofficial status is more intrinsic to the individual, is earned through personal achievements and attributes, and tends to go with him, granting him more lasting or permanent prestige. Further, unofficial status carries with it no authority-oriented status symbols. For the mature and accepted member of the work group, earned status (official or unofficial) is its own reward and needs no visible symbols. The flaunting of symbols, particularly the official reminders of inequality, is symptomatic of immaturity and serves only to undermine feelings of dignity and worth in persons who have lower official status—persons on whom those of higher official status depend for their continuing success.

Most people want to belong to a group and to be able to take pride in it. This belongingness and pride of membership constitute an opportunity and an advantage for the organization with a favorable company or product image. Attractive grounds and buildings and prestigious products are often symbols of status in a community and a source of pride at all levels of the organization. The attitude of the individual to his work group offers the key to filling jobs that would otherwise have low status, the key to getting people who will do the less attractive work. More important than the status of the job is the prestige of the group for which the job is done. Physicians and nurses, for example, have to do things that would disgust unskilled workers who did not see these actions in their professional context; yet the prestige of people in medicine is generally high. Hence, the prestige of the physician's work group and his needed contributions to it make such jobs acceptable. If the prestige of a person's group is high and he earns status by his membership in it, the unpleasant aspects of the work he has to do are of little importance.

Communication

The type and quality of communication within an organization are usually functions of the size and predominant managerial style of the organization. One consequence of the growth of an organization is the tendency to formalize communications. In the small organization, informal face-to-face communication usually finds natural expression, and managers who do not actively prevent it have the benefit of a well-informed work force. However, as the organization expands, relationships become more formalized and communications begin to lag.

A typical bureaucratic response to communication breakdown is the creation of the AVO (avoid verbal orders) and other formalized reporting processes for committing communications to paper. Though seemingly a harmless beginning, traffic in interoffice memos expands exponentially. The memo writer routinely prepares copies for his and the recipient's supervisor, and "for good measure" to others whose responsibilities are at least remotely related. These memos and their copies evoke responses in a reciprocating and exponential volume, to earn for the organization the self-imposed title of "the paper mill." The formalized communication process tends to reinforce an authority-oriented chain of command, quashing the spontaneous interactive process natural to the small organization and necessary for the functioning of a goal-oriented cohesive work force.

Apart from reasons associated with the size and complexity of the organization, communications may lose efficiency because of their defensive application against reductive managerial styles. When the interpersonal trust factor is low, "official" memos are written to provide instruction, obtain compliance, request approval, justify actions, and report progress. Informal oral commitment is no longer adequate, and rejected or unheard viewpoints find expression in the form of "letters to the file" as protection against the vagaries of the future. The massive flow of protective paperwork becomes known as the "paper umbrella."

Concomitant with organizational growth, computer technology is expanded and management systems applications are increased. The flow of memos, forms, and computer printouts increases, jamming in-baskets, filling file cabinets, and gradually encumbering the administrative process. The conformity demanded by these formalized systems takes its toll in freedom of action, administrative flexibility, and constructive expression of talent. As communications continue to fail, formalized communications increase in volume, only to increase the opportunity for, and the likelihood of, further breakdown.

Printed media seldom solve communication problems. No matter how formalized the organization, people rely on both formal and informal communication for job information. Attempts to "manage" information by publishing more communications tend to reduce the total percentage of information assimilated. In addition, the formalized management of information evokes reactive behavior and fosters the development of a reactive and hostile grapevine.

Stability

Organizational stability is a key climate factor, particularly for satisfying employee's security needs. Stability has many ramifications; for many employees it means trust in management, confidence that they will have a job as long as they do good work, or confidence that they will have advance knowledge of changes that may affect them. Ability to cope with instability is often a function of a person's role in the change. Unexpected or misunderstood changes may contribute to a climate of instability, but the same changes when evolved through understanding participation can enhance organizational stability.

When people who are being affected by change have a hand in the management of the change, they are better prepared emotionally as well as intellectually to cope with it. In fact, predictable and constructive change is a welcome respite to the monotony of inescapable stability.

Instability is often a function of short-range planning. Layoffs, for example, are often followed in the near future by active hiring programs. Worse yet, a layoff in one part of an organization may coincide with an active hiring program in another segment of the organization. The coordinated efforts of managers in planning retrenchments can do much to preserve stability. Normal turnover may siphon off between 20 and 40 percent of a work force per year. An imaginative and active program for transferring, retraining, and upgrading can make this normal turnover an opportunity for upgrading and, when necessary, a constructive substitute for layoffs. Other actions for dealing with retrenchment include temporary reassigning and lending of employees within the organization, the splitting of shifts into half-day assignments, reduced hours, educational leave, rescheduling of vacations, early retirement, and other-company placement. Some companies have resorted to business diversification as a strategy for sustaining both the stability and the vitality provided through additional job opportunities.

MANAGEMENT SYSTEMS[3]

A "management system" is a process of people interacting to apply resources to achieve goals. Management system designers tend to place major emphasis on hardware and software (technology), but the primary emphasis must be on the human factor. Computers, machines, buildings, materials, and money lie idle and lifeless in the absence of humans. Hence, all management is the management of human effort. The materiel with which people interact may be organized to facilitate their efforts and to inspire their commitment, or it may be organized in a way that impedes their efforts and evokes their opposition.

[3] Much of this paper is abstracted from documents co-authored with Charles L. Kettler, Coordinator of Texas Instruments' Management Systems Development Committee, and A. Graham Sterling, Manager of Control & Administration in Texas Instruments' Materials Group.

When people encounter difficulty in the pursuit of goals, there is a tendency to blame "the system." For example, problems encountered in terminating a book-of-the-month club membership, in changing a mailing address, in getting a charge account error corrected, in clearing an expense account, or in getting an accounts receivable balanced are usually attributed to "the system." Physical aspects of systems are convenient scapegoats at the "customer-complaint desk," and systems' administrators (users) often attribute their own limitations to restrictions imposed by the system. Attempts to remedy a system, of necessity, lead back to the system designer.

Role of the Management System Designer

The system designer can often defend his applications of software and hardware, and then assert that the system failed only because people misused it. Within that point of view lies the crux of most management system problems.

The system designer is correct in diagnosing systems failures as human failures. But he usually fails to recognize that his responsibility embraces the human factor—that the system designer's role is one of facilitating human processes, and that helpful systems function as extensions of man, not man as an appendage of systems. Furthermore, the system designer often overlooks his responsibility for seeing to it that the system user is adequately trained to administer the system. Systems failures sometimes result from designer permissiveness in allowing the user to divest himself of the responsibility for helping design the system. Because of sheer job pressure, the user may welcome the staff man's takeover.

Sometimes system users try to participate in the design of their system, and the system designers may even urge them to do so. But the system user frequently encounters the same problem in talking to the system designer that the foreman sometimes encounters when he tries to talk to the personnel psychologist—in neither case is the staff man's jargon fully understood. The system user may be as confused by the designer's use of such terms as "SYSGEN," "time-sharing," "syntax-directed," "bombout," and "real-time" as the foreman was by the psychologist's use of "emotional stability," "exophoria," "IQ," "manic-depressive," and "ego drive." In both cases, the staff man has failed to adapt his terminology to the boundaries of his customer's language.

A system user can no more divest himself of responsibility for system design than the foreman can delegate the handling of grievances and job instruction to the personnel department. When system designers and personnel managers permit this type of disengagement, the results almost always are ineffective systems and inept foremen.

Informal Systems

Systems may be formal or informal, simple or complex, but all come into existence because of needs of individuals or groups at any level of the organization. For example, the office check pool (based on the highest poker hand to be found in paycheck serial numbers) is an informal and unofficial system that forms almost spontaneously, and is perpetuated by a combination of social, financial, diversion, and risk-taking needs of the members. "Management" may perceive the check pool as a violation of company rules on gambling, and may try to develop a system for stopping it. Attempts to quash the check pool may be implemented through a system of posted notices, newspaper inserts, public pronouncements, and supervisory instruction, all reinforced by specific or veiled threats of punishment. But, if the need to perpetuate the check pool is strong enough, or if the joy of circumventing authority is great enough, the pool system goes underground, thereby satisfying rebellion needs provoked by management edict, and perhaps increasing the system's value in satisfying social (group cohesiveness), diversion, and risk-taking needs.

All systems are circular and give feedback to the user. Check pool members contribute their dollars and obtain feedback in terms of observed payoff to the highest "poker hand." Attempts by management to intervene merely activate a countersystem for evading detection, which gives the members feedback in terms of not getting caught or, if their system fails, in getting caught. Similarly, management's control system for preventing participation in the check pool gives feedback to management in terms of official reports of conformity or violation. Feedback may or may not be valid.

Formal Systems Development

More formal and complex management systems are developed and refined through a continuous circular process that may be defined in terms of seven phases, as we shall see. Though any phase, and particularly phase 5, may lead directly back to any preceding phase, a system's development generally follows a circular evolutionary process, diagrammed in Figure 4-5.

PHASE 1. *Goal setting* is initiated in response to a felt need to create a new system or modify an old one. Goals are expressed quantitatively and qualitatively in terms of end results desired and resources available.

PHASE 2. The *concept study* is a systematic consideration of how to achieve the stated goals, and the long- and short-range impact of the system on the user, on other systems, or uninvolved bystanders, and on the community, in terms of social, economic, and legal considerations. The concept study ends with the selection of one of several alternative concepts to achieve the established goals.

PHASE 3. *Specifications* define the details of how the system will implement the concepts to achieve the goals. They are established in terms of costs, time schedules, personnel,

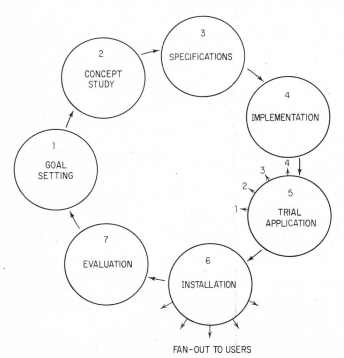

FIG. 4-5   Seven phases of system development.

machines, equipment, materials, facilities, responsibility, and evaluation criteria.

PHASE 4. The system is *implemented* by committing hardware, software, manpower, services, space, and budget; by designing trial applications; and by defining error signals.

PHASE 5. *Trial applications* are made with real or simulated data on representative samples of users; errors are corrected; the system is refined; and management and user commitment is confirmed. Phase 5 may lead directly back to any previous phase.

PHASE 6. The system is *installed* by instructing users, transferring system management to users, informing affected publics, establishing review schedules, and monitoring initial applications. Systems with potential for broad organizational application should be "fanned out" immediately to other operations to maximize system payout.

PHASE 7. The system is *evaluated* by measuring performance against goals, impact on other systems, deviations from design, and identifying goal adjustments required.

A Specimen Management System

The job-posting system, described on pages 157 to 160 as an internal staffing system, can serve as a model to illustrate the cyclical and evolutionary process for developing a management system.[4] Job posting existed as a simple and informal process at Texas Instruments for several years. In its earliest form it consisted of dittoed lists of job openings which rarely crossed organizational and geographical boundaries. Feedback to management through the grapevine and the attitude survey, described on pages 203 to 212, reflected inadequacies in the job-posting system in terms of ambiguous ground rules and reductive supervisory practice.

System shortcomings included allegations that favoritism was a basis for many promotions, seniority was disregarded, education was emphasized to the exclusion of experience, qualifications for job openings were not specified, and advancement opportunities were restricted to the departments in which the opportunities occurred.

[4] Described by Mark Shepherd, president of Texas Instruments, in his EIA presidential address at the Industrial Relations Conference in San Diego, Calif., April 22, 1969.

Supervisory practice complaints alleged that supervisors withheld job opportunity information, sometimes resented transfer requests, refused or delayed transfers, and too often gave priority to outside applicants.

In terms of the system development cycle illustrated in Figure 4-5, these reactions to the job-posting system represented an informal phase 7 evaluation of an ongoing system. This feedback precipitated the formation of an official task force to improve the system.

Preliminary work by the phase 1, goal-setting task force confirmed the phase 7 evaluation described above and further noted the following shortcomings in the existing system:

1. Job openings were published too infrequently.
2. Many job openings were not posted.
3. Posted openings were primarily for lower job grades.
4. Dates for posting and closing job openings were not specified.
5. Job postings were not easily accessible to all.
6. Job specifications were too sketchy.

The systematic evaluation of the existing system was a major basis for defining the goals for its improvement. However, since most of the feedback was from the employees as the primary users of the system, it was necessary to broaden the scope of the goal-setting process to include balanced consideration of the goals of the organization and the impact of job-posting on other systems. The system development task force was comprised of a heterogeneous membership of line and staff persons, chaired by a seasoned industrial relations generalist.[5] Though the permanent membership of the task force numbered about eight persons, *ad hoc* involvement of people from all levels and major functions of the company who became actively involved in the development of the system totaled approximately 900. The involvement process employed here in many respects paralleled the group insurance task-force strategy outlined on pages 176 to 180.

The task-force strategy led routinely and naturally into the phase 2 concept study. Though it was recognized that job posting could lead to increased internal mobility, the advantages of the system appeared to outweigh its disadvantages greatly:

1. Its role in facilitating promotions, transfers and reassignments

---

[5] A. E. Prescott, Manager of Internal Staffing for Texas Instruments, chaired the job-posting system task force whose achievements are outlined in this paper.

would support the company's promotion-from-within policy, and thereby lead to better utilization of manpower and the retention of talent within the organization.

2. It would reduce the loss of people from the work force due to faulty placement or work-force reduction and, hence, would lead to increased organizational and community stability.

3. It would facilitate the placement of people returning from leave of absence, as well as the upgrading of persons who improved their qualifications through skills training and educational programs.

4. It would lower interdepartmental mobility barriers and, thus, lead to broader unification of the total work force and implementation of equal-opportunity policy.

5. It would provide information and a procedure to enable individuals to assume greater responsibility for furthering their own career development, and would correspondingly reduce their dependence on supervision.

Phase 3 specifications were established in terms of overhead, hardware, software, and manpower costs. Evaluation criteria were established to include employee (user) reaction as measured through attitude surveys, frequency of usage, and grapevine testimonials; and impact on the organization in terms of reduced turnover and staffing costs, disruption of work standards and schedules, and general acceptance by supervision.

Phases 4 and 5 of the system were implemented through the joint efforts of a skeletal staff of corporate and division personnel applying the system in Texas operations. Space, personnel, and budget had been allocated by Corporate Personnel, with concomitant pledges of support from the divisions. Immediate and favorable reaction to initial applications resulted in early commitment of support from top management to expand the program to all domestic operations and appropriate opportunities in international operations that might be staffed from domestic operations. Much of phase 5 had been accomplished earlier through the application of the informal and local job-posting systems that had preceded the initiation of the present system development cycle. To the users, the most apparent changes were the more comprehensive coverage of the job opportunity bulletin, illustrated in Figure 5-2 on page 158, and a simple procedure for actuating the system.

Phase 6 was formally and officially completed when capital, overhead, and expense budgets were approved, administrative staff and support personnel were trained, and the system was described in the company newspaper. Approximately 10 percent of the domestic work force utilized the system for promotion and transfers during the first year. More than 20 percent of the positions filled were for salaried-exempt classifications. Administration of the program followed the procedure illustrated in Figure 5-3 on page 159.

General reaction to the system, particularly from the users' viewpoint, was favorable. However, a gradual groundswell of dissatisfaction, largely from operating managers, brought phases 7 and 1 into formal and rigorous application. The central task force was reactivated with nineteen members to determine whether or not to continue the system and, if it was to be continued, to identify and correct problems leading to dissatisfaction with the system. Nine geographically deployed division task forces, involving 125 system users from all levels and functions, compiled a list of problems and possible solutions, and forwarded them to the central task force. The central task force consolidated the division recommendations and returned them to the divisions for review, revision, and ratification. Finally, the central task force consolidated the division revisions for corporate review.

The company president and operating vice-presidents held a day-long meeting to review the system with its problems and possible solutions, and to decide whether or not to continue it. The review, aided by testimonials from line and staff managers, revealed the following problems associated with the job oportunity system, and the modifications adopted.

Problems identified by the phase 7 analysis:

1. Large numbers of bids by a few individuals delayed the candidate evaluation process and feedback to bidders.
2. Bids were submitted on jobs in the outdated monthly bulletin by persons who were not aware of updated interim weekly bulletins posted on bulletin boards.
3. Lateral transfers filled many positions representing promotional opportunities from lower job grades.
4. Profitability of some operating departments was reduced by the discontinuity and instability caused by frequent transfers.
5. People were transferring before achieving their competence

levels, depriving managers of a fair return on training or security clearance investments.

6. Some supervisors were engaging in "gamesmanship" by delaying transfers or negotiating under-the-table transfers under the pretense of following official job-posting procedures.

Dissatisfactions arising from the job opportunity system illustrate a common phenomenon; namely, a system for removing dissatisfactions has the potential itself for being the focus of new or even worse dissatisfactions than the ones it was intended to remove. This principle is illustrated in connection with the discussion of paid suggestion systems on pages 174 to 175.

Modifications incorporated into the system by the new phase 1 activity:

1. Limit concurrent job bids per person to two, except for individuals made available for reassignment.
2. Simplify coding of new job postings.
3. Permit lateral transfers only when
   - progression on the present job is blocked;
   - the job family or salary schedule is being changed;
   - the change is part of a planned career development program;
   - the change is necessary to assign displaced personnel.
4. Effect temporary "transfer-out moratorium" if necessary to protect vital understaffed work groups.
5. Require 6 months on the job for nonexempt personnel and 12 months for exempt, before bidding on new job.
6. Provide continuing education and information to users regarding the system and its revisions.

These changes were communicated back to the work force via informal one-to-one and group discussions, the employee newspaper, and revisions of procedure handbooks. The changes found routine user acceptance, as they were developed through peer representation at all levels. However, many managers, while recognizing and accepting the long-range merits of the system, still resent the short-range disruptions caused by increased work-force mobility.

Characteristics of Effective and Ineffective Systems

This evolutionary process, perpetuated by feedback from the users, represents an ideal model of an effective self-correcting management system. Tracing the evolution of the job-posting system through its seven developmental phases reveals characteristics common to most effective systems. Because of their involvement in the evolutionary process, users understand and agree with its purpose. It is a system *they* can actuate simply by submitting a completed job bid to their personnel department, without fear of supervisory reprisal. Actually many people actuate the system with one or more covert inquiries. It is primarily their initiative that enables them to discover opportunities; and because the system minimizes dependency on, or intervention by, supervision, the user is in control all the way. Finally, the system gives the user direct feedback in terms of a disqualification or acceptance notification. In summary, a management system is considered effective when the people whose job performance is influenced by the system:

1. Understand its purpose
2. Agree with its purpose
3. Know how to use it
4. Are in control of it
5. Can influence its revision
6. Receive timely feedback from it

Stated negatively, as a basis for understanding system failure, it may be generalized that a management system is not effective when the people whose job performance is influenced by the system:

1. Do not understand its purpose
2. Disagree with its purpose
3. Do not know how to use it
4. Feel they are unnecessarily restricted by it
5. Feel it is hopeless to try to change it
6. Receive inadequate feedback from it

The Key Role of the User

It is noteworthy that the conditions for effective and ineffective systems noted above are almost exclusively functions of systems users' attitudes and perceptions. This observation is illustrated by comparing the behavior of two groups of machine operators toward their respective assembly lines.

One group, in a paper carton factory, was idled for a few hours (with pay) while industrial engineers introduced improvements into their line. The operators clustered near the coke machine, laughing, drinking cokes, and smoking. When the engineers completed the installation, they briefed the operators on the changes, and asked for questions. Receiving no questions, they assumed the installation would be an improvement. But the system actually reduced the line yield, and hence, the line was less effective than before. The engineered changes had altered role relationships on the line, and even before giving it a fair trial, the operators had conspired, perhaps unconsciously, to make the system fail.

In contrast, a superintendent and a foreman in an electronics assembly department involved the operators in planning and balancing their own assembly line and setting their first week's production goals. They achieved their Friday evening goal on Wednesday and went on almost to double their first week's goal. From an engineering point of view, the electronic assembly line was not as well designed as the paper carton line, but it worked because the operators made it work.

In summary, it may be generalized that people's attitudes and perceptions are the primary causes of all systems successes and failures,

- Enabling poorly designed systems to succeed, and
- Causing well-designed systems to fail.

Lost in the Maze

Management systems become increasingly complex by a spiraling process. Computer technology, expanding exponentially, provides physical ability to store, retrieve, manipulate, transmit, and display data at increasingly faster rates and lower costs. This capability, serving the mainstream and support functions of an organization, accelerates the organization's growth and complexity, at the same time increasing its dependency on massive and complicated networks of systems and their meticulously detailed and coordinated subsystems. System-imposed conformity, in combination with bigness-induced depersonalization, evokes alienation and apathy or hostility. Thus, systems themselves, depending upon how they were developed, have a primary role in generating the attitudes and perceptions that cause them to succeed or fail.

Qualifications of Systems Designers

It was noted earlier that system designers, recognizing the importance of the users' attitudes to the system's success, have taken the initiative in familiarizing themselves with their users' operations, or have attempted to involve users in the development of their systems. It was also noted that these cooperative efforts were often discouraged by the job demands of the user or the system designer's jargon. Moreover, it was illustrated in the job-posting system that sensitivity to the human factor—the causes of commitment and alienation—is an essential ingredient for developing and managing effective systems. Thus it is apparent that system designers must apply three types of competence in developing workable systems:

1. Technical knowledge of electronic data processing and related technology.
2. Knowledge of the functions or operations to be served by the system, and the proposed system's relation to, and potential impact on, other systems.
3. Sensitivity to the factors evoking human commitment and alienation in the development and administration of management systems.

Management's Role

The hardware and software available for facilitating modern management systems have almost unlimited potential, to be exploited or limited by the people who interact with them. People who man the work force also have untapped potential, to be utilized or limited by the systems they interact with. If synergistic relationships are to exist between people and their systems, human development and system development must be guided by persons who understand both people and systems.

Thus, formalized and effective management systems cannot be established as the warp and the woof of the organization if system development is relegated to staff functions. Many organizations try it, just as they try to delegate the planning function to staff personnel. Neither will succeed, of course, as planning and control functions are mainstream processes which must be managed by the persons who are to implement them.

Simply stated, a manager is responsible for managing materiel, manpower, and technology to achieve organizational goals. The manager's responsibility in managing management systems is to see to it that system development is not an isolated, uncoordinated, or unilateral process but, rather, a joint or task force effort, appropriately balanced with systems technology, mainstream user participation, and human effectiveness expertise.

THE AMERICAN ABROAD[6]

The accelerated infiltration of American business into the widely divergent cultures of the world has given prominence to the problem of defining the roles of American managers and technicians abroad. Though some countries are becoming "Westernized," most are maintaining at least some vestiges of their unique cultural characteristics— some with unbending determination. Hence, the manager in the multinational organization must acquire greater competence in dealing with problems of intercultural conflict.

This section offers guidelines to American managers and technicians sent abroad to establish, or improve the effectiveness of, international operations. Detailed guidelines are needed for each culture, of course, and the principles outlined herein are intended only as general guidelines for Americans on assignment in countries whose social and economic development is below the United States level. This section is based on the assumption that principles of autonomy and delegation apply in the developing countries which host the international operations no less than they do in America. Further, failure to observe these principles abroad may impair organizational effectiveness even more because of the additional issues of economic sovereignty, cultural integrity, and national pride which are at stake.

Hence, this section supports the central theme that organizations should be managed by indigenous personnel. When expatriates serve as managers, their presence should be a consequence of routine cross-cultural job mobility in a multinational organization, or an administrative expedient, and not the transplanting of home-office personnel to mold local operations into replicas of home-country organizations.

---

[6] This section is based on the author's experience of almost 5 years in Iran and on visitations to the international operations of Texas Instruments. The text incorporates suggestions from Iraj Ayman, Franco Bertagnolio, Stewart Carrell, Pierre Clavier, Bill Dees, Manuchehr Derakhshani, Derek Lawrence, Gernot Mueller, Hermann Peusens, Robert Pierson, Louis Pierson, John Powell, Homayoun Sahba, Ben Schranil, Don Wass, and Stephen Wilcock, most of whom are, or were, citizens of countries outside the United States. Though many American managers also agree with these principles, this section does not include the dissenting views of American managers whose managerial styles abroad and at home inspired its writing.

Therefore, managers and technicians on location outside the United States are presumed to be on transitory assignment with the primary mission of developing their local counterparts to take over operating responsibilities. In the balance of this paper, the term "adviser" connotes the expatriate on duty outside his country, whether he be a professional manager or a technical expert, and the term "counterpart" refers to the local national(s) to whom he must transfer his managerial or technical competence.

Other-culture Characteristics

Many of the factors in the foreign culture also exist at home, of course, and in this sense they are not new. However, in the amplified form in which they are sometimes encountered, they present new challenges to the adviser; and it may be the first time that his success is so strongly dependent upon an understanding of these factors.

The Welcoming Façade   Americans arriving in a foreign country usually receive courteous and respectful treatment. The businessman and the appropriately dressed and behaved tourist are typically received with sincere friendliness. However, when the visitor takes up temporary residence in an extended business relationship with the local citizens, he may find that some of this behavior is a façade.

People in certain host countries seem to have developed a propensity for "rolling with the punches." This trait is an understandable consequence of a long history of hosting occupational troops and foreign advisers, many of whom were regarded as necessary evils to be tolerated for the sake of satisfying international agreements, protecting sovereignty, appeasing home-office officials, receiving financial or technical assistance, or stimulating commerce. Host-country officials tend to give advisers polite and courteous treatment, provide them with pleasant facilities, and avoid open disagreements, but they may show little initiative in implementing recommendations. It is easy for an adviser to be lulled into thinking he is receiving whole-hearted support and understanding when, upon his departure, the most tangible evidence of his visit is an English-language report which is routed dutifully to selected readers and finally filed in the archives with earlier foreign advisers' reports.

The National Inferiority Complex   A "national inferiority complex" is one of the common self-ascribed traits in developing countries. However, inferiority feelings are sometimes disguised under a façade of "superiority." National inferiority feelings may have several roots. A common factor is the forced dependence of developing countries upon foreign capital, leadership, and political support. Another factor may be a country's minor role in world affairs, particularly for its foreign-educated citizens, whose sojourns abroad have sensitized them to their country's oblivion to the rest of the world. Unscrupulous and inept local leadership, with their consequential intellectual, social, economic, and moral impoverishment, may be key factors.

Americans abroad in key industrial roles may perpetuate inferiority feelings by their failure to respect local customs and values, to delegate responsibility to local personnel, to provide equitable compensation structures, to provide realistic opportunity for multinational assignments, or to develop indigenous personnel for key positions. Even when granted official autonomy, local managers in American international operations often feel they are being deprived by home-office authority of opportunity to succeed through their own initiative and competence. Though they may believe their association with the parent organization offers rich opportunity for realizing their personal and professional goals, they often feel subjected to unnecessary amounts of arbitrary and overbearing behavior by American bosses. They welcome and acknowledge the technical competence of the American adviser, but his manner of dispensing it may unintentionally reinforce their feelings of inferiority.

Fatalism   "Outer-directedness" and "fatalism" are terms to describe the feeling that life is controlled by forces outside one's influence. Though less common in Western cultures, many citizens in the Middle East, for example, preface statements of plans or aspirations with *ensha 'allah* (God willing). It is felt that plans come to fruition through chance factors or the influence of supernatural powers. Religion plays an ambiguous role, ranging from unquestioning acceptance of orthodox religion by the illiterate villager to agnosticism by many of their educated leaders and urban residents. Outer-directedness or fatalism, if not understood, can be a source of frustration to the adviser whose personal philosophy is more often based on self-reliance.

In some cultures (and in some organizations in all cultures), the selection and placement of persons for desired positions, particularly government offices, is said to be based more on nepotism and political alignment than on merit. In such cases, organizations are believed to be dominated by powerful networks of friends and relatives who protect and advance each other to the exclusion of outsiders. Regardless of the validity of this allegation, the presumed influence of nepotism in itself breeds fatalism and stifles initiative. Exceptions to this generalization are seen in "obligation cultures" of the Far East where networks of family, social, and political relationships are the media through which achievement needs are satisfied, and which have at least temporarily fostered successfully competitive organizations.

Other factors contributing to fatalism and despair include lack of confidence in management, the nearness of militant and unstable neighboring countries, lack of deep faith or common values, lack of vocational opportunities, health hazards, and unemployment.

Little evidence of realistic long-range planning exists in many of the developing countries. This is apparent in the personal life of the citizens, in business enterprise, and in public administration. Few seem willing or able to prepare for the inexorable realities of old age and death by subscribing to life insurance or financial security programs, or to budget living expenses in accordance with a realistic appraisal of personal incomes. Business and government planning more often reflect attempts to justify expenditures of funds rather than to achieve defined long-range goals. Workable plans for 5- and 10-year programs and strategies in business and government are virtually nonexistent.

Education for Status and Conformity   The low status of manual vocations in many developing countries is a hindrance to industrial progress. Unwillingness to "get one's hands dirty" is one manifestation of a class-consciousness syndrome. Those who can afford education usually aspire to government office positions or professions with established high-status levels. It is difficult to attract talented people into blue-collar vocations, and thus skilled and semiskilled workers must come from the ranks of other craftsmen, laborers, and minority groups. However, recent progress in literacy and vocational training, plus accelerated acceptance of modern consumer products, is bringing into prominence new classes of craftsmen. The increasing need for mechanics, plumbers, electricians, machinists, and radio and television repairmen has raised the income of craftsmen, enabling them to buy the symbols of status. Their increasing affluence and sheer numbers are forming a new middle class which is giving its members, as individuals and as a class, more social acceptance and favorable recognition in their society.

Some of the educational processes in many cultures, including the United States, seem more suited to the development of followership than leadership qualities. Success in school is often based more on memory work than on logical and analytical reasoning, grades being influenced strongly by the student's ability to quote the instructor and memorize textbooks. Little opportunity is provided for students to begin bridging the gap between theory and practice by solving relevant problems, participating in laboratory experiments, and conducting original research. Heavy emphasis has been placed on perpetuating classical curricula. Students learn to "second-guess" the instructor, giving him the answer they think he wants, thereby establishing a survival pattern that naturally perseveres into relationships with supervisors in business and government.

Requisites for Intercultural Competence

The adviser's professional role is influenced by the fact that he is also a guest in a foreign country. It is easy for the visiting expert, particularly if he has had little foreign service experience, to be misled by the ingratiating behavior often encountered in host countries. The politeness, flattery, ceremony, hospitality, and generosity of his hosts may make it easy for the naïve adviser to assume an authoritarian order-giving role, or a passive and capitulatory role. He may fail to see beneath the expressions of humility and servility what is sometimes a deep-rooted hostility, but more often an underlying and normal desire for recognition, reciprocity, equality, and independence.

Competence of Advisers The American's success is determined by his successful fulfillment of two roles—his role as a competent technician and his role as an acceptable personality. His spoken word has little impact if his "language of action," on and off the job, conveys a conflicting message. He is seldom judged by the standards of his fellow countrymen, or even by the standards by which the local citizens evaluate each other, but rather by standards which fit their conceptual image of what the American should be.

The ideal adviser is a cosmopolitan—willing and able to adapt himself to the local culture. His job success is considerably enhanced by his tolerance for and readiness to adapt to local values, living patterns, foods, and social customs. He should be able to identify with people of various socioeconomic levels and participate in their local events, and nothing in his behavior or remarks should reflect disapproval or disparagement. His behavior should reflect acceptance of, respect for, and confidence in the country and its citizens.

The adviser's competence in the local language is an asset, perhaps more for the attitude it conveys than for the actual language facility. No matter how broken his grammar, or thick his accent, if his use of the local language represents attempts to learn more about and adapt to the culture, it is usually well received. Language facility does not, of course, assure success, as some advisers, assigned because of language facility, have failed because of undesirable personality traits or technical incompetence. Hence, sensitive regard for the feelings of others is more important than language fluency per se.

The adviser's behavior should reflect the staff man's philosophy of staying out of the limelight. He must make his abilities known and available in a manner that will encourage the local people to use them, and will result in progress, recognition, and a sense of achievement and security for having done so.

The above characteristics of the American adviser are listed as ideals, recognizing that they exceed the qualifications that can be realistically imposed on all persons who must serve as advisers. Many advisers are appointed or requested because of their technical competence and availability, and to insist on their meeting all the above qualifications would leave their positions unfilled. However, the above qualifications, coupled with the total content of this paper, can serve as guidelines in selecting and training American advisers.

Competence of Counterparts   The counterpart's freedom to act independently and responsibly in behalf of his organization has a direct bearing on his ultimate success in carrying on in an executive or technical capacity after the departure of the adviser. If the adviser has influence in selecting his counterpart, care should be exercised that the candidate is not in any way disqualified for full support by local people. "Un-American" as these criteria may be, socioeconomic status, minority group membership, personality, his role during the adviser's visit, as well as technical competence are factors that may have a bearing on the counterpart's acceptance and support by local people, particularly after the departure of the adviser when the counterpart is left to his own resources.

Ideally, the counterpart's experience and education should have some relationship to his work. In the case of complex technologies, experience and education are, of course, highly relevant. However, a high correlation between the person's past experience and his ultimate administrative responsibility is not always necessary or even desirable. Nor is level of education a reliable predictor of success, other than the support it incurs through local values. James Lee[7] found that high school graduates in developing countries tend to display a higher degree of motivation than college graduates—perhaps due to the absence of the degree laurel on which to rest.

The prospective counterpart's motives are important considerations. Does he see his job as an opportunity to qualify himself for a meaningful role in a local organization, is he simply seeking to improve his English language facility, or is the job a steppingstone to emigration or a job in another company? Scarce as candidates are in most countries, compromises in selection standards are not the answer. His aspirations should be aligned with company interests and in balance with his potential achievement level. He should have enough intelligence and language facility to be trainable, but not vastly more than is required for his ultimate job.

A source of talent often overlooked may be found in the ranks of host-country personnel in the United States enrolled in universities, on extended business assignments, or recent immigrants who would welcome opportunities to return to their home country in meaningful roles. Many find such assignments attractive, particularly under the condition of more liberal compensation plans and the diplomatic protection of American citizenship. However, the Americanized returnee, who becomes known as the "150 percent American" because of his tendency to use invidious comparisons, may be poorly qualified for native country assignment.

The assessment of aptitudes of multilingual people often presents a unique problem which can mislead the inexperienced test interpreter. Nationals who have received much of their education and other language facility in other countries tend to be handicapped in both languages. Their second-language competence seldom qualifies them to compete on mental ability tests on an equal basis with people of the other culture. At the same time, their educational leave from their country often arrests the development of their native-language facil-

---

[7] James Lee, "Developing Managers in Developing Countries," *Harvard Business Review*, pp. 55–65, November–December, 1968.

ity. Hence, lacking complete facility in either language, their aptitude test scores in either language usually underestimate their true talent. Apart from the aptitude test handicaps, a local citizen with a "foreign" accent or substandard fluency in his own language may not be fully effective in business relationships.

Importance of the Host-country Language   The host country's language is the everyday language of the people in which school textbooks and newspapers are printed and through which local business is transacted. However, in some countries the problem is complicated by the existence of various dialects. Though an "official" language may be prescribed, legislation seldom succeeds in effecting the countrywide adoption of a common language. American management in this situation must secure agreement with the indigenous work force on their "company language of business" which will respect governmental policy, be sensitive to local sentiment, and serve the long-range needs of the organization and its members. Too often English is automatically presumed to be the official language without giving adequate concern to factors that might alter this presumption.

Use of the local business language in the definition of management systems and programs contributes in several ways to the development of the counterpart, the organization, and the country:

- The writing or translation process tests the counterpart's knowledge of the subject and gives him an opportunity to clarify questions in conference with the adviser.
- Use of the local business language results in the development and standardization of a technical vocabulary.
- Use of the local business language prepares the counterpart to communicate more fluently with his countrymen.
- Use of the local business language assures the message of a wider and more understanding readership in the local setting.
- Nationals are able to take a more active role in discussing, evaluating, modifying, and implementing a system defined in their own language.

The conference room or classroom is a special situation involving the adviser and counterpart for which the above principles also apply. It is a common practice for foreign advisers to give presentations or lectures with the assistance of interpreters. The local participants themselves frequently request this method of instruction to improve their foreign-language facility. But hearing the message in the foreign language may contribute little to their understanding of the subject matter, and because much technical terminology has no ready–made translations, it may actually interfere with their ability to apply the subject in their own culture. Since a culture is circumscribed by its language, there are many technical subjects which cannot be learned until terms are translated, coined, defined, or transliterated for use in the local language. The technical aid missionary innocently perpetuates the problem by teaching classes in the local setting in his own language. The local citizen who has returned with a new degree acquired abroad is ultimately required to make his effectiveness felt locally through his own language, and he may find his language inadequate to convey ideas learned in the foreign language. Hence, much can be gained by going through the tedious procedure of preparing presentations in the local language, developing the necessary vocabulary, and preparing indigenous people to present the information.

The language barrier sometimes works to the disadvantage of the counterpart despite the conscientious efforts of a competent adviser. For example, when advisers are not fluent in the local language, it is necessary to develop all ideas, programs, and correspondence first in the adviser's language and then translate them into the local language. Even if the counterpart contributed most of the ideas in developing a program, the very fact that it appeared first in English and then was translated into the local language creates an impression that the nationals are borrowing a foreign idea. The mechanics of translation are such that a local reader can usually discern that the style is not spontaneous or natural and that it is a translation of a foreign proposal. The counterpart's success in writing a meaningful and intelligent proposal or system in his own language is, of course, a direct function of his technical competence and often a measure of the success of the adviser.

Relationships that Fail   The counterpart-adviser relationship is a subtle and crucial one which, if properly developed, takes the counterpart through a process of training and personal development which enables him to carry on independently after the departure of the adviser. It is not a static relationship, but one that undergoes continuous and progressive change. In the beginning, it may have many characteristics of the instructor-student or supervisor-subordinate relationship. But the adviser must avoid crystallizing and prolonging this dependency relationship, however appropriate it may have seemed initially, if the counterpart is ultimately to step into a leadership role.

Sometimes the adviser-counterpart relationship is destined to at least initial failure by the manner in which the adviser is introduced to his assignment. Consider, for example, the impact of the following note sent to a manager of a European subsidiary by his supervisor in the States:

> TO: Hans F. Wilhelm
> FROM: J. T. Johnson
>
> Dear Hans,
> Herewith I am asking you to list the problems you have in running your business and send this list to Jim Smith so that he will be able to plan a program for himself and you. Jim will visit you two weeks from now and will stay for approximately six months to help you increase your personal effectiveness.
>
> Regards,
> J. T. Johnson

The understandable defensiveness of the recipient naturally failed to evoke the cooperation essential to the counterpart-adviser relationship. The alienation of the counterpart (behind a façade of tight-lipped courtesy and respect) put the adviser in a position of taking unilateral actions which were neither as appropriate nor as well accepted as they could have been through a jointly initiated and developed strategy.

Advisers, even when appropriately introduced to their mission, are sometimes insensitive to the benefits of participation, and launch a program of their own creation without "wasting time" by explaining it to their counterparts or involving them in the development of the proposal. Consequently, many counterparts never fully understand their adviser's program, or if they do finally understand it, the time lag between the adviser's conception and their understanding of it deprives them of the opportunity to contribute to its development. Thus the counterpart role in developing a program is often confined to the translation of words and partially understood or unintegrated ideas for which he feels no commitment. Not only does this type of relationship fail to develop the national into an able associate, but it actually develops and reinforces conformity behavior and feelings of subordination and inferiority.

Many counterparts never get beyond the interpreter-translator role. Retention of the counterpart in such a role reflects an assumption that the counterpart has no ideas of his own, thereby contributing to his feelings of incompetence and dependency. The adviser commonly concludes after a few cursory and unsatisfactory trials that his counterpart can have no ideas of his own, not realizing that this innovative impoverishment has been reinforced by his own behavior.

The typical role of the counterpart manager is one that rarely affords him opportunity to acquire the abilities of his in-residence American adviser. From the time he meets the adviser at the airport, as instructed by the home office, the local manager may find himself serving as a "detail kid" or office boy for the American, becoming his echo through his translating and interpreting activities. He arranges appointments and transportation, and performs many other routine administrative and clerical duties. This self-perpetuating pattern of servility and desire to please sometimes even extends to the performance of personal services for the visiting manager after working hours. Through this gradual conditioning process, his personality becomes submerged and dominated to the extent that his creativity and initiative are replaced by blind conformity.

The Development of Counterparts

When the American adviser completes his tour of duty, the program he has initiated or rejuvenated sometimes deteriorates or collapses. This failure is not intentional, of course, but usually stems from the expert's lack of familiarity with principles and techniques for developing the people who are to perpetuate and support it.

The Counterpart as a Peer   The richest opportunities to develop local managers, and at the same time to develop sounder programs, are frequently overlooked. For example, it is not unusual to find a group of home-office managers in conference on location developing policies and programs without the participation of local personnel. Not only does this practice deprive the planners of the type of guidance that only indigenous personnel can provide regarding laws, practices, resources, customs, and other cultural factors, but it also results in the development of programs not fully understood by the people who are to implement them. On occasions when counterparts are included in meetings, the adviser usually dominates the conversation and decision making, the counterpart merely parroting him in the local language. The counterpart's prestige and self-respect are undermined by this pattern.

The counterpart's role in business meetings is critical to his development. Generally speaking, local personnel should outnumber expatriates in planning meetings and financial reviews, and the local language should be the primary medium of communication. With little preparation, the counterpart's role in a meeting can be changed from what appears to be that of a mere assistant or interpreter to that of a responsible and qualified executive or technician. The counterpart himself can assume the major role in the meeting, if he is coauthor of the subject matter for the meeting, or at least is thoroughly briefed prior to the meeting. The following advantages result from this approach:

1. The counterpart acquires essential knowledge in the process of preparing for the meeting;
2. His commitment to the program, resulting from his role in developing it, enhances its chances of success;
3. His use of his own language enables him to evoke more participation and commitment from local personnel;
4. His initiative and freedom from dependence on the adviser enhance his status in the eyes of his countrymen;
5. The relegation of foreign advisers to a more appropriate "adviser" role tends to bolster the self-confidence of local managers and their willingness to accept responsibility.

The adviser's conduct at all times should reflect a sincere conviction that his counterpart is socially his equal and organizationally his superior. From the beginning of the relationship, the adviser must show respect to his counterpart as ultimate administrator of their developing program. Though the initiative is in the hands of the counterpart, he must, of course, be preconditioned to integrate the goals of the local plant with the needs of the total corporation. The adviser and counterpart must finally agree on the objectives of the program through candid and continuous interchange of ideas between them. Agreement should not be obtained by authority from any source, but rather from consensus gained through open exchange of information among all participants. Ideally, plans, programs, and proposals are developed first in the local language, and are translated into the adviser's language only as an expedient for involving him or for transmitting plans and reports to the home office.

The Adviser as a Trainer   If the primary role of the American adviser is to develop nationals to meet their responsibilities, he is first and foremost a trainer with full awareness of the principles of training outlined on pages 187 to 203. His ability to train others requires competence both in his field of specialization and in knowledge of learning processes. Though learning takes place naturally as a consequence of involvement in the managing process, the training process defined by the professional trainer—prepare, present, perform, and follow up—can be a helpful frame of reference.

The *preparation* phase of the long-term relationship is one in which the adviser and his local counterpart get acquainted, become adjusted to each other's idiosyncrasies, assess physical and human resources, and jointly develop appropriate plans. In the *presentation* stage, the adviser develops a peer relationship with his counterpart, while instructing or assisting him in various skills, knowledge, and procedures. He will participate with the counterpart, for example, in balancing a production line, designing a system, planning a financial review, conducting a market survey, setting up a cost accounting system, and preparing a proposal. It may be appropriate for them to visit an effective operation together, in the United States or in other international operations. The adviser should realize that his style in giving instructions or leading conferences is also usually emulated by the counterpart. In the *performance* stage of the relationship, the counterpart begins to take the lead in managing, calling on the adviser when he elects to do so. If the adviser-counterpart relationship is based on authentic relationships developed early, the adviser can help the counterpart to benefit from successes and failures through feedback and discussion. This critique is effective only if it is a candid and informal, but mutually respectful, two-way process. The final or *follow-up* step begins with the phase-out of the adviser. An adviser on a 2-year assignment should aim to begin his phase-out 3 to 6 months before departure—to be on hand if needed and to participate in or monitor periodic progress reports. Ideally, the follow-up relationship is continued after the adviser's return home by occasional exchanges of information by mail and, when requested by the counterpart, return consultation trips.

Opening New Plants   The foregoing principles are guidelines for advisers serving already established plants. However, they are equally valid when planning the establishment of new plants. Presumably the opening of new operations provides opportunity to start off with a clean slate, with the advantage of forward planning. In practice, the opening of new plants often occurs as a crash effort with little benefit from advance planning. As a consequence, the advantage presumed to be gained by the hasty implementation of a decision is often lost in the costs of coping with unanticipated problems and administering inappropriate systems, and in the alienation of nationals through inept supervision by transplanted Americans. The appointment of an expatriate manager, particularly for a sustained period, not only undermines the initiative of the subordinate indigenous managers, but it also handicaps the organization with a leader unacquainted with the host country's culture. It also sometimes leads to the local manager's emulation of American habits or styles of management which are unnatural to him and, hence, tend to alienate him with his countrymen.

Ideally, the opening of a new plant should be preceded by the recruitment of several high-potential managers from the host country for assignment in at least one of the company's successful operations for a period of from 6 to 24 months, to serve in one or more broad operating roles. During their assignment with the parent organization, they should have opportunity to participate with officers and high-level managers in long-range planning activities and in planning the mission, location, and layout of the plant they are destined to manage, and to visit other international operations. Also, during this home-office assignment they should be able to recruit additional personnel from their home country to be given technical training in the parent organization. This strategy would enable managers, in opening and managing new operations, to establish long and short-range charters compatible with the long-range goals of the parent organization, would prepare them to cope with technological problems, and would help free them from overdependence on American managers.

In practice, the ideal lead time usually does not exist to select and prepare indigenous managers to open and manage plants. The American typically moves in on the assumption that it is too late to find local leadership on short notice, and that this problem can be deferred until the plant is operating successfully. The survival and apparent financial success of operations initiated through this crash strategy would seem to defend it. However, the development of a competent and committed indigenous work force, necessary for sustained organizational effectiveness, is deferred until local leadership and ego involvement find expression.

When an American manager or specialist is sent abroad, he should be a winner by usual home-office standards. He should have distinguished himself by his achievements as a comptroller, manufacturing manager, sales manager, systems analyst, etc., in terms of his technological competence in his area of specialty and his knowledge of company procedures and philosophy. The marginal performer who is sent abroad because he has exhausted home-office opportunities cannot be expected to overcome his characteristic shortcomings and, in addition, to display the skills of an international diplomat.

An organization reflects the personality and management style of the top executive and the people reporting directly to him. Organizations tend to attract and develop, through a multiplier process, individuals whose values and style of management match those of the organization's leaders. Hence, selection of the manager to head up a new organization is tantamount to programming the management style and effectiveness of the organization.

Protecting the Local Manager's Autonomy   Once a manager is established in charge of an operation with self-influenced goals and criteria for evaluation, and opportunities to update his charter through involvement in company and division planning activities, he is much better prepared professionally and emotionally to manage his operation. Every effort should be made to grant organizational status to managers of autonomous operations, with titles reflecting appropriate status in the local culture. Criteria based on factors such as gross sales, return on investment, share of the market, profitability, and growth rate could be a basis for elevating an operation to a group or division status and for promoting a plant manager to officer status (e.g., president of a Swedish subsidiary, assistant vice-president or vice-president for Italian operations). This increased status would then be both a measure of and an incentive for his effectiveness as a manager.

Having succeeded in granting autonomy and opportunity for responsibility to the plant manager, the role of the adviser becomes more appropriately centered around dispensing technical advice rather than authority, and he acts in this consultant role at the request and under the direction of his client, the local manager. The local manager has the freedom to terminate the adviser's assignment without fear of reprisal. The key point here is that the adviser is seen less as a threatening authority figure and more as a source of help to be utilized as defined by the local line manager in achieving his organizational goals. Since the operating manager is measured against company standards through a philosophy of self-direction and self-control, he will naturally seek to utilize technical assistance, from whatever source, in a manner which will best achieve his organizational goals.

chapter five

The Role of the Personnel Function

HISTORICAL TRENDS[1]

The function of Personnel, as it has evolved over years, has assumed a variety of roles in its relations with the line. Though somewhat evolutionary in the order presented below, all roles tend to persevere and find recurrent expression in contemporary organizations.

1. *Counterbalancing influence.* Personnel counterbalances line management's emphasis on production with emphasis on human relations.
2. *Authority-directed experts.* Personnel experts exercise authority over line on personnel matters.
3. *Bureaucratic control.* Personnel systems and policies guide line management in personnel matters.
4. *Missionaries for participation.* Personnel emphasizes participation as the goal of the organization.
5. *Change agent.* Personnel specialists interact with line managers

---

[1] This view of historical trends is adapted from a working paper by John Paré, vice-president for personnel, Steinberg's Limited, Montreal, P. Q., Canada.

to define conditions for mutual achievement of organization and individual goals.

The change agent role is gradually evolving as an ideal model for the personnel specialist. However, the other roles are being perpetuated through the conditions and assumptions that brought them into existence. Each of these roles is discussed below in terms of the forces that brought them into existence, and their usual impact on the organization.

The Counterbalancing Influence

The counterbalancing function of Personnel arose from line management's neglect of, or need to unload, certain of its responsibilities. Line managers typically considered personnel problems as less important than, and not clearly related to, their primary job of getting out production. They appeared to divide management problems into two distinct categories and two separate responsibilities:

1. *Production problems.* Line management is responsible for the planning and controlling of materiel and systems: making the decisions, giving orders, assigning responsibilities, and seeing to it that people get the job done.

2. *People problems.* Personnel is responsible for handling complaints, grievances, and discipline; negotiating labor agreements; administering salary and benefit programs; training supervisors; establishing work rules; and building employee morale.

This split in management responsibilities reflects an assumption that the needs of people and the needs of production are mutually exclusive, and that efficiency in operation results from arranging conditions of work to minimize interference from human factors. The personnel man understandably reacted to the line manager's apparent insensitivity to human factors by emphasizing human relations, often with little regard for production goals.

The Authority-directed Experts

Traditional organization theory holds that authority must be commensurate with responsibility. When line management relinquished its responsibility for human relations problems, Personnel began asking for, and obtaining, authority over the line in these matters. Since authority was seen as the primary means of influencing behavior, this development was only logical: an individual cannot be held responsible for things he cannot control. Thus, use of authority by the personnel department crept into the line-staff relationship, widening the emerging split between the two management functions. Personnel assumed responsibility for recruiting, hiring, placing, and training line people; handling grievances and labor negotiations; and administering wages, salaries, and supplemental benefits.

This jurisdictional split not only creates a major cleavage in the line-staff relationship but is also impractical, as it is impossible, for example, to separate the function of assigning work from the function of processing grievances that arise from the work assignment.

In the ensuing struggle for power, line managers came to regard the personnel function as a "burden" and a "threat" rather than as a source of help. Rather than cope with this conflict, line managers typically severed contact with Personnel, leaving the staff experts out of touch with operations. As a consequence, personnel specialists became preoccupied with their narrow specialities to the point that they seemed to be talking to themselves and appeared to be unconcerned with the welfare of the business as a whole. Under these conditions, personnel programs and procedures seemed to become more "ivory tower" and less practical as solutions to line problems.

Bureaucratic Control

Line management's reaction to the authority which Personnel was exercising over human relations activities caused management to reconsider the line-staff relationship. It was apparent that another tenet of traditional management theory, the principle of "unity of command," was being violated: every individual must have but one boss.

Line management faced the dilemma of lacking insights and skills to resolve the increasingly complex human relations problem, but finding themselves dependent on the personnel "experts," whose specialities made them essential to the organization.

The solution was to set up the personnel department as a "coordinative" function, replacing the direct control by the staff specialist with standard personnel practices. These practices are expressed through the media of job descriptions and evaluations, organization charts, policies, programs, manuals, rules and regulations, and a variety of formalized procedures for detailing personnel activities. Line management had final authority for adopting or rejecting the policies and programs formulated by Personnel—but Personnel was responsible for obtaining line conformity once the policies and programs had been adopted. In effect, the role of "coordination" proved to be merely camouflaged authority. From the line manager's point of view, the staff man exercises as much authority under the bureaucratic form of personnel administration as he does in the authority-oriented role.

Missionaries for Participation

The "policing" role played by Personnel under the above theories caused the Personnel function to be regarded by lower and middle line management as a source of arbitrary, though sometimes candy-coated, authority. Mutual distrust, if not open hostility, characterized line-staff relations, and both groups began to question the use of authority as the exclusive means of managerial control. The influence of partially understood behavioral theory led managers to abandon the principle of authority and to adopt the principle of participation. Based on the assumption that "people support only what they help to create," Personnel sought ways to involve line people more and more in problem-solving activities.

The fundamental error of this approach is in seeing participation as the goal rather than as a means for achieving goals, as decision making then becomes stalemated by the reluctance on the part of both line and staff to reach any decision until the full support of the line is assured.

Change Agent

The primary purpose of Personnel as a change agent is to maximize the achievement of organizational objectives through the soundest utilization of its human resources. This requires the understanding and support of company goals by all members of the organization. It depends on collaborative commitment of individuals and groups to achieve these goals. It requires that the members of the organization identify and remove those barriers in the culture of the organization which prevent the company from reaching its objectives.

Personnel, in this role, provides specialists, advisers, consultants, trainers, counsellors, and researchers to support a goal-oriented philosophy which calls for a reunification of the two categories of management (production and human relations) under the line manager.

High concern for quality of decisions and production must be fused with high concern for people on the assumption that maximum efficiency can be best sustained through committed people who recognize a "common stake" in the achievement of organization goals. The proper fusing of these two high concerns brings about not only a better utilization of talent by the line manager, but a significantly different relationship between line management and the Personnel function. Many of the responsibilities which Personnel has acquired over the years must now be built back into the line. Personnel's charter is built upon the foundation of "a code for human effectiveness," defined in Figure 5-1, and of course the credentials of the personnel man must be reestablished in the light of his new role as change agent.

Credentials of the Personnel Change Agent

The personnel man's realm of competence is knowledge of the requirements for human effectiveness, as defined in Chapter 2. He acts selectively in the roles of educator, researcher, consultant, adviser, counselor, mediator, coordinator, conference leader, and public relations specialist in implementing the Personnel philosophy and systems defined in the balance of this chapter.

- The staffing function, as defined on pages 152 to 164, requires the support of a personnel specialist who not only knows the sources of manpower from employment agencies, universities, technical schools, and community, but more importantly, can prescribe an appropriate balance between internal and external staffing practices. He prepares line managers by briefing them on sources of personnel and techniques of evaluation, coordinates their recruiting itineraries, and compiles company-wide manning tables and recruiting statistics. He instructs line managers in new-employee indoctrination procedures, including anxiety reduction, orientation to physical facilities, supplemental benefits and compensation systems, and company philosophy.
- The personnel specialist provides guidance in the development of performance review systems which place emphasis on the individual's initiative in setting his own goals and measuring his own performance, as described on pages 164 to 169. He instructs supervisors in the hierarchical process of problem

Organizational effectiveness requires human effectiveness. The effectiveness of the organization is measured in terms of return on investment, and the effectiveness of its members in terms of realized potential. The organization will prosper most when its members accomplish their personal goals through the achievement of organization goals.

Guiding principles:

- People achieve more when their job is worth doing and challenging enough to rouse their interest; when they see the results of their achievements and their impact on group goals; and when their job results in advancement, personal growth and self-respect.

- People act more responsibly when they are involved in setting their own goals, are accountable for their own behavior, and share in the responsibilities and rewards for accomplishing organization goals.

- People work better when there is mutual trust, respect, concern, and integrity among them as human beings, regardless of the level of their job.

These principles are implemented by:

- Creating an organizational climate which enables people at all levels to communicate freely and naturally with each other -- keeping them informed about the organization, their jobs, and their relationships to customer goals.

- Designing jobs that involve people at all levels in planning and controlling their own work, and provide opportunity for individuals to make an impact on, and see how their accomplishments influence, the achievement of organization goals.

- Designing management systems sensitive to the needs of the people influenced by the systems and, where feasible, providing opportunities for persons at all levels to have a hand in developing and managing these systems.

- Providing pay and benefits competitive with the better managed organizations in local communities and comparable industries, and by compensating individuals through a system which places more emphasis on merit than on automatic progression.

- Maintaining equal opportunity practices which meet the spirit as well as the letter of the law in enabling individuals to compete and succeed on the basis of merit.

- Maintaining pleasant, convenient, attractive and safe physical facilities.

FIG. 5-1   A code for human effectiveness.

solving and goal setting, the characteristics of meaningful goals, and the use of feedback rather than criticism as a basis for developing responsible behavior.

- The compensation specialist has expertise in motivation and management systems. He chairs panel task forces which conduct and interpret salary surveys, analyze jobs, and develop compensation systems and benefit programs. He briefs supervisors on the multiple roles of pay, as illustrated on pages 169 to 171, and defines the conditions and techniques which optimize the impact of compensation systems.

- Though all personnel specialists are trainers, the training expert has a special role in guiding line managers and other personnel specialists to support a self-development philosophy through appropriate processes for changing knowledge, skills, and attitudes, as defined on pages 187 to 203. He assists line managers in meeting their responsibilities as trainers and makes it possible for them to assess their personal effectiveness by introducing them to "mirror-holding" self-improvement processes such as the managerial grid, sensitivity training, motivation seminars, and attitude surveys.

- The personnel change agent helps managers to understand attitudes as a readiness to respond, to understand that attitudes are learned and provide a basis for predicting behavior. Attitude surveys, as described on pages 203 to 212, afford a means of anticipating and preventing undesirable behavior before it occurs. Involvement of job incumbents at all levels in the process of interpreting survey data is a way of surfacing and coping with frustrations. The change agent helps managers to learn that attitudes are not improved by coercion, persuasion, manipulation, or bribery but, rather, from the language of authentic relationships, meaningful goals, and facilitative systems.

- The labor relations specialist promotes a philosophy which discourages the application of the traditional strategies for outwitting or fighting unions. Rather, he becomes an interpreter of people's behavior so that managers can take appropriate action in dissipating and constructively harnessing the tensions which might otherwise find unproductive and reactive expression. His role is elaborated on pages 224 to 225.

STAFFING

The purpose of the staffing function is to find, attract, and utilize qualified people in such a way that their talents will find expression in the successful pursuit of organizational and personal goals. Common staffing practice reflects the assumptions that the richest source of talent is outside the organization, that the company is responsible for matching individuals to jobs, and that staffing is a staff responsibility. The theme of this paper is that both organizational and individual goals can be achieved better when staffing is based on a different set of assumptions:

1. The richest source of talent is inside the organization.
2. Individuals should be permitted to pursue and move into growth opportunities.
3. Staffing is a line responsibility.

External versus Internal Staffing

All organizations are, of course, composed of members brought in originally from the outside. However, an organization can be said to be staffed internally when most job openings above the lowest job grades are filled through a process of upward mobility from within. It is staffed externally when job openings above the lowest levels are filled primarily by newly hired employees.

Proponents of external staffing hold that the injection of "new blood" is needed at all levels and that staffing from within is a type of inbreeding that results in human and technological obsolescence. Moreover, they reason that hiring in at higher levels attracts stalemated high achievers from other organizations.

Advocates of internal staffing counter with the view that external staffing fills jobs with people who, in a broad sense, failed to make adequate adjustments in other organizations. Hence, managers are often hiring other organizations' rejects. They point out that external staffing, by restricting upward mobility, quashes initiative and results in stagnation, frustration, and higher voluntary separations. Internal staffing, in contrast, stimulates hope and ambition, encourages self-development, and leads to realized potential, personal commitment, and reduced turnover. More importantly, it is noted that a sound promotion-from-within practice affords opportunity for retaining the impatient high achiever whose aspirations might otherwise lead him away from the organization in quest of growth opportunities.

External staffing, as a primary strategy, is a costly and wasteful circular process. At a conservatively estimated rate of 20 percent turnover per year, an organization loses the equivalent of 100 percent of its work force in 5 years. These separatees are, of course, replaced by people who (except for first-job applicants) were for many of the same reasons separated from other organizations. Thus organizations are victims of an insidious and expensive process of exchanging employees with each other.

Though managers tend to see recruited replacements as superior to the separatees, this is largely selective perception, and the real beneficiaries are the job hoppers. Some, in fact, have found that the only way to improve their job status in their own organization is to move to another organization and return in the status of a newly hired employee. All organizations and, hence, society in general, lose by this escalatory process that accelerates inflation and undermines the organization's competitive ability in the world market.

Though the merits of internal staffing generally outweigh those of external staffing, the relative effectiveness of one strategy over another is determined by the policies and practices through which they are implemented. Neither strategy is pure, nor should be, as some promotions and transfers occur in the external staffing strategy; and, of course, replacements are hired to fill lower-level jobs vacated by internal staffing. Moreover, the exceptions which enable outstanding organizations to attract and hire limited numbers of high-level talent do not vitiate the principle of internal staffing, provided most of the openings in middle management and above are filled through promotions.

A company policy that supports practices of promotion from within is a language of action helpful in retaining talent on the work force. The hiring of the majority of top management and supervisory people from other companies is no less damaging to the morale and ambition of members of the work force than the sending of managers into multinational subsidiaries to manage indigenous personnel. In both cases, the managers are seen as outsiders, insensitive to the needs of the local people, taking jobs which rightfully belong to them.

Hence, an ideal environment for staffing a work force is one that duplicates as nearly as possible the opportunities which people traditionally feel they can find only outside the organization. They must know from the language of action that job openings are visible to them; that they can, without fear of reprisal, apply for the jobs; and that, when they are accepted, they will encounter no difficulty in cutting across job classifications and departmental lines to fill the jobs. Equal-opportunity principles exist not only in regard to the traditional criteria of race, gender, and age, but particularly in regard to their status in the organization.

Staffing Reflects Management Values

An organization's staffing function is implemented by a philosophy of management that attracts and retains individuals who, in a circular fashion, reinforce and perpetuate its philosophy. For example, some persons are attracted to the organization that is guided by a strong source of authority and detailed procedures. Though conformity is demanded, it is also rewarded by job security and peer acceptance. Others are attracted to the less formal organization where initiative and talent find spontaneous expression. Though freedom can result in failure, it often leads to a sense of achievement and opportunity for high achievers to gain visibility. As each of these two types of persons adapts to his organization and progresses upward to positions of administrative influence, he develops relationships, systems, and policies which reflect his values. Of course, he hires people whose values match or reinforce his own, and promotes and rewards those who most nearly fit his self-image, or who will not interfere with his style of managing.

Though conformists tend to hire conformists, it does not naturally follow that individualists always hire nonconformists. Uncommon men often inadvertently surround themselves with bright but stable personalities who become satisfied with implementing their mentor's innovations. Thus, brilliant or strong individualism may quash less forceful expressions of individuality. Hence, all organizations run a greater risk of attracting and developing too many conformists than they do of promoting too much individuality.

An organization's management philosophy and its supportive staffing policies are often reflected by the personnel recruiter. The larger the organization, the more likely the recruiting function is to be delegated to professional recruiters, who tend to select candidates whose values match their own, or match their perception of the requisitioning supervisor's personality. The line manager generally tends to be more goal- or achievement-oriented, but his recruiters and other personnel specialists tend to be more maintenance-oriented. Though the personnel man's maintenance orientation can be explained in terms of his forced preoccupation with maintenance problems unloaded by line managers, it does, nonetheless, color his strategy for attracting job candidates.

For example, professional recruiters frequently advertise jobs as pleasant and easy, and as offering generous pay, supplemental benefits, and a congenial environment. In the screening interview, these factors are also stressed, along with detailed descriptions of the compensation system, retirement plan, group insurance, recreation program, and advancement opportunities. The candidate is invited to the company, all expenses paid, where he is taken on a whirlwind tour that steers him away from the less attractive sectors of the organization; he is entertained at an expensive restaurant and is made to feel like "king for a day."

If he accepts the job, he soon encounters reality. Confronted with the ambiguity and pressure of multiple assignments, long hours, the confusion and encumberment of bureaucratic systems, and the anonymity of the masses, he feels he has been deceived. He may rise to the challenge and thrive, or he may recoil and withdraw in disenchantment. He may leave the organization in search of the nonexistent job described in his employment interview. He is branded by the organization as a "maintenance seeker," though, in fact, it was the organization's recruiting strategy which attracted him by emphasizing maintenance factors.

A far better recruiting strategy would be to advertise the difficulty of the challenge, the opportunity to learn, and the long hours, and perhaps even to understate the value of the maintenance factors. During the company visit, off-site entertainment would be minimized, but the candidate would be shown the work place, the goals to be achieved, and the jobs to be done. An informal dinner meeting at the end of the visit with informed company representatives to discuss the company and answer questions could be quite relevant for the achievement-oriented candidate. Although such a strategy might eliminate more candidates, those who were attracted and hired would be prepared for the challenge of reality. Moreover, their first encounter with the organization would not be an act of deception.

Internal staffing not only has more potential than external staffing as a strategy for increasing human effectiveness within the organization, but it also actuates a more achievement-oriented recruiting strategy for supporting that effectiveness. Internally staffed organizations offer growth opportunities where individual talent, effort, and achievements are rewarded, while external staffing tends to lure more persons looking for the ready-made opportunity. However, the success of either staffing strategy depends heavily on the systems through which it is implemented. The key factor here is whether the system is managed by someone above the user (company-managed system), or whether by the people who use the system to do their job (user-managed system).

Company-managed System

Company-managed staffing systems usually reflect management's concern with three of its traditional responsibilities: utilizing talent, satisfying the needs of its employees, and maintaining rigorous control over its management systems. Unfortunately, these responsibilities are in some respects contradictory and tend to be implemented through paternalistic methods which reflect invalid assumptions about people's needs and processes for satisfying them. Consider, for example, the manpower inventory as a company-managed system.

Manpower inventories are initiated for the purpose of enabling management to match employee talent with job opportunity. They usually utilize EDP-based systems for storage and retrieval of vocational information about employees. Cards are keypunched from forms completed by job incumbents listing their educational achievements, job experience, aspirations, and other special skills or achievements such as foreign-language facility, patents, publications, and honors. Job openings are matched against skill and education descriptors, and the records of potential candidates are referred to the hiring supervisor.

Though occasionally useful for locating rare skills, manpower inventories are found in practice to have several fundamental shortcomings. For one, they are never updated completely in terms of changing skills, aspirations, and membership in the work force.

Second, the sensitivity and accuracy of the system are limited by the translation of personnel data to machine language. Third, qualified candidates are often eliminated by supervisory reluctance to free them for reassignment. Fourth, the system, particularly when managed through big-company bureaucracy, seldom gives feedback to the members in terms of availability of opportunities, frequency of review, and probability of candidacy. The manpower inventory's impact as a management control system for limiting self-initiated action is perhaps its most harmful characteristic. The system casts the member in a conforming, passive, and dependent role, responding to initiative from management to administer the system and "find" them when needed. Systems of this type do nothing to inspire the initiative of the individual and his responsibility for his own effectiveness and growth. Misled by an assumption that paternalistic management has his interests at heart and is looking out for his welfare, he may drift into obsolescence or retirement waiting for management to point the way.

User-managed System

Consider for contrast the consequences of a user-managed, or employee-oriented, system. A system is considered user-managed when it is actuated by the lowest-level used in accordance with the criteria of an effective system, as defined on page 126. The user actuates the system to satisfy a personal goal, and it is important to him that he know how to use the system and that he incur no risk in doing so. The job-posting system described on pages 121 to 125 and in Figures 5-2 and 5-3 is an example of a user-managed staffing system.

The Texas Instruments job-posting system is based on the company philosophy that individuals are responsible for their own development. A philosophy of self-development is a platitude and an excuse for company dereliction if realistic opportunities are not provided to enable members to meet this responsibility. Job posting is one of the most effective systems for making self-development a realistic expectation.

The system, to support an internal staffing strategy, must give present employees advantage over outsiders. For example, present employees may have one week's opportunity before outside applicants are considered. Job requirements are defined in terms of

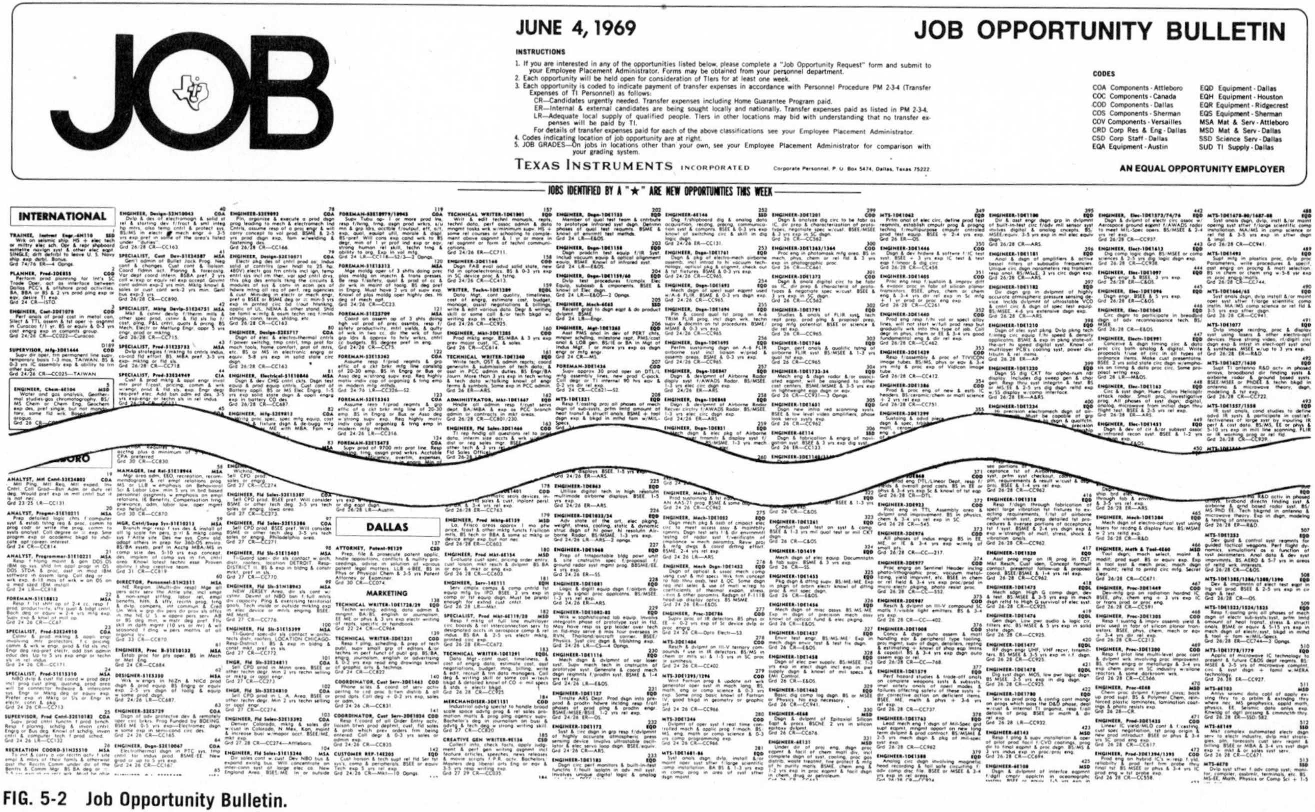

JOB OPPORTUNITY BULLETIN

JUNE 4, 1969

INSTRUCTIONS

1. If you are interested in any of the opportunities listed below, please complete a "Job Opportunity Request" form and submit to your Employee Placement Administrator. Forms may be obtained from your personnel department.
2. Each opportunity will be held open for consideration of Texas for at least one week.
3. Each opportunity is coded to indicate payment of transfer expenses in accordance with Personnel Procedure PM 2-3-4. (Transfer Expenses of TI Personnel) as follows:
   - CR—Candidates urgently needed. Transfer expenses paid.
   - ER—Internal & external candidates are being sought locally and nationally. Transfer expenses paid as listed in PM 2-3-4.
   - LR—Adequate local supply of qualified people. Tiers in other locations may bid with understanding that no transfer expenses will be paid by TI.

   For details of transfer expenses paid for each of the above classifications see your Employee Placement Administrator.
4. Codes indicating location of job opportunity are at right.
5. JOB GRADES—On jobs in locations other than your own, see your Employee Placement Administrator for comparison with your grading system.

CODES

COA Components-Attleboro	EQD Equipment-Dallas
COK Components-Canada	EQH Equipment-Houston
COD Components-Dallas	EQR Equipment-Ridgecrest
COS Components-Sherman	EQS Equipment-Sherman
COV Components-Versailles	MSA Mat & Serv-Attleboro
CRD Corp Res & Eng-Dallas	MSD Mat & Serv-Dallas
DSD Data Systems-Dallas	SnD Science Serv-Dallas
EQA Equipment-Austin	SuD TI Supply-Dallas

AN EQUAL OPPORTUNITY EMPLOYER

Corporate Personnel, P.O. Box 5474, Dallas, Texas 75222

TEXAS INSTRUMENTS INCORPORATED

— JOBS IDENTIFIED BY A ★ ARE NEW OPPORTUNITIES THIS WEEK —

INTERNATIONAL

DALLAS

MARKETING

FIG. 5-2   Job Opportunity Bulletin.

education, skill, and experience requirements; job grade; and location. Monthly listings of all job openings are published, distributed, and posted, and interim openings are posted weekly.

Any employee can actuate the system by completing a form designating his interest in a posted job, and submitting this job bid to his personnel department. Notification of his supervisor at this point is optional with the bidder.

His bid is screened along with others by personnel and, if not eliminated, is referred to the requesting supervisor who screens, interviews, and selects a candidate (or decides to consider outside applicants). The selected candidate is offered the job by the requesting supervisor, and if he accepts it, he notifies his own supervisor of his acceptance of the new job. The requesting supervisor initiates the personnel transfer paper work, and the individual is released to his

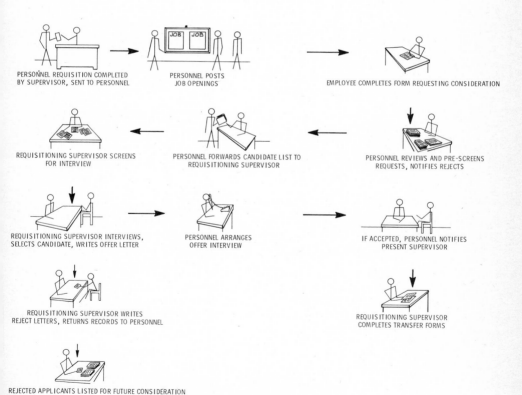

PERSONNEL REQUISITION COMPLETED
BY SUPERVISOR, SENT TO PERSONNEL

PERSONNEL POSTS
JOB OPENINGS

EMPLOYEE COMPLETES FORM REQUESTING CONSIDERATION

REQUISITIONING SUPERVISOR SCREENS
FOR INTERVIEW

PERSONNEL FORWARDS CANDIDATE LIST TO
REQUISITIONING SUPERVISOR

PERSONNEL REVIEWS AND PRE-SCREENS
REQUESTS, NOTIFIES REJECTS

REQUISITIONING SUPERVISOR INTERVIEWS,
SELECTS CANDIDATE, WRITES OFFER LETTER

PERSONNEL ARRANGES
OFFER INTERVIEW

IF ACCEPTED, PERSONNEL NOTIFIES
PRESENT SUPERVISOR

REQUISITIONING SUPERVISOR WRITES
REJECT LETTERS, RETURNS RECORDS TO PERSONNEL

REQUISITIONING SUPERVISOR
COMPLETES TRANSFER FORMS

REJECTED APPLICANTS LISTED FOR FUTURE CONSIDERATION

FIG. 5-3 Job posting.

new job. The releasing supervisor has up to 3 weeks to post the vacated job and select and train a replacement. In practice, many jobs are filled immediately from a reservoir of qualified bidders on file from previous bids. Hence, several bidders may be released simultaneously for their new assignments.

The job posting-system is of the most dramatically successful methods of operation that can be adopted, simply because the user benefits from use of the system. Individuals in quest of growth, responsibility, and change are far more sensitive and perceptive search mechanisms than the programmed computer which performs the search function for the manpower inventory. More importantly, the individual is now responsible for his own growth opportunities and can initiate self-development actions suggested by job-posting specifications and bidding rejects. Participation in Texas Instruments' educational assistance program increased approximately 80 percent after installation of the formal job-posting system.

The system synergistically serves the needs of the user and the organization. Talent now finds more complete and positive expression through promotions, transfers, and reassignments. Though short-term inconvenience is caused by increased turnover, long-term gains are netted by the organization when high-talent transferees find outlets for their competence inside the organization rather than devoting most of their energy to outside activities or looking for a better job. Job posting also benefits the organization as a system for coping with cutbacks in work force, placing graduates from training programs, upgrading educational assistance participants, and placing persons returning from leave.

Other significant, but less tangible, benefits of job posting include a reduced dependency relationship between the job incumbent and his supervisor, higher *esprit de corps* among the members of the work force, the requirement of excellence on the part of supervision to avoid "escape bidding" by members of his group, and greater community stability.

Other staffing systems which provide interface with job posting become more user-oriented. Training, for example, is more often selected by the job incumbent and keyed to his perceptions of opportunity on the work force rather than being a management prescribed program which not always has realistic relationship to job opportunity. Training for training's sake gives way to learning as a means for attaining a personal goal.

Similarly, aptitude testing, long perceived as a mysterious tool of management for selecting and rejecting candidates for jobs and training programs, can become an aid to the individual in helping him understand his strong points and limitations. With the insights offered by aptitude tests, he can direct his aspirations and remedial learning activities and thus assume greater responsibility for his own self-development. However, the use of aptitude tests has become complicated by misapplications, absence of uniform professional standards, and legislative restrictions. Despite these limitations, aptitude tests are potentially among the most potent tools available for furthering the philosophy of self-development.

Aptitude Testing

The use of aptitude tests improves the probability of selecting qualified job candidates. However, tests are not perfect predictors of job success, and occasionally they eliminate qualified applicants who perform poorly on tests, or select unqualified applicants who perform well on tests. Unfortunately for the society which stresses equal opportunity as a cornerstone of its philosophy, tests tend to eliminate larger percentages of minority groups. In some cases the selecting out of minority-group candidates is a result of not having included these groups in the test validation studies, in which case the tests are valid predictors of job success only for candidates from within the culture in which they were validated. Even when tests are properly validated as predictors of job success for all groups, it is sometimes reasoned that minority members should be exempt from standardized predictors on the basis that these individuals are innocent victims of social injustice which handicaps them in both test performance and job performance. In any event, aptitude tests, regardless of their validity, are not widely supported as a selection device.

Paradoxically, part of the problem of aptitude testing stems from the fact that tests are too potent as predictors. The psychologist's apparent ability to predict behavior from tests often leads to the disregard of interview impressions, biographical data, and job history. Overreliance on the psychologist stems in part from the argot he uses in describing characteristics, interest patterns, skills, and intelligence of the candidate. Not fully understanding "psychologese," the manager often capitulates and permits the psychologist to make selection decisions. This practice makes him the user of a system that he does not fully understand, and aptitude testing becomes a crutch, displacing other proved predictors and common judgment in matters of personal selection and evaluation.

Much of the mystery can be removed from testing if the user realizes that all tests, regardless of their labels, can be grouped into four families of human characteristics: capacity, achievement, interests, and temperament.

Capacity tests are of two kinds—mental and physical. *Mental* capacity is measured by various intelligence tests in terms of factors such as verbal fluency, numerical facility, space relations, inductive and deductive reasoning, detail perception, reasoning speed, and memory. *Physical* capacity refers to capabilities such as eye-hand coordination, manual dexterity, hand steadiness, sense of balance, visual acuity, depth perception, and color vision.

Achievement tests are measures of knowledge and skill. *Knowledge* achievement tests are typified by measures of knowledge of mathematics, geography, astronomy, EDP machine language, and principles of management or economics. *Skill* achievement tests are typified by measures of ability to type and take shorthand, operate a desk calculator, write a computer program, lead a conference, or operate a lathe.

Interest tests measure vocational or avocational interests, usually through multiple-choice questionnaires or inventories. *Vocational* interest measures may describe a person's preferences for job activities such as computational, persuasive, scientific, or mechanical; or in terms of vocational titles such as mechanical engineer, chemist, clergyman, business manager, or athlete. *Avocational* interest questionnaires measure off-the-job interests in terms of activities or topics such as oil painting, sports, reading, flying, coin collecting, bird watching, historical events, music, politics, or religion.

Temperament tests, depending on their degree of sophistication and the competence of the administrator, measure surface or subconscious personality. *Surface* personality traits are usually described from responses to questions about parents, siblings, friends, enemies, teachers, supervisors, sex, religion, social situations, dishonesty, fears, and aspirations. This kind of test is often transparent and tends to evoke responses that the individual believes to be correct or desirable. Even when the respondent attempts to be completely candid or honest, the questionnaire may only tap the respondent's conscious personality. As a measure of surface personality, such a test might be valid. For example, such a test might accurately describe one person as an optimistic extrovert and another as a depressive introvert. In terms of everyday observations, and under normal conditions, these may be valid descriptions. However, a test which measures subconscious personality might reveal quite different personalities. The *subconscious* measure is more subtle, perhaps inducing the respondent to project his personality into the interpretation of ambiguous pictures and patterns, thereby giving surface expression to subconscious feelings. Such a test, coupled with a depth interview by a psychologist, might show, for example, that the happy-go-lucky extrovert is really wearing a façade, beneath which is much sadness and despair stemming from alienation and misfortune. The façade makes everyday living bearable to him, and it also becomes the pattern by which his acquaintances may know him. The depressive introvert might harbor a subconscious need to be in the limelight or to be an empire builder, and his behavior might also be a façade imposed by an overdeveloped conscience or a reaction to despair. The paradoxical swing from depression to euphoria, or vice versa, when inhibitions are lowered with alcohol, is sometimes an expression of this phenomenon. It does not logically follow, of course, that surface personalities are always in conflict with subconscious personalities; usually they are not.

None of the tests described above should be administered or interpreted by untrained personnel. All are subject to misinterpretation, especially in the hands of the professionally untrained, and particularly the measures of mental capacity and temperament.

When adequate safeguards are provided against the pitfalls noted above, and when tests are properly validated, administered, and interpreted within the balanced context of other predictors, they represent one of the most effective and democratic systems for uncovering hidden talent. People in manual occupations, for example, may have talents untapped by previous roles or submerged by conformity to social norms. Self-discovery through aptitude tests may provide the spark of aspiration and encouragement needed to lift talent from dormancy or to transform it from reactive to constructive expression. Aptitude tests can also perform the merciful mission of redirecting unrealistic aspirations, enabling individuals to recognize and accept reality, and thereby prevent the later trauma of vocational failure.

The application of aptitude tests should not be aimed at labeling people as successes or failures but, rather, should support the concept that all people have aptitude to succeed—but in different roles. Some have a greater variety of aptitudes than others, but opportunities exist for all to succeed. Particularly in the situation of a tight labor market, or in the implementation of a promotion-from-within policy, tests offer a potent key to the location of talent and a stimulus to self development.

In practice, aptitude tests, as vocational guidance instruments, often represent greater deterrents than catalysts, particularly when they are administered under the direction and control of management authority. No matter how fairly the testing process is administered by management, it increases the dependency relationship of the individual to those above him, and represents one more bureaucratic suppressor to initiative.

However, by transferring the initiative for aptitude testing to the individual, the assessment process can become a developmental personal experience. While it is appropriate for the organization to provide access to, and refund the cost of, aptitude testing, much in the same spirit, and for the same sound business reasons, that educational assistance is offered, the use and control of test scores must be proprietary with the individual. The psychological consultant releases aptitude data only by voluntary authorization of the examinee. Thus test scores become constructive aids to self-development, and are optionally withheld or released as the examinee chooses in applying for promotional opportunity.

PERFORMANCE REVIEW

Douglas McGregor's[2] "uneasy look at performance appraisal" stemmed from his observation that performance reviews more often harmed than helped the relationship between the individual and his supervisor. Much of the negative impact of performance review, according to McGregor, resulted from the common practice of criticizing people during performance reviews, based on the traditional

[2] Douglas McGregor, "An Uneasy Look at Performance Appraisal," *Harvard Business Review*, pp. 89–94, May–June, 1957.

assumption that it was the supervisor's job to identify the individual's failures, shortcomings, and weaknesses; communicate these to him; and advise him how to overcome them.

The Traditional Approach

The process of appraisal and criticism in industry is a natural extension of authority-controlled relationships learned elsewhere, such as those often existing between parents and children in the home, teachers and students in the schools, or superiors and subordinates in the armed forces. Traditional job-performance rating factors, illustrated in Figure 5-4, are similar to school report card factors and provide the basis for supervisory judgment and criticism. Objective observation of the traditional performance review process shows that some people do in fact improve as a result of criticism, but most do not change at all, and a few actually perform less well.

Some managers, perceiving the ineffectiveness of criticism, have concluded that the ineffectiveness is not so much to be attributed to criticism itself as to the tactless application of criticism. Hence, much effort has been devoted to the definition and application of "constructive criticism." Attempts to be constructive in applying criticism were usually of the sugar-coated variety, which only tended to make people more wary and defensive. For example, the "sandwich technique" of

	L H
Quality	⊢—⊢—⊢—⊣
Quantity	⊢—⊢—⊢—⊣
Initiative	⊢—⊢—⊢—⊣
Loyalty	⊢—⊢—⊢—⊣
Cooperativeness	⊢—⊢—⊢—⊣
Creativity	⊢—⊢—⊢—⊣
Stamina	⊢—⊢—⊢—⊣
Dependability	⊢—⊢—⊢—⊣
Potential	⊢—⊢—⊢—⊣

Achievements during past six months

Six-month goals

Long-range goals

Traditional rating factors, completed by the supervisor.

Goal-setting factors, completed by the job incumbent.

FIG. 5-4   Traditional versus goal-setting performance review forms.

criticism, which finds recurring expression in various organizations, is based on the assumption that criticism is constructive if sandwiched between two compliments. Though such a process no doubt makes criticism more bearable, repeated applications tend to condition individuals to become wary of compliments.

Goal-setting Approach

The application of McGregor's theory Y philosophy to performance review takes the emphasis away from the sole use of authority and places more of the responsibility in the hands of the job incumbent. The focus is placed on goal setting and feedback, rather than criticism. The goal-setting form, also illustrated in Figure 5-4, enables the job incumbent to detail his achievements and goals as a basis for planning and review with his supervisor in accordance with the procedure detailed in Figure 5-5. A discussion of his achievements—e.g., lessons learned, recommendations for the future—usually results in self-evaluation by the job incumbent, an acceptance of his shortcomings, and commitment to do better in the future. In such a format, failures and accomplishments can be a basis for learning.

Interdependence of Goals   Individual goal setting seldom stands alone. As organizations grow in size and complexity, and interdependence among individuals and functions becomes encumbered by bureaucratic restrictions, the complexity of individual goal setting becomes more apparent. It is the leader's responsibility to see to it that people with interdependent jobs engage in mutual problem solving and goal setting. This provides the basis for avoiding conflict and overlap, promotes cooperation, and establishes a foundation for setting individual goals.

For example, a manager of a technically oriented manufacturing organization may decide to launch a goal-setting performance review process in the engineering functions on the assumption that well-educated, goal-oriented engineers can establish goal-setting patterns to be emulated by individuals in other functions. But goal setting by individual engineers can find only limited application unless opportunities are created for coordinating the efforts of engineering with other functions. The engineer is a change agent whose success depends on his interface with other functions, such as research, manufacturing, quality assurance, procurement, and sales. Representatives of these functions compose the team that is to develop and

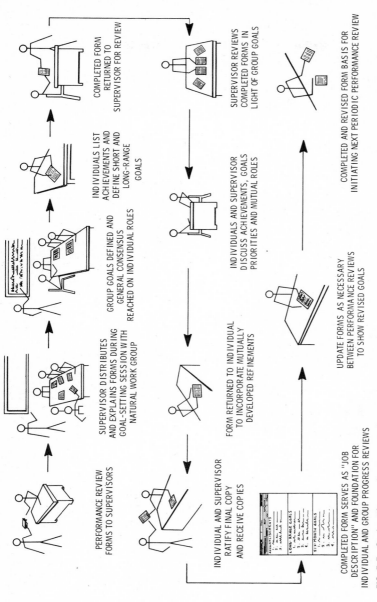

PERFORMANCE REVIEW
FORMS TO SUPERVISORS

SUPERVISOR DISTRIBUTES
AND EXPLAINS FORMS DURING
GOAL-SETTING SESSION WITH
NATURAL WORK GROUP

GROUP GOALS DEFINED AND
GENERAL CONSENSUS
REACHED ON INDIVIDUAL ROLES

INDIVIDUALS LIST
ACHIEVEMENTS AND
DEFINE SHORT AND
LONG-RANGE
GOALS

COMPLETED FORM
RETURNED TO
SUPERVISOR FOR REVIEW

SUPERVISOR REVIEWS
COMPLETED FORMS IN
LIGHT OF GROUP GOALS

INDIVIDUALS AND SUPERVISOR
DISCUSS ACHIEVEMENTS, GOALS
PRIORITIES AND MUTUAL ROLES

FORM RETURNED TO INDIVIDUAL
TO INCORPORATE MUTUALLY
DEVELOPED REFINEMENTS

INDIVIDUAL AND SUPERVISOR
RATIFY FINAL COPY
AND RECEIVE COPIES

UPDATE FORMS AS NECESSARY
BETWEEN PERFORMANCE REVIEWS
TO SHOW REVISED GOALS

COMPLETED AND REVISED FORM BASIS FOR
INITIATING NEXT PERIODIC PERFORMANCE REVIEW

COMPLETED FORM SERVES AS "JOB
DESCRIPTION" AND FOUNDATION FOR
INDIVIDUAL AND GROUP PROGRESS REVIEWS

FIG. 5-5 Goal-setting performance review.

167

implement a strategy for delivering a superior product or service to customers at competitive costs. Hence, group problem solving–goal setting by this natural work group, as illustrated in Figure 5-5, is necessary to obtain consensus on a common goal and the definition of individual roles in supporting the team effort. After the group goal is defined, individual goal setting can be realistically undertaken.

A discussion of short- and long-range goals between the individual and his supervisor enables them to obtain a consensus on priorities, and to jointly plan strategies for achieving them. The involvement of the supervisor is also necessary to enable the individual to dovetail his goals with his peers' goals and the broader departmental objectives. A successful goal-setting performance review experience between the individual and his supervisor will result in mutually acceptable roles for achieving mutually defined goals.

Dimensions of a Goal   An understanding of the characteristics of a goal is vital to this type of performance review. A marketing manager who defined a goal as "increasing his share of the served available market" had not set a goal. However, he had set a goal when he specified that he would progress from 7 to 15 percent of an $80 million served available market with a particular line of products by December of the coming year. Goals have both quantitative dimensions and target dates. Long-range goals also need intermediate checkpoints to enable the individual to know whether he is on schedule and to give progress reports to others who need feedback. When a goal of this type has been set, the performance review is not a mechanism for judging and criticizing the individual. After agreement on the goal, the supervisor's intervention should normally occur only upon request, usually when the job incumbent needs assistance to stay on target. In this format, the performance review is transformed from a system of control by authority to a system for mutual direction and control by the job incumbent and his supervisor.

Feedback versus Criticism   The performance review as a developmental experience depends also on an understanding of the distinction between criticism and feedback. Sometimes the only distinction lies in the eyes of the perceiver. Criticism is usually perceived as an arbitrary value judgment dispensed by authority of management prerogative. No matter how fair or objective this judgment, it is often resented because of its resemblance to oppressions or indignities experienced at the hands of other authority figures. Feedback, in contrast, more often has the characteristic of being candid, immediate, and uninterpreted transmission of information. For example, when a salesman has alienated a customer, prompting the customer to fire off a letter of complaint to the sales manager, it may be more constructive to give the letter to the salesman to draft a response than to wait till performance review and pontificate to the salesman on the flaws in his personality and sales strategy. Needless to say, feedback serves best in a climate of trust and interpersonal competence where candor and leveling can take place. The use of criticism is one of the potent factors in destroying such a climate.

Like all systems, performance review as a system is at the mercy of its users. Qualified and committed people can achieve good results with a poorly designed form and ambiguously defined procedures. Unqualified and uncommitted people will cause performance reviews to fail no matter how sophisticated the system.

COMPENSATION

Pay commonly serves the following functions, arranged to correspond roughly with man's hierarchy of needs.

- Pay satisfies maintenance needs.
- Pay is a measure of status.
- Pay is a scorekeeping system.
- Pay buys freedom and opportunity.

As a *maintenance factor,* money pays for food, shelter, clothing, education, transportation, and the costs of government. As a society's affluence increases, its citizens' maintenance needs are broadened to include a myriad of leisure-time pursuits, supplemental benefits, services, and symbols of status. The maintenance needs of an individual are sometimes defined as the goods and services that enable him to keep up with the Joneses. The illiterate farmer in the isolated Iranian village was not dissatisfied, until he visited Tehran! Similarly, an underprivileged American finds little consolation in the fact that he is living better than the middle class in an undeveloped country—he measures his maintenance needs according to standards surrounding him. Labor unions, through collective bargaining, have stressed "equal treatment" and reinforced the role of compensation as a maintenance factor in providing adequate wages, hours, and working conditions.

Pay is a *measure of status*—personally, vocationally, and socially. Engineers, scientists, managers, college professors, and other professionals scan salary survey data to determine their vocational progress and status, within and outside the organization. Individuals in work groups may gain or lose prestige, if only in self-image, according to their relative standing in the group in regard to monetary increases, awards and penalties, and pay level. Organizational status is reflected as a gross dichotomy in differential pay systems for hourly and salaried employees, and is a function of job grade at all levels. Social relationships and pay status are inextricably related in the community.

Money is a *scorekeeping system,* particularly for those who have no more tangible measure of achievement. The loss of one-half his fortune would not be felt by the multibillionaire, unless he was informed of his loss. Yet, the name of his game is making another million—much as the checker player uses checkers for scorekeeping. Silas Marner had no plan for converting his gold into goods or services, but the money itself afforded him a measure of achievement and satisfaction, and the gold coins were the units for measuring his most prized possession. Employees on piecework quickly learn to translate labor standards into monetary equivalents as a basis for measuring job performance. For employees whose impact on job goals is otherwise obscured, the pay increase, or lack of it, determined through the judgment of the supervisor may be the only feedback received. Pay is often the scorekeeping system for giving substance to allegations of favoritism or fairness.

Some desire money for the *freedom and opportunity* it buys. Money provides freedom from drudgery, monotony, pettiness, fear, and other conditions that are seemingly unbearable and are otherwise inescapable. Money provides opportunity to seek higher goals, multiply achievements, buy power or influence, grow personally and professionally, and realize the American dream. The risk takers—mineral explorers, stock market or real estate speculators, gamblers, inventors, entrepreneurs—when their goal is spectacular financial gain, are often seeking or experiencing freedom and opportunity.

The above categorization of pay is primarily a system of emphasis, as money in any given instance might serve any or all of the four functions described. In addition, it must be recognized that these categories are somewhat arbitrary and oversimplified. Almost every individual becomes highly motivated by the prospect of acquiring a large amount of money—and he does not need to analyze his motives for wanting it. Money itself has come to symbolize all that money can buy, and also there is a bit of Silas Marner in most of us. But this classification system underscores the fact that money does not serve the single, simple function that seems to be implied in traditional approaches to wage and salary administration.

Compensation, in the form of both pay and supplemental benefits, is often more potent as a dissatisfier than as a reinforcement of motivation. Dissatisfaction with compensation arises more often from the pay system itself than from the absolute level of pay. A pay system based on merit is preferred to one based on tenure, but only if the merit system is understood and equitably administered.[3] Hence, pay is a dissatisfier when it fails to satisfy the purpose for which it is sought, particularly if the pay system has the characteristics of an ineffective system as defined on pages 125 to 126.

Cash Compensation Systems

Dissatisfactions are minimized when *pay increases* and *pay levels* are perceived to be equitably related to performance. However, when majority rules, as it often does, particularly when collective bargaining is the medium of leverage, automatic progression is the usual result. This deemphasis of merit in favor of tenure usually reflects a lack of confidence in the merit system, or the people who administer it. Dissatisfactions arising from automatic progression are probably no more numerous than the dissatisfactions stemming from a merit system. However, merit systems more often dissatisfy the low achievers while automatic progression systems dissatisfy the high achievers whose commitment is more essential to the success of the organization. Compensation systems, in addition to those for administering wages and salaries, are often intended to emphasize or reward merit. When they fail, it is not because they reflect merit but, rather, because they fail to reward merit at all levels of the organization or their merit features have become encumbered with, and overshadowed by, bureaucratic dissatisfiers.

Discretionary bonuses can be reinforcements of positively motivated behavior if administered on the basis of fair and understandable cri-

[3] Michael Beers and Gloria J. Gery, "Pay System Preferences and their Correlates," *Proceedings of the 76th Annual Convention of the American Psychological Association*, San Francisco, 1968.

teria, and can provide proportionately greater awards to higher achievers. Unlike pay increases, they can be exercised without distorting rate ·structures; but like other forms of merit pay, they may be dissatisfiers to low achievers. In practice, they may evoke dissatisfactions from high performers because of real or imagined discrimination. One common form of discrimination is the failure to award bonuses at the lower levels in accordance with criteria meaningful at lower levels. In a climate of trust, discretionary awards, like other merit systems, can be a positive reinforcement of commitment; but in a climate of distrust, because they are by definition discretionary with supervision, they can intensify hostility and alienation.

Stock options have long been awarded to employees, primarily at the upper levels, as a form of compensation presumed to increase the recipient's proprietary commitment to the success of the organization. Also, stock options, until modified by Federal legislation, offered tax advantages, particularly at the upper levels where increasing tax rates diminished the incentive value of salary increases.

Stock options have not commonly been made available to people at the lower levels, apparently as a result of two implicit assumptions. It is traditionally assumed that, since the reins of the organization are in the hands of the managers who occupy the drivers' seats, managers are the ones who must be motivated. After all, they are the decision makers who make things happen, and it is natural for them to identify with the success of the organization. In contrast, it is reasoned that people at the lower levels of the organization are pretty much limited to what they are told to do, and stock options would have little value in changing their perspective and commitment. Further, it is assumed that people at the lower levels are not sophisticated enough to comprehend stock price fluctuations, or that they are not able to afford, or willing to accept, adverse price trends.

These assumptions are partly valid and are understandable consequences of the tradition that has circumscribed the responsibility, perspective, and security of people at the lower levels of the organization. However, these assumptions are being invalidated by the efforts of enlightened managements, who are obtaining better expression of talent and commitment through job enrichment and goal-oriented supervision; and by the impact of increasingly affluent cultures, which are providing better-informed and more independent job candidates. Whatever value stock options may have at upper levels can now be realized as well at the lower levels.

One successful and progressive corporation has made stock options available to all employees through payroll deductions—stock certificates to be delivered when paid for, at the market price in effect when payroll deductions were authorized. As a hedge against price decline or urgent need of cash, the plan permits the individual to receive his deductions plus interest instead of stock certificates. To the extent that stock ownership increases proprietary commitment, and to the extent that this commitment is permitted to find constructive expression, stock options can yield a better return to the organization.

Profit sharing, in a gross sense, is a merit pay system as it returns to members of the work force the consequences of their collective, individual, and group effort. It reinforces the feeling of a joint stake in the success of the enterprise, and leads to the development of proprietary interest in the utilization of company resources. Through this system more people come to understand criteria of organizational effectiveness and the interdependence of individual and organizational goals. When all members of the group benefit from profit sharing, group involvement in increasing profits is encouraged. Profit sharing constitutes a lesson in economics, supporting the free enterprise system.

Most profit-sharing plans fail to achieve their full potential because of the inadequacy of their feedback processes. One problem stems from the reluctance to explain, or the difficulty of explaining, to the participants the rationale of the decision making which distributes much of an organization's profits for research, expansion, dividends, and taxes. Participants would feel less dependent on the arbitrary judgments of the top decision makers if they understood and could estimate the amount of the profit-sharing fund from openly shared financial data.

A second problem is caused by the delay in feedback. Traditionally, profit-sharing funds are announced at the close of the year, based on annualized profits. For most people, whose job goals and achievements are planned on a shorter time span, the annual report is poorly correlated with their individual or group's successes and failures.

The system would be more sensitive to the needs of the participants and their families if fund distributions corresponded to the normal monthly, quarterly, and annual financial reviews. For example, each month a supplementary profit-sharing check (or statement explaining its absence) based on perhaps 25 percent of the estimated profit-sharing fund earned during the month could be distributed as take-home pay with the paycheck. At the end of the quarterly financial review, an additional check reflecting 25 percent of the profit-sharing fund calculated for the quarter could be distributed as take-home pay. Finally, after the year-end review, the remaining 50 percent of the profit-sharing fund (adjusted for annualized calculations) could be distributed, or credited to a deferred account for estate planning as most plans do for the entire fund. Individuals should have the option of crediting monthly and quarterly funds to their deferred accounts, but they should receive feedback reports with the same frequency.

A profit-sharing system having the above features would satisfy most of the conditions of an effective system as described on page 126.

Piecework is a merit pay system, intended as an incentive, usually at the lower levels of the organization. Good in theory, the system often breaks down in practice because of management's manipulative motives in creating the system. Further, piecework is usually based on standards engineered by people who understand the needs of people no better than the job incumbents understand the rationale of the incentive system. Hence, workers find themselves at the mercy of a management system which they do not understand, administered by persons whom they do not fully trust. Because job content is in constant flux in most factories and offices, standards are quickly outdated, and the revision of standards by whatever method is often interpreted by incumbents as acts of exploitation. People in piecework jobs soon learn that standards are based on normative data, that when too many members of the group exceed the bogey (100 percent of standard), industrial engineers will raise it, thereby penalizing all members of the group. Consequently, peer pressure keeps the group below the danger point, and engineered labor standards thus inadvertently become a system for perpetuating mediocrity and undermining the company's ability to compete.

The *paid suggestion plan,* as a merit pay system, satisfies a few, but for most it inevitably acquires greater potential for dissatisfaction than motivation. Soon after its initiation, a system usually begins bogging down in administrative indecision. A backlog of suggestions accumulates as a consequence of their sheer volume, inability to assess them, unwillingness to implement them, redundancies, and the difficulty of giving negative feedback to suggestors. Moreover, paid suggestion systems often disqualify industrial engineers, supervisors, and other members of management on the basis that these people are hired as innovators, and should not receive additional pay for their suggestions. Persons so disqualified are understandably tempted at times to "beat the system" by engaging in unethical collaboration with qualified suggestors. And, of course, breaches of ethics usually lead to compromise and deterioration of the trust factor in the organizational climate. Unequal treatment also reinforces the concept of two classes of people: the worker, hired and paid for his fast and efficient hands; and the professional, hired for his creativity.

Though the paid suggestion system may evoke collaborative efforts to beat the system, as noted above, it tends to quash group collaboration in problem solving. Because the system is designed to reward *individual* creativity, individuals understandably protect their ideas by concealing them from others. A paid suggestion system can be designed to encourage both individual and group effort by giving it some of the characteristics of a profit-sharing plan. If all suggestion awards were placed in a common pool and distributed as a flat percentage of base rate to all in the group, individuals would have a natural incentive to see their ideas elaborated and improved through the efforts of others. Peer pressures thus would not be directed aggressively against the system but, rather, constructively toward enlarging the fund, thereby adding synergistic support to organizational goals.

Supplemental Benefit Systems

During the first half of the twentieth century in the United States, the cost of supplemental benefits as a percentage of total compensation has risen from less than 10 percent to over 30 percent. Some of these benefits are required by law, some were won through collective bargaining, many were granted through paternalism, and others were provided by enlightened management. Though aimed initially at remedying deficiencies in wages, hours, and working conditions, they have been increasingly broadened to support the expanding maintenance needs of an affluent society. Increasing costs of supplemental benefits, as overhead costs, ultimately work to the detriment of employees as they reduce the organization's ability to compete in the world market.

The evolution of supplemental benefits illustrates the overriding strength of tradition in blinding management to the changing needs of people. In earlier decades, when many people did in fact suffer from thwarted maintenance needs, management learned that satisfying these was a sound business investment. To many managers, supplemental benefits are still seen as key incentives in stimulating effectiveness. Employees are often blamed for their seemingly insatiable demands for increased supplemental benefits, when it was and is management's perceptions and invalid assumptions about people that escalated these benefits to their excessively high levels. As noted earlier, preoccupation with maintenance factors in today's society is more often a symptom of thwarted motivation needs than of unsatisfied maintenance needs. But most managers do not know how to provide the conditions necessary for satisfying motivation needs. Though the motivation needs of people are best satisfied through the medium of meaningful work itself, these needs can also be partially satisfied through people's involvement in the management of their supplemental benefit systems.

Consider *group insurance* as a specimen supplemental benefit. Traditionally, a group insurance system is masterminded by personnel experts within constraints designated by top management. The mission is to provide the most attractive program for the greatest number at the lowest cost. In effect, Personnel through armchair logic evolves a system to satisfy the presumed needs of their customers— the employees of the organization. Following the development and ratification of the program by top management, it is given the hard sell by the personnel department, who point out to the people the benefits and advantages of the new system over others. Though inflationary trends may have increased the price of the package, they are assured that they are getting more for the price than before. The ardor and eloquence of management in selling this system usually makes it suspect. The system might in fact be superior, but employees feel a vague suspicion about management's need to convince them of its merits. They have learned that "the big print giveth and the little print taketh away." They are hearing the "big print" and wondering about the unspoken "little print." The greater the gap between management and labor the less likely employees are to believe that management is acting in their behalf. It is understandable that a group insurance program is often the issue of collective bargaining where the employees feel that their rights are being protected by their peers in the bargaining process.

In short, it can be said that employees typically do not see the group insurance program as *their* program but, rather, as management's program. The labeling of the program as the "employees insurance plan" is a form of paternalistic deception which has evoked and always will evoke resentment when attempted. In a very real sense, employees are the customer and the user of the system. The group insurance program will succeed or fail according to the criteria listed on page 126.

As the customer, employees must have an opportunity to define the purpose of the group insurance system; they will then understand and agree with its purpose. They must know how to use the system and apply it to their own situations. They must receive timely feedback regarding their own personal involvement, as well as regarding its adequacy to the population of customers being served. Finally, they must be able to initiate actions to adapt or revise the system to increase its effectiveness. The primary system user thus has the opportunity to influence the development, administration, and revision of a system designed to serve him as a customer. To do this responsibly, he must, of course, be fully informed on matters pertaining to policy and legal guidelines, economic trends, and financial and service resources available for this system. Just as every manager must manage his budget, so must those who influence the management of this system.

A group insurance system that will minimize dissatisfactions and satisfy the needs of the largest number must be evolved through full participation by panels of employee representatives, as illustrated in Figure 5-6. If possible, these panels should be selected by a flexible process that taps groups naturally related through work roles, union membership, or fluid communication channels. Perhaps the first assignment of the panel is to evaluate the membership in the light of the assignment and to suggest revisions. Though panels will naturally include professional and management personnel in their memberships, individuals are not involved as agents of management or labor or any other ingroup.

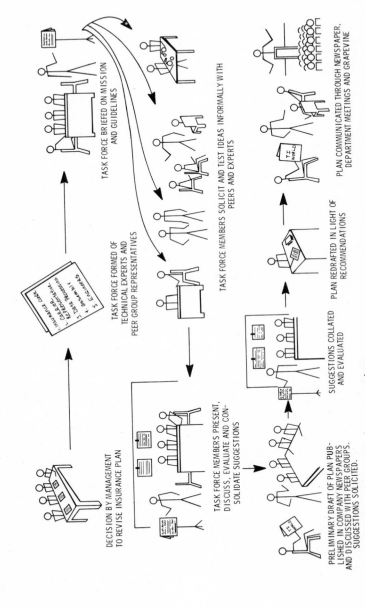

DECISION BY MANAGEMENT
TO REVISE INSURANCE PLAN

TASK FORCE FORMED OF
TECHNICAL EXPERTS AND
PEER GROUP REPRESENTATIVES

TASK FORCE BRIEFED ON MISSION
AND GUIDELINES

TASK FORCE MEMBERS SOLICIT AND TEST IDEAS INFORMALLY WITH
PEERS AND EXPERTS

PLAN REDRAFTED IN LIGHT OF
RECOMMENDATIONS

PLAN COMMUNICATED THROUGH NEWSPAPER,
DEPARTMENT MEETINGS AND GRAPEVINE

SUGGESTIONS COLLATED
AND EVALUATED

TASK FORCE MEMBERS PRESENT,
DISCUSS, EVALUATE AND CON-
SOLIDATE SUGGESTIONS

PRELIMINARY DRAFT OF PLAN PUB-
LISHED IN COMPANY NEWSPAPERS
AND DISCUSSED WITH PEER GROUPS.
SUGGESTIONS SOLICITED.

FIG. 5-6 Development of group insurance system.

Qualification for panel membership is based on either technical competence needed for designing and administering the system, or ability to represent the members of natural work groups or segments of the organization. Technical competence factors, for example, would draw membership from systems designers, carrier representatives, data processors, legal staff, and particularly the company insurance clerks who have day-to-day contact with the users. Employee representation considerations would include members who would represent the interests of the young and the old, short- and long-tenured, married and single, male and female, unskilled and skilled, professional and managerial individuals, who collectively comprise the work force and are to be served through the system.

Panel memberships are crucial to the successful development of a system to serve the entire population. All organizations have bellwethers who are tied into the fluid communication process because their personality characteristics make them the natural, informal, and trusted unifying agents of natural peer groups. To prescribe membership simply through prescheduled and formalized appointments, elections, rotation, or lottery would not usually achieve representativeness. The informal nomination and election process, with flexible guidelines for periodic review and revision, is more likely to keep the panel attuned to its constituency's grapevine.

The effectiveness of such a working task force depends on the full disclosure of all information that would be available to corporate systems planners. The first meeting of the panel task force should be a briefing session, to define the mission and administrative guidelines, and to determine the adequacy of panel membership with respect to technical know-how and work-force representation. The briefing session is conducted informally by the panel itself, utilizing the technical competence represented in the group.

Orientation should include brief reviews of historical data, economic trends, benefit trends, experience with previous plans, comparative survey data, reasons for developing a new plan, reasons for working through panels, support services available, and budgetary guidelines. Financial limits and administrative restrictions should be fully defined; indicating those which are primarily guidelines that could be modified in the light of sound business logic developed by the group.

The group should be goal-oriented rather than authority-directed, to facilitate free and natural exchange of information. The chairman of the task force is usually a corporate insurance administrator, but chairmanship may be transferred or rotated to other members at the group's option.

The panel should conclude the first meeting with a clear understanding that they are responsible for building the company group insurance package, with the freedom and responsibility to discuss the issues informally with their peers on the job. Though no group insurance plan would ever satisfy all members equally, this process is better for four reasons:

1. It is more likely to result in a system attuned to the most important needs of the greatest number of users.
2. The ego involvement of authorship, and concern for the needs of the users, increases employee identification with the system.
3. The resultant evolutionary, self-correcting system places less of a drain on high-level administrative talent in coping with dissatisfactions.
4. The group insurance system, being widely visible throughout the organization, is a language of action symbolizing management by competence rather than management by authority.

Pay Systems as Dissatisfiers

Apart from the roles of pay itself discussed earlier, pay systems, like supplemental benefit systems, have potential as either distractors or reinforcers of satisfaction derived from work itself. Take-home pay of employees in industry is generally influenced directly or indirectly by at least seven systems:

1. Financial reviews
2. Job evaluation
3. Performance appraisal
4. Wage and salary surveys
5. Cost-of-living index (Bureau of Labor Statistics)
6. Federal income tax (Internal Revenue Service)
7. Social security (Department of Health, Education, and Welfare)

The first four systems are usually designed and administered by the employer, and the last three by an arm of the Federal government. All these systems have potential for dissatisfaction, but the employing organization can influence their administration to reduce or eliminate their negative impact on employees—certainly the first four more than the last three, but all can be influenced.

Typically, these seven systems impact the paycheck in the following manner. Top management of the organization during the year-end *financial review* makes a forecast of profits for the coming year. This forecast is a partial basis for allocating funds for pay increases at the beginning of the year. However, before funds are finally allocated, consideration is given to the results of the company *survey of wages and salaries* in comparable industries and communities, and any changes in the *cost-of-living index* published by the Bureau of Labor Statistics. Considering these three inputs, management allocates a fund that the company can afford, usually expressed as a percentage of total payroll—such as "an average of 5 percent increase across the board." The actual distribution of this average percentage is, of course, delegated to successive levels of supervision down the line so that actual increases range from zero (or perhaps a reduction in pay) to varying amounts above 5 percent.

The distribution of pay to individuals is influenced by *job evaluation* and *performance appraisal.* Job-evaluation systems establish pay levels or rate ranges for each job, based on comparative analyses of jobs in terms of a wide variety of factors such as skill and knowledge requirements, accountability, creativity, health hazards, and amount of supervision required. Job evaluations determine the relative values of jobs within the company, and these evaluations are in turn coupled with rate surveys to establish the actual rate range for the job. Once a rate range is established through job evaluation, an individual's personal rate within that range, and any subsequent increases, are usually established by the judgment of his supervisor who typically compares him with his peers in terms of preselected factors such as quantity and quality of work, initiative, creativity, cooperativeness, and responsibility.

Finally, the individual receives his paycheck from his supervisor and notices on the check stub that the payroll department has deducted amounts for Federal income tax and social security, as required by law. These are the minimum deductions; he may have his paycheck further diminished by payroll deductions for state taxes, union dues, charity donations, savings bonds, insurance premiums, retirement pension, and credit union loans. And though most of the items in this expanded list of deductions are authorized and theoretically optional, in practice they are to him as insidious and inescapable as the legally required deductions.

Thus, the average employee perceives his paycheck as a product of mysterious processes controlled by unknown, arbitrary authority figures in Federal and state governments, management and supervision, payroll and personnel departments, and the union. In a climate of security and trust, his dependency relationship is bearable, but in a climate of insecurity and deception, he responds with apathy or aggression.

Why Pay Systems Fail

Dissatisfactions arising from pay stem largely from ineffective application of systems that influence pay. No matter how intrinsically well designed the system, if it does not satisfy the conditions of effective systems, as defined on page 126, it will not win acceptance and satisfaction.

In reviewing the seven basic pay systems, it is apparent that not all conditions for effectiveness can be satisfied directly for each system. However, three conditions are satisfied for all seven systems if people understand and agree with the systems and receive timely feedback from them. The other conditions (which enable individuals to use, control, and adapt the systems), usually cannot be satisfied directly, but this is not always necessary as long as individuals know how the system is used, how and who controls it, and when and why it is adapted to new situations.

The financial review deals with information traditionally reserved for top management in the name of management prerogatives. The logic defending this practice reflects the assumptions that people at the lower levels are not responsible, honest, and intelligent—that they will use the information inadvertently or maliciously to the detriment of the organization. Management will cite cases in point where individuals have surreptitiously gained and misused information—or where rumors based on mismanaged information have caused anxieties, loss of morale, disruption of work, and disaffection. Members of top management often fail to realize that they have fulfilled their prophecy by practices which alienate lower levels of management.

The withholding of information reflects a lack of trust; and the evasiveness of managers when asked for information is often perceived as deception, thereby dividing the organization into two camps—people at the upper levels and people at the lower levels— neither of whom trust each other. Since job success requires access to relevant information, unofficial channels are developed by lower levels. This, of course, causes management to tighten controls on company information. The ultimate and often unrecognized consequence of this circular process is that much of the energy at the lower levels of the organization is dissipated through apprehension, random activity, and efforts to outwit the censors.

Thus, when top management announces the amount of funds available for pay increases, the climate is rife with suspicion, cynicism, and a readiness to challenge the decision and to demand more. It may be that management has strained company resources to make the allocation, but in a climate of mutual mistrust where deception is expected, truth evokes suspicion.

Hence, a well-meant change in policy to disclose financial information to explain the allocation of funds for pay increases does not immediately win the understanding support of the people influenced by the allocation. This is still the language of words dispensed by top management, couched in terms unfamiliar to nonmanagers. When people fail to respond with gratitude and, instead, react with suspicion, management asserts with righteous indignation that it is a waste of time to try to help ungrateful people. The language of words is inadequate; what is needed is the language of action.

But the scope of the financial review is broader than the compensation system. It is also the basis for planning company growth, developing marketing strategies, discontinuing or adding products and services, investing in buildings and equipment, financing research, planning tax strategies, declaring dividends, and performing various correlated functions. Moreover, compensation is only one of the topics considered in the financial review, and the annual pay increase is only one of several subtopics of compensation for which decisions must be made. Other topics under compensation might include stock options, discretionary bonuses, profit sharing, collective bargaining trends, group insurance, retirement plan, subsidized eating facilities, and other supplemental benefits which are part of the total compensation package. Of the four company systems listed as having direct impact on compensation, it is apparent that the financial review is the only one dealing with compensation as a subsidiary function—the other three have an impact on compensation directly as a primary function. Two strategies are required to transform these systems into a language of action that will evoke understanding and acceptance.

Making Pay Systems Succeed

One strategy is to utilize the relationships that exist naturally in all organizations, to involve horizontally and vertically related groups in the problem-solving–goal-setting functions of the organization. This means cutting across functional lines wherever it is to the organization's advantage to do so. And it means extending the vertical slices from the top to the bottom of the organization through the successively delegated responsibilities. An example of this strategy is described under "problem solving–goal setting" on pages 81 to 87.

The other strategy is the formation of task forces which, during the process of achieving specific missions, disregard functional and hierarchical relationships within the task force, relying on the influence of competence rather than the influence of authority. This strategy is illustrated on pages 176 to 180, in describing the development of a company group insurance program.

The financial review and performance appraisal systems are best administered through the *natural-relationships strategy*, whereas job evaluations and wage and salary surveys may be achieved better through emphasis on the *task-force strategy*. These two strategies are not mutually exclusive, as the success of one requires the support of the other; and it is only as a matter of emphasis when one strategy is recommended over another.

The financial review, administered through the natural-relationships strategy, begins by broadening the number and depth of individuals who participate in the top management planning and control functions. The planning function, described on pages 50 to 52, illustrates this base-broadening process. Each manager presents to his peers and top management a plan developed through iterative problem-solving relationships with the members of his organization. The ratification of the plan is the basis for the manager to give feedback to the members of his organization in terms of plans, goals, and problems. This is a unique opportunity for people to comprehend the organization's financial status and plans for utilizing profits or coping with deficits. This feedback is communicated to all members of the manager's unit through periodic (quarterly or monthly) "depart-ment meetings" and through the individual goal-setting process of the performance appraisal as described on pages 164 to 169.

Hence, individuals at the bottom of the organization, through the problem-solving–goal-setting process, aid their supervisor in solving problems and setting his goals. He, in turn, with his peers, assists his supervisor in the problem-solving–goal-setting process until the pres-ident of the organization is ultimately presented with the goals and strategies of the people reporting to him. But the president and his economic researchers and marketing planners have concurrently been providing information downward, giving direction to the prob-lem-solving–goal-setting process of the natural work groups and task forces below. Hence, approved plans and strategies finally converge in the year-end (as well as quarterly) financial review and are melded into the corporate plan and goal. The natural-relationships strategy is neither a top-to-bottom nor a bottom-to-top process but, rather, a multidirectional reciprocative process with fluid flow of information in all directions and opportunity for purposeful involvement at all levels of the organization.

The performance review is an expression of the natural-rela-tionships strategy. All organizations, and each of their progressively subdivided units, exist for the purpose of achieving goals. Responsi-bility inheres only in individuals—not in organizations or groups. However, individuals, alone or collectively, set goals and organize manpower and materiel to achieve these goals. In the goal-oriented organization (as contrasted to the authority-oriented organization) in-dividuals earn the opportunity to survive and succeed by their ability to achieve their goals. The goal-setting performance review process is described on pages 166 to 169.

The key distinction between performance review through goal setting and performance review by authority is the involvement of the job incumbent in the goal-setting system in defining his goals, the strategy for achieving them, and the criteria for measuring his achievement. In contrast, in the authority-oriented system, evalua-tions are often influenced by criteria which may not be predeter-mined or even known to the job incumbent, except that he senses that he must do whatever his intuition tells him is necessary to win the favor of the boss. Evaluation in the goal-setting system is based more objectively on the comparison of an individual's achievements against ratified goals and, hence, is in effect a self-appraisal system. The relating of pay decisions and bonuses to achievements of self-influenced goals is far more acceptable than the seemingly arbitrary dispensing and withholding of merit pay based on the judgments of authority figures using ambiguous criteria of merit.

Administration of wage and salary surveys and job-evaluation plans is facilitated by the task-force strategy, following the group insurance process described on page 178. Panels made up of technical experts and peer representatives are briefed, in this case, in the theory and practice of pay administration, in compensation problems and conditions unique to the organization, and in procedures for evaluating jobs and conducting compensation surveys. The key to this process is the full and candid disclosure of any information needed or wanted by members.

Panels bring to these systems broader talent and keener awareness of the perceptions of the employees, including real and imagined inequities, thereby improving the validity of the systems by making them more responsive to the needs of the users. Of equal importance is the panel's role in gaining understanding and acceptance of the systems and their application through the peer-based fluid communication process. As was pointed out on pages 126 to 127, systems' successes and failures are caused largely by the attitudes and perceptions of people influenced by the systems.

The remaining systems—cost-of-living index, Federal income tax, and social security—can now lose much of their mystery and, hence, much of their oppressiveness. These systems provide guidelines for management committees and are explained as part of the briefing curriculum for panel task forces involved in job evaluation and wage and salary surveys. Panel members learn, for example, the distinction between merit pay and cost-of-living adjustments, and managers become aware of the negative impact of attempting to inflate "merit increases" with cost-of-living adjustments. Company newspapers and bulletins, department meetings, and the grapevine are natural media for explaining these systems and announcing changes in them.

The combined impact of the natural-relationships strategy and the task-force strategy can create a substantially different perception of the paycheck. Though few individuals would be able or have occasion to define all the factors impacting their pay, the networks of formal and informal involvement processes supported by open and fluid communication practices make information available if wanted and do much to minimize the dissatisfactions seemingly inherent in pay systems.

TRAINING

Training in industry is undertaken to increase organizational effectiveness by changing the knowledge, skills, and attitudes of people at work. However, the term "training" reflects a process that is intrinsically unsound as a strategy for changing people. Most learning and growth result not from training programs but, rather, from living itself, particularly in those life roles directed toward the attainment of personal goals. Hence, the focus of training should be on "learning opportunities."

People are motivated primarily by their personal goals, and will take the initiative in acquiring knowledge and skills necessary to attain them. They are motivated by organization goals only if they feel that attainment of them will result in the achievement of their personal goals. Beyond the subsistence level, the attainment of most personal goals leads to the satisfaction of growth, achievement, responsibility, and recognition needs. In the industrial organization, these needs are satisfied through the guiding principles and strategies outlined in Chapter 2. Training, within this context, is not a program, but a variety of job-related activities supporting a way of life at work.

The Changing Focus of Training

The knowledge explosion, which has accelerated change in technology and human values, has placed a two-pronged focus on technical training and managerial effectiveness. In regard to technical training, for example, engineers and technicians, whose technology once served a lifetime, now require constant updating just to stay employable. Large blocks of skilled and semiskilled workers are continuously rendered temporarily obsolete by product and process evolution. The manager's technology of planning, organization, and control systems requires continuous updating.

The philosophical underpinnings of scientific management are also changing. Hence, managerial competence is taking on a new meaning. Since increasing numbers of people in business organizations are reacting adversely to direction and control by authority, and are expecting and seeking opportunity to influence their organizational goals and the methods for achieving them, managerial training to guide this initiative must now apply to every member of the work force. If every employee is to be a manager of his job, as defined on pages 69 to 95, he must be granted much of the same knowledge and freedom previously reserved for top-echelon people who formerly assumed the full burden of organizational responsibility. The focus of training, then, is on both technical and managerial training, and is for all levels of the organization.

A Pitfall of Paternalism

If individuals are to experience sustained growth and maturity, their training must result from their own initiative. A trend has developed, however, particularly in big industry, which has gradually conditioned people to look to the organization for guidance and support in furthering their careers. It is not uncommon to find massive training programs which routinely schedule people at all levels of the organization, from top management through semiskilled ranks, for participation in courses prescribed by someone in line or staff management. The fault with such a system lies not so much in the content of the courses as with the source of initiative it represents. In essence, it undermines self-responsibility by conditioning people to be outer-directed, to wait for initiative and cues from authority figures. It leads to dependency relationships and complacency based on the feeling that "management" knows what is best for them and will see to it that they are trained and utilized effectively. The fallibility of such a system is discovered by many individuals late in their careers when they awaken abruptly to the realization that life has passed them by and that retirement is around the corner. Only then do they discover their own dereliction in abandoning self-responsibility and their company's dereliction in encouraging them to do so. Hence, paternalism is a deceptive, though innocently set, trap which takes the initiative away from the individual, but fails to replace it with an alternative that satisfies his long-range goals.

Training Processes

Training activities which cast participants in passive listening roles, such as films and uninterrupted lectures, are less likely to result in change than processes employing active learning techniques, such as those listed in Figure 5-7. Most effective training programs are not training programs as such but, rather, systems which involve individuals in the pursuit of meaningful goals. The developmental roles of a number of these systems or processes are summarized below with page references, where relevant, for more complete descriptions of the systems themselves.

- The *planning process* described on pages 50 to 53 offers rich opportunity for managerial development. Not only does it perpetuate the development of upper and middle managers, but its involvement of managers at lower levels in defining goals, strategies, and budgets prepares them for advancement and

---

1 –   In-basket. Situational test for simulating a person's responsibility in handling letters, memoranda, phone calls and other material collected in his in-basket.

2 –   Role playing. Real or hypothetical problem–solving by a number of individuals in simulated roles.

3 –   Management games. Teaching of business strategy and counter–strategy by involving small teams of players in competitive manipulation of business variables.

4 –   Sensitivity training. Small trainee-centered groups in permissive atmosphere coping with frustration and interpersonal processes through unstructured methods, usually with occasional intervention by skilled observer-trainer.

5 –   Programmed instruction. Individual self-instruction through machines or textbooks which present organized instructional material requiring responses and feedback.

6 –   Group discussion. Used in conjunction with lectures, films, readings and day-to-day job activities for developing better understanding, acceptance and application of subject matter; usually stimulated by the use of overhead, directed, relay and reverse questions.

7 –   Task force. Small groups of persons, usually representing a variety of relevant functional skills and responsibilities, in pursuit of specific organizational goals.

8 –   Problem analysis. Involvement of individuals in identifying and defining barriers to organizational effectiveness and prescribing remedial action.

9 –   Listening. The practice of showing courtesy, respect and acceptance in providing time and opportunity for individuals to be heard.

FIG. 5-7   Active learning techniques.

determines their candidacy for promotion. Moreover, their participation in the formulation and implementation of higher-level goals provides a model for involving their natural work groups in similar problem-solving–goal-setting strategies. Planning-conference presentations of the open-forum type dispense information that enables conference participants to avoid conflict and overlap and to discover opportunities for mutual support. The public presentation, in terms of performance against last year's goals and the definition of new goals, places the responsibility for establishing goals and strategies and assessing achievements on the shoulders of the goal setter. The presentation is a timely and original "lecture" on innovativeness in strategic planning, organization of resources and control processes, offering learning opportunity to conference participants. Hence, the planning process leads to the development of managerial skills and knowledge, and in itself represents diverse models for managerial effectiveness.

■ *Strategy management,* defined on page 52, offers managerial training to task-force leaders whose strategies support broad business objectives defined in the long-range planning conference. A strategy manager's competence is a function of his ability to identify and influence resource personnel throughout the organization, whose combined talent will enable him to define and implement strategies for supporting longer-range objectives. Perhaps the most developmental aspect of the strategy manager's assignment is the requirement that he organize and gain commitment from human resources without the use of official authority. Since his strategy teams cut across organizational lines, he cannot exercise organizational control over them. Hence, his successful attainment of strategy goals requires the development of leadership skills, as defined on pages 97 to 105.

■ *Work simplification*[4] is the downward extension of planning,

[4] Work Simplification has been introduced into many organizations, but under a variety of titles, including "job management," "methods change program," "deliberate methods change," and "improvement program." Whatever the label, the process defined here had its origin in the innovations of Allan H. Mogensen, whose encounter with reactive creativity in the 1930s led him to develop Work Simplification as a process for transferring traditional industrial engineering functions to job incumbents. The evolution and definition of Work Simplification are described in Auren Uris, "Mogy's Work Simplification Is Working New Miracles," *Factory,* p. 112, September, 1965.

organizing and control functions which enables people at lower levels to apply their talents, individually and collectively, in managing their own jobs. It replaces traditional time and motion study on the assumptions that:

1. Most people have creative potential for improving their own jobs.
2. Improvements are best made by those who perform the job.
3. Self-initiated change is positively motivational, while change imposed by authority is usually resented and opposed.
4. People satisfy social and achievement needs through co-operative work-improvement activities.

Employees learn work simplification through standardized company programs, taught by professional trainers or their supervisors. Classroom sessions, which usually total about 20 hours, provide principles and techniques of time-and-motion economy, flow-process charting, cost analysis, and human relations, and the sessions also include an on-the-job project for applying newly learned techniques. Development occuring through work simplification broadens employees' perspectives to enable them to perceive their job and the organization through the eyes of a responsible manager.

■ *Problem solving–goal setting,* defined on pages 81 to 87 as a job-enrichment process, is an evolutionary outgrowth of the work-simplification process and, in many respects, duplicates the corporate planning model. The problem-solving–goal-setting process on the production line, for example, is initiated for specific purposes, such as reducing costs, increasing quality, and shortening schedules, and involves natural team members such as operators, engineers, inspectors, and foremen. Participants gain a better understanding of their goals, their problems, and their interdependent relationships, and work cooperatively in solving problems and setting goals. The process develops interpersonal competence across functions and levels and increases goal orientation.

■ Results of the Texas Instruments *improvement survey,* described on pages 203 to 212, afford opportunities for people at lower levels to become involved in the solving of problems traditionally considered to be management problems. Through their task-force assignments, they acquire freedom and knowledge that enable them to work from the perspective of the manager, and in formulating recommendations they grapple with the obstacles not usually comprehended at the lower levels. Though task-force membership directly involves only a small percentage of the work force, their informal impact on the grapevine evokes the involvement of most of their peers. Hence, this program broadens employees' management perspective and develops a greater sense of responsibility at the lower levels.

■ *After-hours training opportunity* offered through company education assistance programs enables individuals to assume the initiative for their own development. The pursuit of specific knowledge and skills, a general education, or a college degree, requires the definition of career goals by the individual, and his commitment in time, effort, and finances to the attainment of these goals. Self-initiated after-hours activities, whether in the classroom or through correspondence courses, is reinforced in an environment of promotional opportunity, as offered by the internal staffing strategy defined on pages 152 to 161. Apart from the doors opened by educational credentials, the intellectual messages received from textbooks and lectures may ultimately have a profound impact on behavior, but usually by a process so subtle and delayed that cause-and-effect relationships cannot be established.

■ *Preemployment training* is becoming increasingly important, particularly at the lower levels, for bridging the gap between the requirements of technology-based organizations and the qualifications of the culturally disadvantaged recruited for entry occupations. Many industrial organizations, in collaboration with the U.S. Department of Labor, have undertaken projects for preparing the disadvantaged for responsible job roles and citizenship. For example, 400 participants in one of Texas Instruments' contracted preemployment programs are exposed to varied experiences designed to enable them to overcome obstacles—social, psychological, and educational skill deficiencies—which have deprived them of meaningful employment. In addition to socialization opportunities provided by the preemployment training environment, they receive up to 280 hours of remedial academic instruction and world-of-work orientation. The educational foundation includes word-attack skills; reading fluency, comprehension, and analysis; fundamental arithmetic skills; and application of math skills to work-related problems in measurement and decimal conversions. Reading assignments and discussion encompass history, civics, basic science, and job-related materials. The goal is to raise the minimum academic achievement level to that of the eighth grade. The world-of-work orientation covers concepts of getting, holding, and advancing on a job; basic economics of family budgeting and planning; and how to use credit intelligently, and to understand employee benefits, taxes, and payroll deductions. Persons entering the work force after completing this training program are, on an average, superior to those hired through the normal selection and placement process, particularly in regard to self-responsible behavior.

■ *Laboratory experiences,* particularly off-site, are sometimes needed if for no other reason than to disengage people from the cultural entrapments within the organization which impede interpersonal competence and distort their perceptions of their roles in the organization. Laboratory experiences have many forms, but always employ some aspect of sensitivity training. Training groups may be composed of members of separate organizations (strangers), members of the same organization, not closely related in function or chain of command (cousins), or members of natural work groups (family). The sensitivity process is guided by ground rules against use of criticism and places the emphasis on understanding and accepting self and others. The trainer's role is largely one of observing and intervening when appropriate to sensitize members to group processes. A successful laboratory generates a climate conducive to interpersonal competence, in which candor and spontaneity have an affirming rather than a threatening impact on members. The assumptions underlying this process are that self-understanding and self acceptance are keys to eliminating the protective façades which prevent authentic human interaction, and that the results of laboratory experiences will be transferred to the work situation to improve organizational effectiveness. In industry it is found that laboratory experiences become more relevant to the job situation when combined with intellectual messages and goal-oriented exercises such as the team improvement laboratory described on pages 87 to 95, the managerial grid described on pages 21–22, or the power structure workshop described on pages 22–23. Though candor or leveling may occur more easily in stranger labs because of the absence of established social or authority relationships which sometimes inhibit progress in family or cousin labs, the ideal in terms of ultimate job success is the development of interpersonal competence within and between natural work groups.

■ *Supervisory skills training* is becoming increasingly critical as rapidly changing technology-based organizations promote technically trained personnel into supervisory responsibilities. Ideally, supervisors should have at least basic orientation in planning, organizing, and control functions, along with principles of human relations and techniques of supervision. However, in practice this orientation is often not undertaken until after the assignment. If not delayed too long, learning while supervising can provide more realistic training, as it enables the individual to reinforce his learning through immediate application of theory.

An innovative program for training new supervisors was instituted by a department manager in Texas Instruments who trained operators to train new supervisors in their department.[5] Some of the first-line supervisory positions were filled by promotion and transfer, but approximately 60 percent of them were filled by new college graduates. Preemployment conditioning of new supervisors in parent-child, teacher-student, officer–enlisted man relationships, caused many of them to approach their first supervisory jobs with the traditional notion that a leader is a person with authority who "can do everything his subordinates can, only better."

Because of his desire to be the infallible leader, the new supervisor understandably felt inadequate in his new role of supervising large numbers of individuals, most of whom knew

---

[5] Earl R. Gomersall and M. Scott Myers, "Breakthrough in On-the-job Training," *Harvard Business Review* p. 70, July–August, 1966.

the operations better than he did. He did not realize that the operators recognized and accepted his limitations and that it would be futile and self-defeating for him to try to conceal them.

To help new supervisors gain early acceptance of their limitations and a better understanding of their supervisory role, a plan was developed for having operators train the supervisor. Working in pairs, operators (who had received trainer training) gave the new or transferred supervisor his first orientation to their assembly line, acquainting him with the pitfalls traditionally encountered by new supervisors and defining his role as it is perceived by the operators. This innovative approach serves three basic purposes:

1. It provides a supervisor with valid information directly from the persons who have the most detailed knowledge of the operations.
2. It provides assurance to the operators that the supervisor is properly qualified and acquainted with their problems. Because they get personally involved in this training, they will seek to make him successful.
3. Most importantly, it reorients the values of the supervisor and lessens the likelihood of his drifting into authority-oriented supervisory behavior. A supervisor who, in his first experience as a leader, learns to expect and seek information from subordinates, and discovers that they are creative and responsible, is favorably conditioned or permanently "reprogrammed" to look to, and rely on, subordinates for assistance in solving problems.

■ *Job skill training,* because of the accelerating rate of technological change, is placing increasingly heavy demands on the organization and the resourcefulness of trainers. Training functions which attempt to provide skills training for the organization find that the staff trainer usually has neither the technical background to cope with diversifying technologies nor the resources to cope with logistics problems stemming from the combination of increasing numbers, changing technologies, and geographical dispersion. Increasingly, then, the professional trainer's role must be that of training line people to become trainers.

A professional trainer in Texas Instruments provided a good example of this more effective role when he was asked by the head of a drafting department to provide a training program for sixty of his draftsmen. The staff trainer involved the department head and his supervisors in the training-needs analysis by asking them to define the drafting skills and knowledge in which the draftsmen were most deficient. When the line managers had completed this preliminary analysis, the training manager taught them how to write multiple-choice test questions covering the areas of deficiency. A test of approximately 100 multiple-choice test questions was developed and administered to all draftsmen in the department. An item analysis of test results showed the primary areas of deficiency for the total department, and specific areas for each draftsman. The curriculum for the training program was designed to emphasize areas of deficiency.

In planning the implementation of the training program, the search for technically qualified trainers led back to the supervisors themselves, who after briefing in training techniques, were the persons best qualified to conduct the training programs within their own departments. Upon completion of the training program, the same multiple-choice test was used again, this time to measure the success of the training program. Draftsmen who failed to meet standards, as measured by the test, were given additional training. Not only did this training program give the draftsmen more valid training, but more importantly, it familiarized the supervisors with the levels of competence and talent in their department, and prepared them for future trainer roles.

■ *Job orientation* is becoming an increasingly critical requirement as people seek to adapt to the complex systems, restrictive legislation, and rapidly changing job requirements of large organizations. Many new employees unquestioningly accept conformity roles simply because they have no realistic expectation of being able to exercise initiative and creativity in the overwhelming environment which characterizes the new world of work. For many, work is expected to be unpleasant and meaningless, having value only as a source of money for buying what they need to buy. Therefore, to say the least, creativity and self-confidence cannot be expected from people conforming to the requirements of what they perceive as an alien and sometimes threatening environment.

A Case Study in Job Orientation

Recognizing the problem of alienation noted above, a manager in Texas Instruments initiated an innovative process for orienting people to their world of work which could serve as a job orientation model for most industries. The study[6] was made in a rapidly growing electronics manufacturing department of Texas Instruments which included more than 1,400 women operators who collectively performed approximately 1,850 different operations on three shifts (the most numerously replicated of these operations having only 70 operators per shift). Approximately 57 percent of the operators worked with microscopes, and all jobs placed a premium on visual acuity, eye-hand coordination, and mechanical aptitude.

The staffing of operations required a continuous training process—training new people hired for expansion and replacement purposes, and retraining transferees and the technologically displaced. The learning curve of ball bonders, as shown in Figure 5-8, was fairly typical for production operators in the department.

Ball bonders required approximately 3 months to reach the "competence" level, at which stage they could independently perform the operation, but had not yet achieved the speed and accuracy ultimately expected of them to reach performance standards established by industrial engineering. The competence level would be about 85 percent of labor standards, while in this department about 115 percent of standard was termed the "mastery" level.

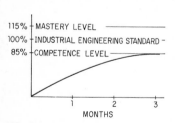

FIG. 5-8 **Learning curve for ball bonders.**

In a process initially unrelated to the training effort described here, the department manager had, during the preceding year, followed a systematic program for interviewing individuals during the morning coffee break. The results of 135 interviews with 405 operators yielded the following facts:

[6] Earl R. Gomersall and M. Scott Myers, "Breakthrough in On-the-job Training," *Harvard Business Review*, p. 194, July–August, 1966.

- Their first days on the job were anxious and disturbing ones.
- "New-employee initiation practices" by peers intensified anxiety.
- Anxiety interfered with the training process.
- Turnover of newly hired employees was caused primarily by anxiety.
- The new operators were reluctant to discuss problems with their supervisors.
- Their supervisors had been unsuccessful in translating motivation theory into practice.

FIG. 5-9   Relationship of anxiety to competence.

Facts uncovered through these interviews underscored the impact of anxiety in inhibiting job effectiveness of operators. It seemed obvious that anxiety dropped as competence was achieved. The relationship between the learning curve and what was believed to be the anxiety curve of operators is illustrated in Figure 5-9.

To supplement information obtained through personal interviews and to gain a better understanding of the characteristics of the anxiety to be reduced, a ninety-two-item questionnaire was developed to measure the following possible causes of tension or anxiety: supervision; job knowledge and skill; social acceptance; physical conditions; orientation; job pressure; regimentation; vocational adjustment; personal problems; financial worries; outside social factors; and opportunities for the satisfaction of growth, achievement, responsibility, and recognition needs.

Administration of this questionnaire to short-tenure and seasoned employees identified three types of tension in the job situation—the first two harmful and the third potentially helpful:

1. The primary source of anxiety, mentioned previously, stemmed from the unpredictable, overwhelming, and sometimes threatening new world of work. This anxiety was higher among new trainees and, according to the manager's interview results, appeared to diminish as competence was gained, as hypothesized in Figure 5-9.
2. Another type of tension, largely unrelated to job tenure, resulted from anxieties about nonjob factors such as personal

finances, domestic problems, professional status, and outside social relationships.

3. The third type of tension was identified as a positive, inner-directed desire for constructive self-expression. This creative tension is the type observed in the job situation that finds expression after job competence is reached either in constructive job-improvement activities or in antiorganization behavior.

Assuming the validity of Figure 5-9, the manager questioned the presumed cause-and-effect relationship between competence and anxiety. Anxiety on the job is characteristically assumed to be the dependent variable, gradually dropping as competence is acquired. Might not the reverse be true? And if so, is it possible to accelerate achievement to the competence level by reducing anxiety at a faster rate? With this question in mind, he developed an orientation program to reduce the anxieties of experimental groups of new employees. Experimental groups were selected from the second shift and control groups from the first and third shifts. Precautions were taken to avoid the "Hawthorne effect" of influencing behavior through special attention.

Control groups went through the usual first-day orientation, which consisted of a 2-hour briefing by Personnel on hours of work, insurance, parking, work rules, and employee services. This session included warnings of the consequences of failure to conform to organization expectations and, though not intended as a threat, tended to raise rather than reduce anxieties.

Following this orientation, it was customary for a bonder to be introduced to her friendly, but very busy supervisor, who gave her further orientation and job instruction. Unfortunately, the supervisor's detailed familiarity with the operations often desensitized him to the technical gap between them, and the following might be typical of what the operator heard him say:

> "Alice, I would like you to take the sixth yellow chair on this assembly line, which is in front of bonding machine #14. On the left side of your machine you will find a wiring diagram indicating where you should bond your units. On the right-hand side of your machine you will find a carrying tray full of 14-lead packages. Pick up the headers, one at a time, using your 3-C tweezers and place them on the substrate below the capillary head. Grasp the cam actuator on the right-hand side of the machine and lower the hot capillary over the first bonding pad indicated by the diagram. Ball bond to the pad and, by moving the hot substrate, loop the

wire to the pin indicated by the diagram. Stitch bond to this lead, raise the capillary, and check for pigtails. When you have completed all leads, put the unit back in the carrying tray.

"Your training operator will be around to help you with other details. Do you have any questions?"

Overwhelmed by these instructions and not wanting to offend this polite and friendly supervisor or look stupid by telling him she did not understand anything he said, the operator would go to her work station and try to learn by furtively observing assemblers on either side of her. But they, in pursuit of operating goals, had little time to assist her. Needless to say, her anxieties were increased and her learning ability was impaired. And the longer she remained unproductive, the more reluctant she was to disclose her wasted effort to her supervisor and the more threatening her job situation became.

Experimental groups participated in a one-day program especially designed to overcome anxieties not eliminated by the usual process of job orientation. Following the 2-hour orientation by Personnel, they were isolated in a conference room before they could be "initiated" by their peers. They were told there would be no work the first day, that they should relax, sit back, and have a coke or cigarette, and use this time to get acquainted with the organization and each other, and to ask questions. Throughout this one-day anxiety-reduction session, questions were encouraged and answered. This orientation emphasized four points:

1. "Your opportunity to succeed is very good." Company records disclosed that 99.6 percent of all persons hired or transferred into this job were eventually successful in terms of their ability to learn the necessary skills. Trainees were shown learning curves illustrating the gradual buildup of competence over the learning period. They were told five or six times during the day that all members of this group could expect to be successful on the job.

2. "Disregard 'hall talk.'" Trainees were told of the hazing game that old employees played—scaring newcomers with exaggerated allegations about work rules, standards, disciplinary actions, and other job factors—to make the job as frightening to the newcomers as it had been for them. To prevent these distortions by peers, the trainees were given facts about both the good and the bad aspects of the job and exactly what was expected of them.

The basis for "hall-talk" rumors was explained. For example, rumor stated that more than one-half of the people who terminated had been fired for poor performance. The interviews mentioned earlier disclosed the fact that supervisors themselves unintentionally caused this rumor by intimating to operators that voluntary terminations (marriage, pregnancy, leaving town) were really performance terminations. Many supervisors felt this was a good negative incentive to pull up the low performers.

3. "Take the initiative in communication." The new operators were told of the natural reluctance of many supervisors to be talkative and that it was easier for the supervisor to do his job if they asked him questions. They were told that supervisors realized that trainees needed continuous instruction at first, that they would not understand technical terminology for a while, that they were expected to ask questions, and that supervisors would not consider them dumb for asking questions.

4. "Get to know your supervisor." The personality of the supervisor was described in detail. Candor was the rule. A description might reveal that:

. . . The supervisor is strict, but friendly.

. . . His hobbies are fishing and ham radio operation.

. . . He tends to be shy sometimes, but he really likes to talk to you if you want to.

. . . He would like you to check with him before you go on a personal break, just so he knows where you are.

Following this special day-long orientation session, members of experimental groups were introduced to their supervisors and their training operators in accordance with standard practice. Training commenced as usual, and eventually all operators were given regular production assignments.

A difference in attitude and learning rate was apparent from the beginning in the progress of the two groups. By the end of four weeks, experimental groups in ball bonding were significantly outperforming control groups, as reflected in Figure 5-10.

Figure 5-11 shows performance curves reflecting results for over 200 members of additional experimental and control groups for assembling, welding, and inspection, along with their absenteeism rates.

A significant effect of the new orientation program is the encouragement of upward communication. Sensitivity of the supervisors is a key ingredient of a climate conducive to natural and informal exchange of information. It was as a result of sensitizing supervisors

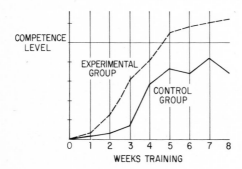

FIG. 5-10   Learning curves of experimental and control groups—ball bonding.

to the importance of listening and maintaining fluid communication channels at all levels that the following incident took place:

An operator approached a supervisor during coffee break and casually struck up a conversation about the "units with little white specks on them that leaked after welding." The supervisor asked, "What little white specks?" The operator pointed out that almost all

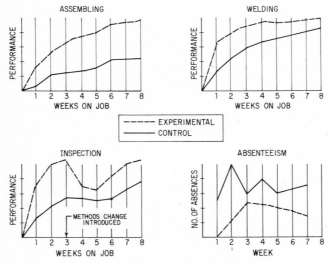

FIG. 5-11   Further comparisons of experimental and control groups.

the units that leaked after welding had little specks on them, a fact unnoted by the supervisor before. Verifying and investigating this fact revealed that units were placed in plastic trays while still hot from a previous process; their heat caused many of them to fuse to the plastic container. Removing them from the container caused the units to pull away a small amount of plastic, thus insulating them during the welding process.

Once this was discovered, the problem was solved simply by delaying the placing of units in the plastic trays until they had cooled sufficiently. This single suggestion reduced rejects to less than one-fourth their previous level for this product—a projected cost prevention of hundreds of thousands of dollars.

The point emphasized here is that casual questions and observations of the type described take place only in an atmosphere of approval, genuine respect, and interest.

On the basis of increased production, reduced turnover, absenteeism, and training time, annual departmental savings in excess of $50,000 were realized. Moreover, as trainees with less anxiety gradually became members of the regular work force, their attitudes began influencing the performance of the work groups they joined. The greater confidence of the new members seemed to inspire greater confidence among their older peers. Their higher performance established new reference points for stimulating competitiveness, and old peers were sometimes hard pressed to maintain a superiority margin between themselves and the newcomers. There was evidence of improvements in quality and quantity, not only among immediate peer groups, but also among adjacent work groups who were influenced through the informal social system in the plant.

ATTITUDE MEASUREMENT

As managers learn that behavior is related to attitudes, they become interested in measuring and changing attitudes. Most large companies have at least experimented with attitude surveys, and many administer them routinely as a part of their ongoing industrial relations program. Unfortunately, attitude surveys are often administered without thoughtful analysis of what their purposes should be. Like many other programs, such as performance review, suggestion systems and communication programs, they are often administered and perpetuated as symbols of progressive management. A traditionally mismanaged attitude survey is described below, followed by a description of a developmental attitude survey system.

The Traditional Way

A typical attitude questionnaire is a form containing approximately 100 items of the type illustrated in Figure 5-12. Forms are administered to employees, usually by an outside consultant, and the percentage of favorable responses to each item is calculated and tabulated by job classification, shift, plant location, or other meaningful categories. The report is generally sent to top management where it is reviewed behind the closed doors of an executive conference room. Though such a report always contains some favorable responses, it inevitably contains some information interpreted by management as "negative," "ungrateful," or "disloyal." Managers who have strong proprietary interests in the company usually find it difficult to accept or understand expressions of anticompany feelings, and are sensitive to intimations that their motives and competence are in question.

	Agree	?	Disagree
The hours of work here are O.K.	( )	( )	( )
I'm paid fairly compared with other employees.	( )	( )	( )
My supervisor has always been fair in his dealings with me.	( )	( )	( )
I have confidence in the fairness and honesty of management.	( )	( )	( )
I work in a friendly environment.	( )	( )	( )
I know how my job fits in with other work in this organization.	( )	( )	( )
My supervisor welcomes our ideas even when they differ from his own.	( )	( )	( )
I'm proud to work for this company.	( )	( )	( )
Favoritism is a problem in my area.	( )	( )	( )
I have very few complaints about our lunch facilities.	( )	( )	( )

FIG. 5-12 Typical attitude survey items.

The inability of managers to agree on the relative importance of the items on the questionnaire complicates their interpretation. If 50 percent complain about the cafeteria, 30 percent are dissatisfied with the hours of work, and 20 percent believe favoritism exists in their department, which is the most serious problem? Simply following percentages could be misleading, as the cafeteria, as a chronic dissatisfier, may be a less serious problem than favoritism. Managers often come to an impasse trying to identify the most serious problems, and when they agree on a problem, they may fail to agree on a plan of remedial action. Their search for guidance often leads to futile attempts to derive insights through detailed statistical manipulation of survey data. Finally, they conclude their review by saying, "I am sure there is an important message here for us that will help us become more effective as managers, and we have personally benefited from the review of survey results. But this stuff is dynamite and we've got to be careful who sees it. If the union gets it, it will come back to bite us." They adjourn their meeting without a comprehensive action plan, make a few token changes with much fanfare, and lock the report in a file cabinet in the personnel department.

Then, to their chagrin, they are reminded that they promised employees feedback of the results. The personnel director or newspaper editor prepares a report for publication in the company newspaper. Though the first draft may be relatively candid and objective, the subsequent purging of "negative" information by upper management results in a delayed and whitewashed report such as the following, published under the headline "Results of Recent Attitude Survey":

> The attitude survey administered in the Ajax Company 7 months ago has been analyzed, and much useful information has been obtained from it. It was gratifying to note that most of you were very positive in your attitudes toward the company, our fringe benefits, the cafeteria and hours of work. Ninety percent of you reflected your company loyalty by saying you were proud to work for Ajax! A few felt there was opportunity for improvement in the administration of the performance review and wage and salary program. Surprisingly, very few Ajaxers were acquainted with their opportunities for advancement, but many had confidence in top management. Some of you felt that favoritism was a problem in your department, but most of you thought your supervisor was qualified for his job.
>
> This information is very useful because it indicates a need to clarify career opportunities in Ajax and policies governing growth with the company, and it stresses our need to continue our efforts in supervisory

training. No company is perfect, of course, but we believe ours is better than most, and we are doing everything in our power to make Ajax the kind of company you want it to be.

We would like to take this opportunity to thank all of you for your useful suggestions, and we hope to ask you from time to time for additional suggestions.

With the publication of this report in the company newspaper, management has "done its duty," and fulfilled the need for feedback. Such a whitewashed report usually deceives no one but the authors. The employees do not react to this insult to their intelligence, only because they are accustomed to it, and had no reason to expect anything better.

Attitude surveys need not follow this traditional pattern. They have potential for serving a number of constructive purposes, provided managers have the courage to disregard some traditional assumptions and practices. Following is a description of an involvement approach which better serves the needs of the organization and its members.

The Involvement Approach[7]

A questionnaire of the type illustrated in Figure 5-12 is administered annually to a 10 to 20 percent sample of employees throughout the company. Profiles, as illustrated in Figure 5-13, are prepared from computer printouts. The heavy solid line shows the company average

[7] A major role was played by Earl D. Weed in developing the concepts and techniques for utilizing attitude surveys as described herein.

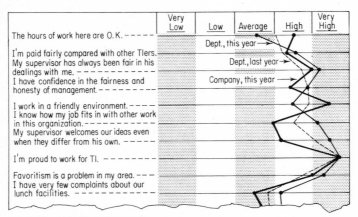

FIG. 5-13   Attitude survey profile.

for this year, and is the same on every profile. The thin solid line is one department's profile for this year, and the broken line is the same department's profile for last year. These profiles, which show the percentage of favorable response for each of about 100 questions, enable the manager to compare his department's results for each item with the total company results and with the previous year's profile. The involvement approach, as depicted in Figure 5-14, follows the traditional process for only the first two steps; the subsequent steps are different.

Survey results are fed back first to department heads, usually three or four levels below the president, rather than to top management. Upon receipt of the profiles (on overhead projector transparencies), the department head discusses them first with the managers reporting to him, noting the highs and lows compared to the company profile, and the improvements and deteriorations since last year. No action plans are made at this time. Instead he calls a group meeting of all members of his department and gives them candid and detailed results of the survey by reviewing the profiles with them on the overhead projector. He then selects a task force of employees (peers) and gives the profiles to this task force for detailed analysis and recommendations. The task force is given a five-point mission:

1. Study the profiles and find out what our problems are.
2. Find out what causes these problems.
3. Recommend what can be done to solve these problems.
4. Where are we already doing a good job?
5. What are the causes of the successes we are now having?

The last two questions were added in response to task-force suggestions that criticisms should be balanced with positive comments about the company. However, in practice these items are rarely used.

Task-force members may be selected by any of several methods: appointed by a manager, chosen by an appointed task-force chairman, or formed by an informal group process. In unionized organizations, the total process should be administered openly with the concurrence and involvement of the union leaders. Task-force makeup should be approved by the union and, where possible, should include union stewards. Task-force members usually number about five, and are authorized to meet as often as required on company time to analyze the results. A member of the personnel department briefs task-force members on the interpretation of profiles, helps them

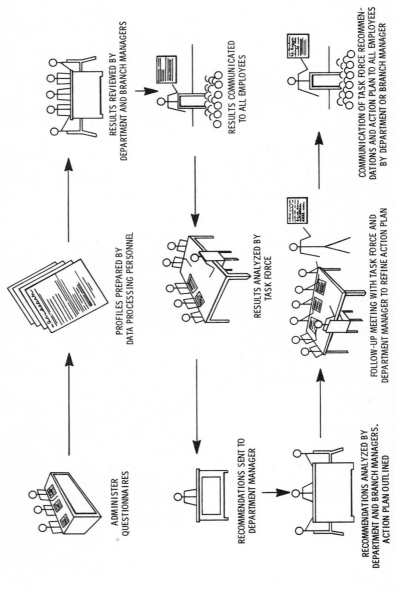

ADMINISTER
QUESTIONNAIRES

PROFILES PREPARED BY
DATA PROCESSING PERSONNEL

RESULTS REVIEWED BY
DEPARTMENT AND BRANCH MANAGERS

RESULTS COMMUNICATED
TO ALL EMPLOYEES

RESULTS ANALYZED BY
TASK FORCE

RECOMMENDATIONS SENT TO
DEPARTMENT MANAGER

RECOMMENDATIONS ANALYZED BY
DEPARTMENT AND BRANCH MANAGERS.
ACTION PLAN OUTLINED

FOLLOW-UP MEETING WITH TASK FORCE AND
DEPARTMENT MANAGER TO REFINE ACTION PLAN

COMMUNICATION OF TASK FORCE RECOMMEN-
DATIONS AND ACTION PLAN TO ALL EMPLOYEES
BY DEPARTMENT OR BRANCH MANAGER

FIG. 5-14 Improvement survey procedure.

nominate a chairman or secretary, restates their five-point mission, and leaves them to function as an autonomous group. Typically, a task force will meet in five or six 2-hour sessions, questioning fellow employees between sessions to gain information and insights in preparation for the next meeting. Personnel representatives visit task forces during the second meeting to answer questions or clarify their assignment and at a later meeting to review recommendations. During the last visitation the group is asked to act as if it were the department manager in examining and determining how and when its suggestions could be put into effect.

Task-force members finally prepare a written report for the department head, summarizing their interpretation of the survey results and recommendations for improvement according to the process diagrammed in Figure 5-14. It is not unusual for these reports to exceed twenty-five typewritten pages. Figure 5-15 lists examples of suggestions summarized from detailed reports. The department head shares these findings with managers under his supervision, and jointly they formulate tentative action plans.

The department head then meets with the task force to discuss their recommendations and to clarify points of misunderstanding. More successful managers combine these last two steps by involving task-force members along with the managers in the development of action plans. This face-to-face meeting is most successful, of course, in an atmosphere of informality, approval, and authentic relationships. Unfortunately, this feedback process is sometimes hampered by the classical circular problem of the more threatening manager having the worst problems and being least successful in getting task-force members to level with him. However, task-force members, as spokesmen for their anonymous peers, usually feel they can articulate complaints without fear of reprisal.

Serious misunderstandings are often clarified through these meetings. For example, one department head interpreted a report as recommending the termination of two foremen. However, in discussing the report with the task force, he was relieved to find that they were not recommending such drastic action, but felt that the foremen should be given a chance to improve. When the foremen received feedback from the department head, they made apparent attempts to improve; and though their efforts were not immediately translated

| Committee Report for XYZ Department | | |
Problems	Causes	Recommendations
1 – New employees are often hired for good jobs that old employees are qualified to fill.	We never know of job openings in other departments, or sometimes even in our own department.	Post job openings on bulletin boards and explain procedure for bidding on these jobs.
2 – Sometimes employees are not told till Friday night that they are expected to work on Saturday.	Foreman doesn't try to predict overtime requirements in advance -- or else he doesn't care if he ruins our weekend plans.	Give at least two days' notice of the requirement to work on weekends.
3 – Salaried people receive less pay per hour than employees in other companies.	Salary comparisons with other companies do not take into consideration overtime pay practices in effect in other companies.	Define the normal work week for salaried personnel which serves as the basis for salary comparisons with other companies.
4 – We sometimes read about company events in local newspapers before we hear about them in the company.	The same information is sent to the company newspaper, it is published only once a month. The local papers are daily.	Let employees hear first about company events through department meetings, newspaper, bulletins & supervisors.
5 – We are often pulled off a job before it's finished and put on another rush job.	Someone up the line panics when a customer complains, and priorities are switched. Sometimes we run out of parts.	Better planning and more consideration on the part of supervision could correct most of this.
6 – Because the attitude survey is done on a sample basis, a lot of people feel "left out."	They think we are playing favorites and don't realize that samples are taken so the line can keep running.	Increase the size of the samples or explain why you can't.

Good features	Why successful
1 – Informality and friendliness among people.	Managers set a good example. We call our managers by first name and don't have to polish the apple.
2 – Free coffee.	Conveniently located, and coffee bars are good places to socialize and meet new friends.
3 – No union.	We are treated fairly and can usually get a fair hearing from someone, if not our supervisor.
4 – Interesting work.	They listen to our ideas and give us a chance to use our heads and change jobs when they get too boring.

FIG. 5-15 Examples from task-force report.

into supervisory competence, their earnest attempts did much to improve their acceptance by their work groups.

Finally, a meeting is held with all members of the department to explain the results of the survey, the committee's recommendations, and actions to be taken—usually in three parts:

1. Actions to be taken immediately, and by whom (department, division, corporate).
2. Actions to be taken at some future, specified time.
3. Recommendations which cannot be implemented, or must be deferred, and the reasons why.

This completes the formal feedback to the people in the department. The manager then communicates his survey results upward, along with the action plan.

The involvement of employees in the analysis of survey results serves many purposes. First, it is direct feedback of survey results from and to those who participated in the survey, unaltered by the value judgments of managers. Experience has shown that it is not "dangerous" to share information of this type with the people. Second, the appeal for help in solving company problems reflects confidence in, and respect for, the individual, a philosophy which is more likely to evoke behavior which earns this trust. Third, this type of involvement is a form of vertical job enlargement which takes the employee out of the restrictive realm of unthinking repetition and affords him an opportunity to exercise his initiative and engage in a creative growth experience. He is dealing with problems generally thought to be management problems. Finally, it is found that recommendations made by the persons closest to the problem are more valid than recommendations armchaired by managers and staff people.

In summary, the attitude survey can serve the manager in four basic functions:

1. It can provide the manager with measures of managerial effectiveness—through trend data with which he can check his progress from year to year, and by enabling him to compare his department with the rest of the company and with other companies.
2. It can identify problems and evolve workable solutions for solving them. Because of their proximity to, or involvement

in, the problems, task-force solutions are usually more valid than those developed by management groups.

3. It can serve as a medium for involving employees in the analysis and solution of problems, thereby contributing to their understanding and acceptance of these problems, their personal and professional growth, their sense of responsibility and accomplishment, and their opportunity to earn recognition.

4. It can provide a learning experience for the manager, giving him insights into the creative ability of people and developing his skill in working with groups.

The procedure described above was designed to serve the large multidepartmental organization. However, it has been applied effectively in small antonomous groups, such as a single unit within a company, or a total small company. Since the primary role of the survey is to provide a medium for involving members of natural work groups in defining and solving their organizational problems, the content of the questionnaire is of little importance. If the items of the questionnaire fail to tap the real problems, as is often the case, the real problems are surfaced through the informal communication processes of the group, and find their way into the task-force recommendations. One survey task force in a drafting department, in reviewing the profiles, decided that the wrong questions were asked. They rewrote the questionnaire, administered it themselves to the total department and developed their recommendations on responses to the new questions. In one respect, this improvised questionnaire was superior, as it had greater validity for the group, and their initiative and authorship evoked a greater sense of commitment than the standard company questionnaire. The main disadvantage of the independent questionnaire is the lack of normative data for comparing profiles with other group profiles. However, the function of comparing profiles is secondary in importance to the group problem-solving process.

LABOR RELATIONS

The administration of labor relations is traditionally based on the assumption that the goals of the organization, as represented by upper-level managers, are naturally in conflict with the needs of its "workers" or "labor" at the lower levels of the organization. The labor portion of the work force is usually made up of hourly paid personnel in production, maintenance, and administrative jobs who are not exempt from the restrictions of the Fair Labor Standards Act. They compose more than 80 percent of the work force in United States business and industry.

In contrast, people in the top layers of the organization are usually identified with the organization, by themselves as well as by others, and bear the label of "management." People in the middle ranks are often uncertain about their identity as management or labor, though they are usually assured they are members of management. In many unionized organizations, management and labor have come to represent two enemy camps whose conflicting goals and philosophies are the basis for the ongoing warfare moderated through collective bargaining. The basis for the management-labor dichotomy is described on pages 63 to 67 and illustrated in Figure 3-4.

Formalizing the Management-Labor Gap

Most formal agreements between management and labor reflect an implied conflict of interest between the two parties. Figure 5-16, excerpted from an agreement between a large aerospace firm and the International Brotherhood of Electrical Workers (IBEW), illustrates some typical prerogatives of management and labor. Though the term "prerogative" is traditionally used in this context to denote management rights, labor rights by definition and comparison are no less prerogatives. The rights of management define time-honored prerogatives stemming from authority vested by ownership. Implicit in this statement is the assumption that these rights are needed to protect the plant from the irresponsible demands or behavior of labor. In a climate of mistrust, the average member of the organization could understandably see this array of management rights—to hire, classify, promote, transfer, suspend, discipline, discharge, lay off, release employees—as threatening. Certainly the specification of these management prerogatives would seem to require the need for a counterbalancing array of labor prerogatives.

To a manager in a nonunion plant, the rights of the union may represent a startling degree of capitulation by management, and a serious limitation on the manager's freedom to manage. However, these rights are protected, or even required, by law in union plants,

Rights of management

The management of the plant and the direction of the working force is vested exclusively in the Company. This shall include and not be limited to the right to hire, classify, promote, transfer, suspend, discipline, discharge for cause, layoff, or release employees for lack of work, provided these rights shall not conflict with this Agreement.

Rights of labor

1 –   The Company recognizes the Union as the exclusive representative of all employees.

2 –   The Company agrees to deduct the initiation fee and monthly Union dues from the pay of employees who authorize such deductions.

3 –   Stewards are privileged to handle grievances in the plant during working hours without loss of compensation.

4 –   The Company will maintain a bulletin board for the use of the Union.

5 –   The Company shall provide the Group Insurance Program as outlined in Appendix "B" of this Agreement.

6 –   The Retirement Plan shall remain in effect as specified in this Agreement.

7 –   Overtime records shall be kept by the Company for the purpose of distributing overtime work as equally as possible.

8 –   When terminating employment, an employee shall be paid for each day of earned sick leave not used.

9 –   An employee who works on a day considered a holiday shall receive holiday pay plus double his regular rate for all hours worked on the holiday.

10 –   The Maintenance Electrician job includes installation and maintenance of electrical systems and equipment; electronic controls and tape making equipment used on machine tools; and installation, maintenance, repair, servicing and alteration of air conditioning and refrigeration systems.

11 –   The Maintenance Electrician job excludes electrical assembly and maintenance work on airplanes and their component parts.

12 –   All job classifications and their descriptions as listed in Appendix "A" shall remain in effect for the duration of this Agreement.

*Excerpts from a 1966 Agreement between an aerospace firm in the Southwest and the IBEW.

FIG. 5-16   Examples of traditional prerogatives of management and labor.

where they are also perpetuated as unquestioned long-standing tradition. Nevertheless, recognizing the union as the exclusive representative of employees does reflect the assumptions that people need a protector against management, and that the goals of the employees are different from the goals of the organization. Moreover, the union's initiative in defining the terms for providing bulletin boards, group insurance, retirement plan, equitable distribution of overtime, and other conditions suggests that these programs were opposed or neglected by management. When the union has established itself as the people's protector, enlightened as well as derelict managers often find themselves on the defensive. The union, with single-minded determination, directs more effort to wresting rights from management than to supporting the health of the company, and pressures management unremittingly to relinquish profits for distribution to its members.

Though management may be only trying to prevent excesses, it often acquires the image of the penurious exploiter. The union, in its unrelenting drive to support its membership, unwittingly impairs management's ability to invest in the future and remain competitive, and simultaneously plants the seeds of indolence, dependency, and disaffection. Now, for example, sick leave has become more than a cushion against the expense of illness; for many the wish to save it for other use has become the main reason for not faking illness. Triple pay for holidays makes holiday work attractive to the worker and undesirable to management, but either alternative—holiday pay or holiday closing—is harmful to the organization and ultimately to its members. The circumscribed definition of jobs reduces the flexibility, versatility, and job satisfaction generally required for a creative and viable work force. Union leadership, while paying lip service to the long-range growth needs of the organization, usually applies pressure for a share of any short-term gain, thereby undermining long-range growth strategies and encouraging defensive financial reporting by the company.

Symptoms of Management Failure

Management brought the problem of unions on itself by earlier exploitation, paternalism, and manipulation. Much of management's failure was incurred innocently by authorizing the management of humans by persons who had only the credentials for managing materiel. Though managers trained in human management are infiltrating organizations in increasing numbers, they are plagued by two obstacles.

One obstacle is a work force of maintenance seekers, the older ones jaded by long confinement to meaningless work, and the younger ones rebelling against conformity pressures imposed by the company, the union, and work itself. Initial or cursory attempts to treat people as responsible adults typically evoke at least temporary suspicion, hos-

tility, or apathy; and few managers have the courage and perseverance to undertake the reprogramming of such a work force.

The second, and often the greater, obstacle is top management,
conditioned to act with authority vested by management prerogative.
The boss, when conditioned to mistrust the enemy below, seldom
affords innovative managers the freedom necessary to effect
significant changes in relationships and work roles. The development
of responsibility and commitment in the work force is a long-range
strategy involving the risk of short-run setbacks. Idealism in the face
of unbending authority invites capitulation—and the aspiring innova-
tor may understandably elect to survive by perpetuating the status
quo. He may justify his capitulation with the rationale that it is better
to survive today in order to win the grand battle tomorrow. Hence, all
but the very courageous take on the protective coloring of the world
about them, and become inadvertent perpetuators of a philosophy
they know intellectually and feel intuitively to be destructive. "But,"
they rationalize, "all organizations are equally handicapped by the
same bad management practices and at least we're not as bad as most
of them."

Union-company stalemates and win-lose strategies are understandable in the light of history. Nineteenth-century management
flagrantly, though often innocently, exercised assumed prerogatives
in motivating people through fear, threats, manipulation, and
bribery. Wage earners living at the bare subsistence levels responded
well to the security of uninterrupted employment. When Henry Ford
opened an automated assembly line in 1914 and paid workers $5 a
day, his plant prospered and the workers were both happy and
motivated. Though his management innovations satisfied many needs
of that era, they embraced two characteristics which became the foundation for latter-day labor problems. One innovation was the
simplification of tasks, forerunner of a trend resulting in a situation
described in one sociological study,[8] in which 83 percent of the jobs in
an automobile assembly plant had fewer than ten operations and 32
percent but a single operation. The average time cycle for these jobs
was 3 minutes, and the learning time was a few hours to a week.

As jobs became more impoverished, pay rates continued upward,
maintaining the automotive industry's leadership in providing

[8] Charles R. Walker and Robert H. Guest, *The Man on the Assembly Line,* Harvard University Press, Cambridge, Mass., 1952.

higher-than-average wages and supplemental benefits. Hence, people's maintenance needs were satisfied better, but their talents were utilized no better, or even less well. In the era of thwarted maintenance needs, the automotive worker with a steady job counted his blessings, taking the monotony of the automated assembly line in stride. But as the total culture achieved greater affluence, improved maintenance factors lost their relative importance in the wage earner's hierarchy of needs. Furthermore, opportunities abounded elsewhere for satisfying maintenance needs, and his security was not jeopardized by changing jobs. The union had successfully protected him against the arbitrariness of management and given him discretionary income to buy goods and services previously beyond his aspirations, and more time to enjoy them. The source of his frustration was thus gradually transferred from maintenance needs to thwarted higher-order needs, or the motivation needs shown in the inner circle of Figure 1-2.

Attacking the Symptoms

The individual who experiences need frustration is not always able to pinpoint the cause. This was true for the factory worker who was culturally conditioned to gain satisfaction by improving wages, hours and working conditions. But union-led victories came to have less value for the benefits they yielded than for the sense of achievement or successful conquest they represented. The opposing teams of management and labor have some of the characteristics of team sports such as baseball, football, or hockey. They are competitively matched by the terms of their agreement and are refereed by the National Labor Relations Board. Workers are vicariously aligned with the union team, and supervisors with the management team. The issues are of relatively less importance than the statisfaction of winning the battle, and the more bitter the relationship between parties, the sweeter the victory. Hence, the vicarious winning and losing of battles provides outlets for frustrations that otherwise have little opportunity for dissipation.

Rebellion against the *status quo,* particularly after World War II, became more frequent and demanding. Whole industries were paralyzed by strikes and other forms of reactive behavior, some of which were directed toward the union management which, in some cases, had become no less a source of oppression than the company management. In frantic attempts to perpetuate their jurisdiction, unions bargained indiscriminately for continuing improvements in wages, hours, and working conditions, baffled by their members' unconcern for interrupted incomes and lack of gratitude for hard-won battles. Hence, the worker, the union, and the company were all victims of their mutual failure to understand the real causes of worker frustration and alienation.

A Gradual Awakening

Allegations of deterioration of worker loyalty and pride in work reached consensus proportions. Only gradually, and among an enlightened few, was an awareness developed of the real causes of disaffection. Discovery of the key to revived human effectiveness stimulated enthusiastic, though often misdirected, efforts to return responsibility and challenge to the job. As the concepts and techniques of job enrichment led to the redefinition of the supervisor's role as discussed on pages 98 to 105, labor relations specialists became aware of their dilemma. They found themselves administering a strategy based on the use of power, authority, and cunning, in the face of an emerging philosophy based on the influence of mutual respect and competence. The "labor skate" or "labor hack," accustomed to the use of compromise and coercion, began to realize he had been dealing primarily with symptoms of problems—and that real and lasting peace could be obtained only by curing the causes. The insights of the behavioral sciences were needed, and the labor-relations specialist had a choice of acquiring these insights, changing vocations, or becoming vocationally obsolete.

Strategies for reorienting labor relations must adapt to the uniqueness of the organization. Certainly the nonunion organization requires a different approach than the union plant. In the unionized organization, the intermediate goal may be to make peace with the union. This is not easy, of course, because in most union-management relationships any act initiated by one party arouses the ire or suspicion of the other. The first goal is to prepare both parties to listen to each other.

Grappling with the Cause

One approach to this first step is through some form of training. Sensitivity training, as noted on pages 193–194, is a process used alone or in combination with problem-solving–goal-setting exercises to enable people to see themselves as others see them, to understand the assumptions which motivate their behavior, and to gain some insights into their own styles of management. Skills of interpersonal competence are developed through this process. A major retail food chain in Canada exposes their managers to various instrumented forms of sensitivity training.

When managers first acquired the skills of candor and leveling, they were frustrated by their continuing inability to develop authentic relationships with union leaders. Union spokesmen continued to be on guard and to maintain at least a façade of mistrust in response to management's overtures of openness. Union officers, at their request, were permitted to participate in the company's instrumented sensitivity training program, which at that time was the managerial grid.[9] When the union leaders had completed the 1-week course, they agreed to participate in an intergroup confrontation with management for the purpose of surfacing some of the causes of mistrust and conflict. In the initial meeting the parties agreed to undertake separately the task of defining what they thought would constitute a sound relationship between them. Each defined their own and the other party's role in this ideal relationship, and convened for comparisons and discussion. Though their lists were different, there were no basic points of contradiction. Avoiding the customary win-lose traps, they carried on candid discussions of their respective roles and images. These working sessions were the basis for reconciling or accepting most of their differences and misunderstandings. Finally, after three decades of traditional labor-management relationships, the ice was broken and the two parties began working together with common goals, developing compatible strategies to satisfy the mutual needs of the organization and its members.

Learning to talk to each other is not the ultimate goal, but it is a necessary beginning toward implementation of a philosophy based on mutual respect. Nor is this first goal achieved easily or quickly. The values of labor leaders and company managers are deep-seated, having been conditioned throughout the professional careers of both. Hence, change requires initiative and time, and follows an evolutionary process which will continue only in a climate of mutual trust.

[9] Robert R. Blake and Jane S. Mouton, *Corporate Excellence through Grid Organization Development*, Gulf Publishing Company, Houston, 1968.

Mutual trust cannot be developed by the language of words, but only through the language of trustworthy behavior by both parties.

The Intermediate Goal

The intermediate, and sometimes the ultimate, goal of labor relations is the harmonious coexistence and active cooperation of the company and the union in the attainment of their mutual goals. For some, of course, the ultimate goal is the synergising of individual and organizational goals to the point that union intervention is unneeded. However, pursuit of the intermediate goal of constructive coexistence offers the best platform for launching a program of constructive union-company confrontation.

Charles A. Myers listed some conditions for constructive coexistence of companies and unions, based on a review of thirteen case studies sponsored by the National Planning Association.[10] Though there were variations among case studies, the following characteristics of the union-management relationship were found in most situations:

1. There is full acceptance by management of the collective bargaining process and of unionism as an institution. The company considers a strong union an asset to management.
2. The union fully accepts private ownership and operation of the industry; it recognizes that the welfare of its members depends upon the successful operation of the business.
3. The union is strong, responsible, and democratic.
4. The company stays out of the union's internal affairs; it does not seek to alienate the workers' allegiance to their union.
5. Mutual trust and confidence exist between the parties. There have been no serious ideological incompatibilities.
6. Neither party to bargaining has adopted a legalistic approach to the solution of problems in the relationship.
7. Negotiations are problem-centered: more time is spent on day-to-day problems than on defining abstract principles.
8. There is widespread union-management consultation and highly developed information sharing.
9. Grievances are settled promptly, in the local plant whenever possible. There is flexibility and informality within the procedure.

[10] Clinton S. Golden and Virginia D. Parker, *Causes of Industrial Peace*, Harper & Brothers, New York, 1955, p. 47.

Unions came into existence primarily as protectors of the less privileged at the lower levels of the organization, and usually continued as a counterbalancing influence against arbitrary management authority. Hence, survival of a union would seem to require continuing conflict between management and labor. However, when a company and its local unions learn to achieve industrial peace through cooperative pursuit of common goals, this attainment alone will not automatically cause the dissolution of the unions. The inertia of traditional management practices, legal restrictions, and conditioned dependency relationships with the union, coupled with active resistance by the parent (usually international) union, make the decertification of a union dependent on extraordinary initiative on the part of both parties. Thus, unions may continue functioning long after they achieve a level of mutual trust that would have prevented their initial formation.

The Ultimate Goal

The ultimate goal of labor relations is the same in both the nonunion and the union groups: namely, building a climate of mutual trust through goal-directed individual and group relationships throughout the organization. The strategy for building such an environment is the theme of this entire book, and is illustrated in some detail in the discussions of meaningful work on pages 62 to 72, the changing role of the supervisor on pages 97 to 105, and the descriptions of personnel management systems on pages 46 to 54. In essence, it is a philosophy of involving talent of people at all levels of the organization in the pursuit of visible, desirable, challenging, and attainable goals through involvement processes in which the influence of competence rather than the application of authority provides direction.

If nonunion organizations are to withstand organization attempts, their members must have conditions comparable with those of their unionized counterparts. However, the traditional maintenance factors of wages, hours, and working conditions are of secondary importance if employees have better opportunities to develop and use their talents in the performance of meaningful work. Their managers cannot practice the techniques of coercion and manipulation but, rather, they must satisfy the conditions of interpersonal competence, meaningful goals and helpful systems as defined on pages 53 to 54. They must defend the rights of the members to the organization with the fervor of union stewards, but as supervisors, they must make the relationship of individual and organizational goals synergistic, or at least compatible.

Handling Grievances

Grievance procedures in nonunion organizations cannot be patterned after the procedures in the union plant, for this would imply and incur the assumptions that precipitated the intervention of unions. In a typical union plant, the grievance procedure moves upward through dual chains of command, engaging the contestants in win-lose conflicts to be resolved sooner or later by fact finding, power pressures, capitulation, and mediation. As noted earlier, this process is based on the premise that management and labor have conflicting goals and hence are incapable of voluntary or natural problem resolution. Such a strategy in the nonunion plant would fail to surface grievances because of the intuitive recognition by the individual that his supervisor has the trump card of authority and that there are no safeguards against the subtle reprisals that might occur if the "management-labor" style of grievance procedure were applied. Hence, simply introducing a traditional union grievance procedure into the nonunion plant not only fails to surface and resolve grievances, but more damagingly, it precipitates and broadens the "management-labor" cleavage associated with alienation.

Grievances rarely spring full blown into existence as a consequence of a single recent event or cause. More often a grievance is an eruption that releases tensions built up from sustained subjection to petty injustices, oppressive restrictions, monotonous and demeaning work, economic pressures, and particularly in the large organizations, frustrations arising from the lack of opportunity to be heard or to obtain wanted information. Emotions displayed in connection with a grievance often seem disproportionate to the stated reason for the grievance. However, taken in the context of the backlog of culminating factors, the grievance is understandable for what it usually is—the final straw which pushed the individual temporarily beyond his threshold of self-restraint. Many grievances are filed by persons who would normally seek more rational resolutions for their problems. However, having locked themselves into a win-lose conflict during a moment of high emotion, their pride and the lingering pressure of previous frustrations formalize the grievance for official processing.

Psychologists in the Los Angeles school system, recognizing that teenager rebellion often has its roots in frustrations arising from the absence of someone trustworthy to talk to about their problems, established a "hot-line" telephone number to call for help. Counselors receiving their calls listened and gave advice, often referring them to others; but most importantly, they were immediately available and did not require identifying information. Most of 7,000 calls received during the first year dealt with boy-girl relationships and conflict with authority, problems not considered "important" by many adults. The availability of an understanding ear when they needed it was a key factor for many in reducing tensions which might otherwise have found harmful expression.

Many grievances in industry are precipitated by the absence of someone who cares enough to listen to employees' problems and give them information or advice when they need it. Their frustrations, like those of teenagers, often result from an accumulation of unresolved minor problems and unanswered questions about such matters as supplemental benefits, job opportunities, interpersonal conflict, and home problems. The large organization needs an "information line" to give immediate and anonymous response to requests for information and complaints about real or imagined injustices. This immediate dissipation of emotion would prevent the ground swell of alienation which infiltrates the organization and ultimately contaminates the vast majority whose attitudes are otherwise characteristically neutral or uninvolved.

The first step in a grievance procedure for the nonunion plant must grant the individual complete freedom to use his judgment in whatever way seems appropriate to *him*. It cannot force him, as a first step, even informally, to take the matter up with his supervisor, because the supervisor may be his problem. He should be able to consult an anonymous information line, his peers, a personnel representative, a technical specialist, or someone above his supervisor. In other words, he must have the freedom of a citizen in a democracy to appeal his case in whatever manner seems appropriate, with confidence that he is not violating rules by doing so and that he will receive a fair hearing. At the same time, sustained circumvention of supervision deprives the supervisor of feedback necessary for his job effectiveness. The anonymous information line could provide constructive suggestions to supervisors without jeopardizing the anonymity of the complaint system.

If the grievance is not resolved through the informal first-step procedures, the second step of the grievance procedure should allow the supervisor opportunity for involvement, perhaps through the "neutral-third-party" intervention of a mutually acceptable member of the organization who informally assists in clarifying the problem and working out a satisfactory resolution. Should the grievance become more formalized, the third person and/or the supervisor may assist the complainant in writing the formal grievance. Grievances not resolved at this level to the satisfaction of the individual and his supervisor may be appealed upward to successively higher levels of management. If not resolved through the management hierarchy, the services of a mutually acceptable outsider serving an ombudsman role might be needed to mediate an impartial and acceptable resolution.

Role of the Labor Relations Specialist

The labor relations man's responsibility must be focused increasingly on preventive maintenance and less on the fire-fighting or counterbalancing role of dealing with problems spun out by inept supervision. Though he must, of course, continue to handle these problems as they are surfaced, his talents are better applied in reorienting supervision to prevent their recurrence. The reorientation problem is not restricted to the lower levels of supervision, but perhaps is even more applicable to middle and upper-middle management's nonverbal communications. The labor relations man must train supervisors to understand behavior as a response to the restrictions and opportunities represented by the job and supervision. In an advisory or educative role he reinforces them as they relinquish outmoded supervisory tactics and gradually internalize the definition of supervision on pages 98 to 105. He is succeeding in his new role when supervisors are able to surface and cope with conflict within their own natural work groups with diminishing reliance on labor relations specialists to bail them out.

In addition to his educative role, the effective labor relations specialist is qualified by his combination of professional competence and responsibility to serve the following ongoing functions:

1. Pulse taking within the work force and the community to anticipate, and prepare strategies against, irresponsible actions of labor unions.

2. Provision of legal advice to supervisors, systems designers, and procedure writers to prevent innocent infractions of rules.
3. Provision of information to local, state, and Federal lawmakers to promote the enactment of sound industrial relations laws.

The nonunion plant offers the most immediate opportunity for the labor relations man to serve his new role, and the qualified specialist can phase naturally into this new role with few transitional changes. In the unionized plant, the strategy is more complex and long-range. He must, of course, continue his fire-fighting functions during the early process of building interpersonal competence between management and union leadership, but 5 years of sustained effort by the company and union may be required before they feel they are working from a foundation of common goals. Having achieved interpersonal competence and compatible goals, the labor relations man can enter more fully into his new educative role of supporting the efforts of natural work groups to manage their own conflict.

Index

Index

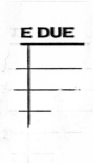